Representing the Troubles in Irish Short Fiction

Michael L. Storey

Representing the Troubles in Irish Short Fiction

The Catholic University of America Press
Washington, D.C.

The paper used in this publication meets the minimum requirements of American National Standards for the Information Science—Permanence of Paper for Printed Library Materials, ANSI Z39.48-1984.

∞

Library of Congress Cataloguing-in-Publication Data

Storey, Michael L., 1942–
Representing the troubles in Irish short fiction / Michael L. Storey.
p. cm.
Includes bibliographical references and index.
ISBN 978-0-8132-3310-9 (alk. paper)
1. Short stories, English—Irish authors—History and criticism. 2. Nationalism and literature—Ireland—History—20th century. 3. Politics and literature—Ireland—History—20th century. 4. Literature and society—Ireland—History—20th century. 5. Romanticism—Ireland—History—20th century. 6. Ireland—In literature. I. Title.
PR8807.S5S76 2004
823′.0109358—dc21

2003007835

For Anna Maria, my *gradh geal*

Contents

Acknowledgments

This project has been realized through the generous support and encouragement of my family, friends, colleagues, students, and institution, as well as the staff of The Catholic University of America Press.

From my institution, the College of Notre Dame of Maryland, I received a sabbatical leave in the fall semester of 1998, which enabled me to write a substantial portion of the text. The College's Council for Faculty Research and Development awarded me study grants that allowed me to devote several summers to the project. To both the College and the Council I am grateful.

I am also grateful to numerous colleagues, both in and out of the English department, who have encouraged me over the years to pursue my research and writing about the subject. I would particularly like to name my good friend and retired colleague, Sister Maura Eichner, who for years taught Irish literature with me. Sister Margaret MacCurtain, Irish scholar, was very supportive of my work while a visiting professor at our college in 1995. After hearing my paper on an aspect of the topic at an IASIL conference in Gotenborg, Sweden, in 1997, Sister Margaret encouraged me to extend the paper into a book.

The clerical work that my student assistants have done over the last five years has been invaluable. In successive order, Jen Perkins, Jess Rapisarda, Kathy Nikolaidis, Guin Phoebe, and Natasha Allen have researched, tracked down, and photocopied materials; typed and proofread text; and helped prepare an index. The staff of the Loyola-Notre Dame Library, especially those who work in the Inter-Library Loan department, have also been extremely helpful to me.

Throughout the book I have used, with permission of the editors, portions of articles that I have published previously in *Éire-Ireland* and *The New Hibernia Review*. Those articles are identified in the bibliography. Dr. Thomas Dillon Redshaw, who was editor of *Éire-Ireland* at the time my article was published in that journal, provided me with helpful suggestions about the subject.

I am especially appreciative of the editorial work done by my daughter, Meg Storey. Meg's ability to ferret out unnecessary and imprecise words and phrases, to straighten convoluted sentences, and to temper my passion for parentheses brought a greater clarity to the text. She also was a careful reader of the sense of the text, pointing out where the argument needed to be stronger or the clarity greater. Members of The Catholic University of America Press, in particular Dave McGonagle, Susan Needham, and Elizabeth Kerr, have also been very generous and helpful in their support and editorial advice.

More than anything, the unfailing encouragement and support of my wife, Anna Maria, has made this book possible.

Abbreviations

Primary works (short story collections, anthologies, and autobiographies) frequently cited have been identified by the following abbreviations. Complete information about these works may be found under Primary Sources in the Selected Bibliography.

AN	*At Night All Cats are Grey*, by Patrick Boyle.
AQ	*Antiquities: A Sequence of Short Stories*, by Val Mulkerns.
BC	*Bones of Contention and Other Stories*, by Frank O'Connor.
BW	*A Belfast Woman*, by Mary Beckett.
CSO	*The Collected Stories of Sean O'Faolain*.
CST	*The Collected Stories*, by William Trevor.
DC	*Death of a Chieftain and Other Stories*, by John Montague.
DP	*Departures*, by Jennifer C Cornell.
DR	*Domestic Relations*, by Frank O'Connor.
EC	*Everything in This Country Must*, by Colum McCann.
FG	*Forgiveness: Ireland's Best Contemporary Short Stories*, edited by Augustine Martin.
FS	*Fishing the Sloe-Black River*, by Colum McCann.
GN	*Guests of the Nation*, by Frank O'Connor.
HB	*The Hounds of Banba*, by Daniel Corkery.
HE	*Heritage and Other Stories*, by Eugene McCabe.
HW	*The Hurt World: Short Stories of the Troubles*, edited by Michael Parker.

MS	*More Stories by Frank O'Connor.*
NM	*Northern Myths*, by John Morrow.
OC	*An Only Child*, by Frank O'Connor.
OS	*Oranges from Spain*, by David Park.
P&S	*Poems and Stories*, by Brendan Behan.
PS	*The Patriot Son and Other Stories*, by Mary Lavin.
S&P	*Stories and Plays*, by Flann O'Brien.
SD	*Shame the Devil*, by Liam O'Flaherty.
SFO	*The Stories of Frank O'Connor.*
SH	*Sixpence in Her Shoe and Other Stories*, by Maura Treacy.
SI	*The State of Ireland: A Novella and Seventeen Stories*, by Benedict Kiely.
SM	*A Season for Mothers and Other Stories*, by Helen Lucy Burke.
SS	*Spring Sowing*, by Liam O'Flaherty.
TS	*Tears of the Shamrock: An Anthology of Contemporary Short Stories on the Theme of Ireland's Struggle for Nationhood*, edited by David Marcus.
TT	*The Tent*, by Liam O'Flaherty.
TV	*Territories of the Voice: Contemporary Stories by Irish Women Writers*, edited by Louise DeSalvo, Kathleen Walsh D'Arcy, and Katherine Hogan.
VM	*Vive Moi!*, by Sean O'Faolain.
WC	*The Wounded Cormorant and Other Stories*, by Liam O'Flaherty.
WD	*Walking the Dog and Other Stories*, by Bernard MacLaverty.
WP	*The Way-Paver*, by Anne Devlin.

Introduction

I

The modern Irish short story arrived in 1903 with the publication of *The Untilled Field* by George Moore. Moore combined contemporary themes of emigration, clerical interference, poverty, and rural loneliness with psychological characterization and narrative economy. In doing so, he severed the modern Irish story from its nineteenth-century roots, particularly the Gothic tales of Sheridan Le Fanu and the loosely-constructed stories of William Carleton, whose model had been the Irish *seanchái*, the famed oral storyteller of Irish tradition. James Joyce's *Dubliners*, published in 1914, further modernized the Irish story through greater artistic economy and precise, realistic representation of Irish life. In the ensuing decades, the Irish short story established itself as the premier national literary genre through collections by Daniel Corkery, Liam O'Flaherty, Frank O'Connor, Elizabeth Bowen, Sean O'Faolain, and Mary Lavin. In the latter half of the twentieth century, Benedict Kiely, Edna O'Brien, William Trevor, Mary Beckett, John McGahern, Bernard MacLaverty, Val Mulkerns, Clare Boylan, Colum McCann, and numerous others brought international acclaim to the Irish short story.

Based solidly in the mode of realism, the modern short story is a veritable chronicle of Irish life, probing every significant Irish social and political issue of the twentieth century: rural poverty and hardship, forced emigration and exile, village provincialism, moral prohibition, clerical interference, marriage relations, sexual and gender issues, divorce and abortion. But no issue has been treated so extensively and so probingly in the modern Irish story as the Troubles. In fact, a reader could gain no better insight into the human aspects of the Irish Troubles than to read the many Irish short stories that deal with that phenomenon.

II

The Troubles, the Irish euphemism for political turmoil and violence, have their roots in Ireland's colonial relationship to England and the political and sectarian divisions in Ireland flowing out of that relationship. The term was first applied to the revolutionary events that took place between 1916 and 1923, a period that included the 1916 Easter Rising, the War of Independence of 1919–1921, and the Civil War of 1922–1923. It was later revived to label the sectarian hostilities that erupted in Northern Ireland in the late 1960s and that continued unabated into the 1990s. A 1994 ceasefire and a 1998 peace agreement (commonly referred to as the Good Friday Agreement) have lessened the frequency of the violence while not completely stopping it. While these two periods (1916–1923 and the late 1960s to the present) are distinctly different in their political situations, they closely resemble each other in the violent and brutal behavior of the hostile factions and in the misery, tragedy, and death brought to many innocent victims. Thus, the Troubles is an apt term for both periods.[1] There is now, however, an excellent possibility that, with successful implementation of the Good Friday Agreement at the beginning of the twenty-first century, the term may be retired once again—perhaps forever.

Political violence in Ireland, especially that committed for and against the cause of independence, is not, of course, a modern phenomenon. Ever since the Norman Earls of England invaded Ireland in the twelfth century, the native Irish and some Anglo-Irish (including the Earls themselves) have resorted to violence in rebelling against the English rulers and their representatives. Over the centuries, nationalists and others seeking to be free of English dominion have taken up arms in violent rebellion, and they, in turn, have been violently subdued. A litany of such events up to the twentieth century would include the armed rebellions of the Munster FitzGeralds, Norman Earls of Des-

1. I use the term "Troubles" throughout the text as the generic term for the hostile events of both periods; at times I also use more specific phrases, such as "the early Troubles" and "the Northern Troubles," to specify one period or the other.

mond, in the 1580s and of the Gaelic chieftains Red Hugh O'Donnell and Hugh O'Neill in the period 1595–1603; Cromwell's massacre of Catholics in mid-seventeenth century; the Siege of Derry and the Battle of the Boyne in the late seventeenth century; the United Irishmen rebellion of 1798; and the Fenian Uprising of 1867. By the early years of the twentieth century, however, not a great deal had changed in the political situation: England still ruled Ireland.

The change—and the Troubles—began on Easter Monday, 1916. A band of rebels, comprised largely of the Irish Republican Brotherhood (IRB), the Irish Volunteers, and the Irish Citizen Army and led by Patrick Pearse, seized the General Post Office (GPO) and other buildings in Dublin and declared Ireland a republic. Overwhelmed by British forces and discouraged by the antipathy of the Irish people, the rebels surrendered a few days later, seemingly having added one more failed attempt in the long history of Irish rebellion. But the British made the great blunder of executing fifteen of the rebel leaders, including Pearse, thereby making martyrs of them and engendering widespread sympathy and support among the Irish people for armed rebellion. This change in public support made possible the War of Independence.

The War of Independence (also referred to as the Anglo-Irish War or the Black and Tan War) began after the Sinn Féin party won the 1918 general elections. Refusing to take their seats in London, Sinn Féin representatives formed Dáil Eireann, the Irish parliament, and in January 1919 declared allegiance to an Irish republic. At the same time, the Irish Volunteers, their numbers having swelled in the aftermath of the Easter Rising, started guerrilla warfare—ambushes, surprise bombings, assassinations, reprisals, and the like—against the British occupation forces and their representatives, including the Royal Irish Constabulary (RIC) and the "Black and Tans," an auxiliary group named for their makeshift uniforms and infamous for their brutality. Led by the brilliant strategist Michael Collins, the Volunteers, renamed the Irish Republican Army (IRA), fought the superior British forces to a stalemate. Negotiations between the Irish rebels and the British in the latter half of 1921 resulted in the Anglo-Irish Treaty. The Treaty promised dominion status (a "Free

State") to twenty-six of the thirty-two counties of Ireland but required partition of the other six counties, populated largely by Protestant loyalists, into Northern Ireland, and an oath of allegiance by members of the Dáil to the British monarch. These key Treaty provisions—dominion status for southern Ireland, the oath of allegiance, and partition of the north—created bitter disagreement between those Irish who welcomed Free State status and those who insisted on a united Ireland and a complete and immediate break with Britain. The leaders who signed the Treaty, including Collins, promoted it as a steppingstone to the ultimate goal of a republic, but Éamon de Valera, President of the Dáil and political leader of the republicans, regarded the Treaty as a British triumph and urged rejection of it.

After the Treaty was ratified by a majority in the Dáil, de Valera led his followers out in protest and defiance. In April 1922, republican "irregulars" seized the Four Courts, the seat of the Irish judiciary, and other buildings in Dublin. When Free State troops forcibly dislodged the rebels the following June, the Civil War began. Driven from the Four Courts, the rebels carried the fighting into the streets of Dublin and out to the countryside, conducting the war in the same guerrilla fashion as the War of Independence had been waged—quick skirmishes, ambushes, and executions. Collins, once the revered leader of the IRA but now commander-in-chief of the Free State army, was ambushed and killed in Co. Cork by the very men he had once led. The tragedy of his assassination was that it was brought about by disagreements over the means, not the ultimate goals, of republicanism. Nevertheless, the Free State forces, backed by British resources, proved superior. Eventually they subdued the rebels, forcing surrender in May 1923. One of the bitter ironies of the war was the Free State execution of seventy-seven rebels—more than five times as many as the British had executed after the Easter Rising. Undoubtedly the single most divisive event in modern Irish history, the Civil War split the country, pitting father against son, brother against brother, and neighbor against neighbor, and left a legacy of bitterness for decades to come.

The period between the end of the Civil War and the onset of hostilities in Northern Ireland in the late 1960s is not usually labeled a time of Troubles, but there were from time to time acts of hostility related to the reunification of north and south, which became the principal remaining nationalist issue of significance. In 1937 a new constitution changed the name of the Irish Free State to Éire and, with the oath of allegiance abolished, set the country on the road to becoming a republic (Éire became a republic in 1949). The new constitution also claimed jurisdiction over Northern Ireland, a claim strongly rejected by the Protestant majority of the north. Thus, the issue of reunification of north and south remained a volatile one, and the Troubles lay just below the surface of Irish life, occasionally flaring up. In 1939, after issuing an ultimatum to the British to depart Ireland once and for all, the IRA carried out a yearlong but ill-planned and ineffectual bombing campaign in English cities. In the early 1950s the IRA raided army barracks in England and Northern Ireland, seizing arms and ammunition, thereby enabling the organization to conduct a campaign on the north-south border between 1956 and 1962 in an attempt to end partition and bring about reunification. The campaign failed.

When violence erupted in Northern Ireland in the late 1960s—thus beginning the second period of the Troubles—the major impetus did not come from the IRA and the immediate issue was not reunification. Rather, it began during a period of civil rights marches, organized by the Northern Ireland Civil Rights Association (NICRA) and its more militant off-shoot, People's Democracy, both made up mostly of Northern Catholics who felt angry and frustrated over being excluded from the economic and social benefits of Northern Ireland. One of the first marches—from Belfast to Derry in January of 1969—was attacked by Protestant unionists while the Royal Ulster Constabulary (RUC) stood by. That event set off a succession of riots in the Catholic areas of Derry (the "Bogside") and Belfast. When the Protestant-dominated RUC and its auxiliary B Specials (organized in 1920 to counter the IRA in the north) did more to incite than allay the violence, British troops were sent into Northern Ireland to restore peace. Although the army was initially welcomed by Catholics, its presence eventually exacerbated the situation and the Troubles escalated.

By then the IRA had become involved, though there was dissension within the organization over what its role should entail. The more militant members insisted on using "physical force" to defend the Catholic areas of Derry and Belfast, while the progressive, socialist-minded leadership, which had recently tried to transform the organization, urged a nonviolent policy that would unite Catholic and Protestant workers in civil rights solidarity against the government of Northern Ireland and its British sponsor, thus potentially eliminating the sectarian element in the Troubles. In 1970 the organization split into the "Official" IRA (those favoring the socialist, nonsectarian approach) and the Provisional IRA (popularly called the "Provos"), which, believing that the issue was clearly sectarian, took up arms to defend Catholics against militant Protestants and began a bombing campaign, targeting Protestant businesses. Militant Protestant groups, including the Ulster Volunteer Force (UVF), originally formed in 1912 to oppose home rule, and the Ulster Freedom Fighters (UFF), a subgroup of the Ulster Defence Association (UDA), began their own violent campaign against Catholics.

The conflict was now seen almost entirely in sectarian terms—the Catholic nationalist minority vs. the Protestant loyalist majority—rather than a class struggle focused on civil rights. Sectarian-motivated violence continued through the 1970s, the 1980s, and much of the 1990s. This period was one long nightmare for Northern Ireland, characterized as it was by virtually incessant acts of terrorist violence: executions, knee-cappings and other mutilations, car bombs, petrol bombs, assassinations of government officials, and pub explosions. These acts were perpetrated by a bewildering array of paramilitary groups, including further splinter groups of the IRA, such as the Irish National Liberation Army (INLA), the Contingency IRA, and the Real IRA, and, on the Protestant side, Ulster Resistance, Loyalist Volunteer Force (LVF), and Tara, in addition to the UVF, UDA, and the UFF. The victims were largely noncombatants, both Catholic and Protestant citizens of Northern Ireland (and occasionally of the Republic), often randomly killed or maimed by extremists in retaliation for an attack on citizens by the other side. In a quarter century of conflict, some thirty-six hundred people in Ireland were killed and thousands of others maimed in Troubles-related violence.

Suffering under such wretched conditions, the people of Northern Ireland, both Catholics and Protestants, have overwhelmingly turned away from the extremist militant factions and moved toward more moderate political parties and organizations that favor peace. This shift in public attitude has given some measure of hope to peace prospects. The ceasefire declared in 1994 by both the IRA and loyalist paramilitaries has held, despite a brief rescission and some egregious violations. The 1998 Good Friday Agreement envisions permanent peace and justice in the north. It calls for an end to more than a quarter century of direct British rule (in 1972 the province's parliament was indefinitely suspended due to hostilities) and for a government in which Protestants and Catholics share power and economic benefits. In exchange, the Republic of Ireland has revoked its constitutional claim to the six counties that constitute Northern Ireland, and the IRA and other militant groups have pledged to give up ("decommission") their weapons. Finally, the Good Friday Agreement incorporates the principle of consent, i.e., that "a united Ireland shall be brought about only by peaceful means with the consent of a majority of the people, democratically expressed, in both jurisdictions in the island."[2] At last, real peace and justice are being given a chance in Ireland.

III

Critical attention to the Irish short story has been strangely paradoxical. On the one hand, the short story has been called Ireland's

2. The wording is from Article 3 of the Irish Constitution, amended in accordance with the Good Friday Agreement. For a succinct discussion of the Good Friday Agreement, see chapter 14 in Jonathan Tonge, *Northern Ireland: Conflict and Change*, 2d ed. (Harlow, England: Longman, 2002).

"national art form,"[3] said by some critics to exceed the Irish novel in achievement. On the other hand, very little in the way of comprehensive study has been done. Only a few books trace the development of the Irish short story, and none of these examines the development of Troubles stories. The most significant and inclusive of these studies is *The Irish Short Story: A Critical History,* edited by James F. Kilroy (1984),[4] but it is now twenty years old. There are, it should be noted, numerous studies of individual Irish short-story writers, including several books each on Frank O'Connor, Sean O'Faolain, Liam O'Flaherty, Mary Lavin, and William Trevor. Many of these works are devoted exclusively or largely to the writer's short fiction, often assessing his or her contribution to the Irish short story. In most, the writer's Troubles stories are given substantial attention, but the focus is always on the place these stories have in the writer's oeuvre, rather than on their relationship to similar stories by other Irish writers or on their contribution to Troubles short fiction.

There is also a growing list of books that examine, in whole or part, the treatment of the Troubles in selected works of Irish literature. The earliest of these, William Irwin Thompson's *The Imagination of an Insurrection: Dublin, Easter 1916* (1967), focuses on the literary treatment of the Easter Rising. Thompson discusses the poetry of those who participated in the rebellion—Pearse, Thomas MacDonagh, and Joseph Mary Plunkett—as well as the poetic and dramatic works of those who observed the Rising from a distance: W. B. Yeats, George Russell (AE), and

3. Ben Forkner, Introduction to *Modern Irish Short Stories*, ed. Ben Forkner (New York: Penguin, 1980), 42. See also Dermot Bolger, Introduction to *The Vintage Book of Contemporary Irish Fiction*, ed. Dermot Bolger (New York: Random House, 1994), xiv–xv. The fact that Bolger, who does not agree with this assessment, feels the need to argue the superiority of the Irish novel to the Irish short story is, in itself, proof of the latter's strong critical reputation; no critic of the American novel would think that that genre required a defense against the American short story.

4. The others are Deborah Averill, *The Irish Short Story from George Moore to Frank O'Connor* (Washington, D.C.: University Press of America, 1982) and *The Irish Short Story*, ed. Patrick Rafroidi and Terence Brown (Atlantic Highlands, N.J.: Humanities Press, 1979), both of which have a narrower scope than Kilroy's book.

Sean O'Casey. Peter Costello's *The Heart Grown Brutal: The Irish Revolution in Literature from Parnell to the Death of Yeats, 1891–1939* (1977) takes a more comprehensive view. Asserting that the Irish revolution was made possible by the ideal image of Ireland set forth in the literary revival, Costello examines drama, poetry, novels, and short stories, including fiction by O'Connor, O'Faolain, and O'Flaherty, inspired by the revolutionary events of the 1916–1923 period.

More recent works examining the literary treatment of the Troubles have tended to be genre specific, with most of the attention going to the novel and very little to the short story. Many of these studies deal with the works of a single poet, playwright, or novelist, but several fruitfully compare works by two or more writers. In dramatic studies, works by Antony Roche and Nicholas Grene stand out. Roche's *Contemporary Irish Drama: From Beckett to McGuinness* (1995) contains a chapter entitled "Northern Irish Drama: Imagining Alternatives," which explores the theme of sectarian conflict in the plays of Stewart Parker, Christina Reid, Anne Devlin, and Marina Carr. *The Politics of Irish Drama: Plays in Context from Boucicault to Friel* (1999), by Grene, examines, in a chapter entitled "Reactions to Revolution," the Troubles-related plays of O'Casey, Denis Johnston, Brendan Behan, Parker, Frank McGuinness and Brian Friel. In poetic studies, themes of Northern Irish politics and violence running through the poetry of Seamus Heaney, Derek Mahon, Thomas Kinsella, John Montague, John Hewitt, Paul Muldoon, and others, have been examined by Edna Longley, Clair Wills, Norman Vance, and Steven Matthews, among others.[5] Matthews' *Irish Poetry: Politics, History, Negotiation* (1997), the most sustained and inclusive study of the topic, traces the development of poetic responses to the Northern Troubles from 1969 to the mid-1990s.

5. See Edna Longley, "Poetry and Politics in Northern Ireland," in *Poetry in the Wars* (Newark: University of Delaware Press, 1987); Clair Wills, *Improprieties: Politics and Sexuality in Northern Irish Poetry* (Oxford: The Clarendon Press, 1993); and Norman Vance, "Contemporary Ireland and the Poetics of Partition: John Hewitt and Seamus Heaney," in *Irish Literature, A Social History: Tradition, Identity and Difference* (Oxford: Basil Blackwell, 1990).

Novels about the Troubles, said by one estimate to number over five hundred, have garnered a great deal of critical attention. In *Great Hatred, Little Room: The Irish Historical Novel* (1983), James M. Cahalan examines and compares several novels treating the Troubles, including O'Flaherty's *Insurrection*, Walter Macken's *The Scorching Wind*, and Iris Murdoch's *The Red and the Green*, all to some degree about the Easter Rising. More recent critical studies include Cahalan's *Double Vision: Women and Men in Modern and Contemporary Irish Fiction* (1999) and *Contemporary Irish Fiction: Themes, Tropes, Theories*, ed. Liam Harte and Michael Parker (2000). As their titles suggest, both studies have a broader perspective than the Troubles, but each devotes space to valuable commentaries on the treatment of the Troubles in Irish novels.[6] *Writing the North: The Contemporary Novel in Northern Ireland* (1998), by Laura Pelaschiar, and *Fiction and the Northern Ireland Troubles since 1969: (De-)constructing the North* (2003), by Elmer Kennedy-Andrews, explore many of the same novelists, including Robert McLiam Wilson, Colin Bateman, Bernard MacLaverty, Danny Morrison, Eoin McNamee, Deirdre Madden, Glenn Patterson, and Jennifer Johnston. There are also numerous journal articles devoted to the Troubles novel.[7]

Additionally, many studies investigate the ways in which literary works contribute to an understanding of the related issues of Irish nationalism, post-colonialism, violence, and the Troubles. David Lloyd's *Anomalous States: Irish Writing and the Post-Colonial Moment* (1993) explores these issues in the works of Heaney, Beckett, Joyce, Yeats, and

6. See chapter 5, "Gender and History in Trouble(s)" in James M. Cahalan, *Double Visions: Women and Men in Modern and Contemporary Irish Fiction* (Syracuse: Syracuse University Press, 1999); Richard Haslam, "'The Pose Arranged and Lingered Over': Visualizing the 'Troubles,'" and Liam Harte and Michael Parker, "Reconfiguring Identities: Recent Northern Irish Fiction," in *Contemporary Irish Fiction: Themes, Tropes, Theories*, ed. Liam Harte and Michael Parker (New York: St. Martin's, 2000).

7. For example, John Cronin, "Ulster's Alarming Novels," *Éire-Ireland* 4 (winter 1969): 27–34; Joseph McMinn, "Contemporary Novels on the Troubles," *Études Irlandaises* 5 (1980): 113–21; Margaret Scanlon, "The Unbearable Present: Northern Ireland in Four Contemporary Novels," *"Études Irlandaises* 10 (Dec. 1985): 145–61; and Alan Titley, "Rough Rug-Headed Kerns: The Irish Gunman in the Popular Novel," *Éire-Ireland* 15 (winter 1980): 15–38.

others. *Literature, Rhetoric and Violence in Northern Ireland, 1968–98: Hardened to Death* (2001), by Patrick Grant, examines the ways that Irish poets, playwrights, and novelists conceptualize the violence of the Troubles and thereby contribute in distinctive ways to the "discourse through which violence can be described and assessed. . . ."[8] In *Literature, Partition and the Nation-State: Culture and Conflict in Ireland, Israel and Palestine* (2002), Joe Cleary discusses how cultural narratives, including novels about the Northern Troubles, affect popular perceptions regarding the sources of conflict stemming from national partitions.

Despite the growing critical interest in the ways in which the Troubles and the related issues of nationalism and post-colonialism are represented in Irish literature, and notwithstanding the fact that nearly every Irish short-story writer of note (except Joyce) in the twentieth and twenty-first centuries—from Corkery, O'Connor, O'Faolain, and O'Flaherty to Flann O'Brien, Lavin, Benedict Kiely, Trevor, Mary Beckett, Bernard MacLaverty, Anne Devlin, David Park, and Colum McCann—has written such a story, until now no book[9] has been exclusively devoted to the treatment of the Troubles in the Irish short story. This book is meant to fill that gap.

IV

In the following study I show that over the last eighty-plus years—from the publication of Daniel Corkery's *The Hounds of Banba* in 1920 to the present—the Irish short story has recorded the shifting attitudes of the Irish toward every aspect of the Troubles: nationalist ideology, armed rebellion and violence, sectarianism, terrorism, and identity-thinking. To record these shifting attitudes, Irish short-story writers have embraced a variety of literary modes and techniques,

8. Patrick Grant, *Literature, Rhetoric and Violence in Northern Ireland, 1968–98: Hardened to Death* (New York: Palgrave, 2001), 3.

9. The only articles exclusively devoted to the treatment of the Troubles in the short fiction of several writers appear to be my own articles, "'Not to be written afterwards': The Irish Revolution in the Short Story," *Éire-Ireland* 27 (spring 1993): 32–47, and "Postcolonialism and Stories of the Irish Troubles," *New Hibernia Review* 2 (autumn 1998): 63–77.

from romanticism and naturalism, to comedy, satire, realism, and irony.

It can be argued that, at times, the writers of Troubles stories were engaged as much in an effort to promote ideology as to reflect public attitudes. Corkery was obviously urging a romantic nationalist ideology in *The Hounds of Banba*, written in the midst of the War of Independence, and later writers, by graphically describing violence in Northern Ireland and thereby evoking an abhorrence of it, may be viewed as advocates of a nonviolent ideology. On the other hand, O'Connor, O'Faolain, and O'Flaherty, in writing their stories after the revolutionary events of 1916–1923, had no interest in promoting or reviving the romantic ideology that had largely faded with the Civil War. Rather, they wished to record how that ideology had been instilled in the Irish and, subsequently, how many Irish, including themselves, had become disillusioned with it. Furthermore, many of the stories of the latter part of the twentieth century, although written in the midst of the conflict, seem to reflect more of an effort to record the causes and effects of the Troubles than an attempt to shape ideology, though an obvious exception is the work of Gerry Adams, whose stories seem a blatant attempt to restore a sense of romantic nationalism. Recent writers, such as Colum McCann and Bernard MacLaverty, seem more intent on envisioning an end, than on promoting an ideological solution, to the Troubles.

This study also demonstrates that the Troubles stories have evolved over the decades in such a way as to show a clear historical and logical pattern of attitudes toward the Troubles: from the embracing of a romantic, idealistic nationalism to disillusionment with it, a satiric disdain of nationalistic fervor, an abhorrence of sectarianism and terrorism, and, finally, an incipient repudiation of sectarian identity-thinking. At each stage, writers adopt the literary mode necessary to express the shift in attitude.

The earliest stories of the Troubles, examined in chapter 1, are written in the mode of romantic nationalism, a mode that employs both the conventions of literary romanticism and the post-colonial themes and techniques adopted by colonized writers to forge a nationalist literature of their own. Romantic conventions, such as the expressed belief in the attainment of the Ideal, daring adventures, and the quest narrative, are designed to evoke the revolutionary fervor, excitement, and idealism that the rebels experienced during the Easter Rising and War of Independence in their pursuit of the ideal Irish nation. A sense of Irish nationalism is attained through the development of the themes of colonial oppression and cultural displacement and through various post-colonial stylistic features, such as the use of Irish English, that promote Irish identity-formation.

The divisive Irish Civil War, erupting as a result of the unsatisfactory Treaty that followed the War of Independence and concluding with the defeat and extensive executions of the republicans, brought to a bitter end the romantic and idealistic aspirations of many revolutionaries. In order to express their disillusionment with the revolutionary enterprise, Irish short-story writers turned to the naturalistic mode inherited from Zola and other nineteenth-century writers. Chapter 2 analyzes stories that portray amoral, brutal and violent characters who are devoid of any redeeming idealistic qualities. Typically, these stories are written in the plain but bleak style of literary naturalism, and they end in bitter irony reflecting the philosophical pessimism of naturalism. Some of the naturalistic stories are ironic parodies of romantic nationalism, portraying and then subverting the quest myth.

In the decades following the Civil War, some Irish writers attempted to view the Troubles with more objectivity and distance and thus resorted to their innate sense of comedy and satire to do so. This development is the topic of chapter 3. If it seems odd that Irish writers would treat such momentous and painful events with humor and satire, it should be remembered that the Irish have traditionally spared no subject—religion, politics, marriage, patriotism—from their wit and withering sense of humor, and so the Troubles were fair game. In these stories, one sees such comic Irish figures as the drunk, the *omadhawn* (or clown), and the rogue, as well as such staple comic elements as the pub joke, farce, comic by-play and absurdities, invective and satire, and black humor.

Chapter 4 examines two types of stories written and/or set in the years from the 1930s up into the early 1970s. The first type depicts shadowy IRA figures engaged in violent operations, such as border raids or the execution of informers. Some of these stories are written in the bleak style of literary naturalism, while others combine realism and irony. The second type treats the simmering sectarian tensions between Catholics and Protestants, mostly in the north but also in the Republic. These stories deftly examine the causes and effects of sectarianism, and they poignantly illustrate how sectarian suspicion and hatred can infect, even destroy, communal relations, love affairs, marriages, and relations between brothers. Written primarily in a realistic style, they also frequently employ irony and symbolism to evoke the insidious and deadly effects of sectarianism.

In the early 1970s when the Provisional IRA and Protestant paramilitaries resorted to terrorism, Northern Ireland became a nightmarish place to live. The response of Irish writers was to create stories depicting that nightmare in all of its horror. Chapter 5 examines stories of violence and terrorism. Written in a style of unflinching realism, the stories graphically present the violence inflicted on the Irish people as a result of sectarian hostilities: bombings in crowded areas, executions, mutilations, decapitation, knee-cappings, and other atrocities. Largely devoid of ideological perspective—the victims in the stories are both Catholic and Protestant—the stories are primarily concerned with conveying the enormous pain and suffering terrorism has brought to the Irish people.

Chapter 6 examines both the portrayal of women as revolutionaries and the contributions of women writers to Troubles short fiction. Through such organizations as Cumann na mBan (Irishwomen's Council) women played significant roles in the early Troubles. Although most played supportive roles—as nurses, cooks, couriers, and the like—some women actually fought side-by-side with the men in the Easter Rising and the War of Independence. Nevertheless, in the early stories—all written by men—female characters are relegated exclusively to supporting roles. Since the eruption of the Northern Troubles, Irish women writers have increasingly treated the theme of the Troubles and have brought more female characters into the stories. With rare exception, however, these female characters are passive victims of the Troubles rather than active participants, that is, combatants or peace activists.

By the 1990s fewer stories about the Troubles were being published. The story of terrorism, so prominent in the 1970s and 1980s, began to disappear, perhaps owing to the decline in actual terrorist acts, perhaps to a weariness of writers and public alike over such graphic descriptions of violence and brutality. Of the Troubles stories that have been written over the last ten years (discussed in the Conclusion to this study), several explore possible ways out of the conflict, including the reconciliation of the divided communities. A couple stories offer another intriguing possibility. They suggest that one consequence of terrorism may be the deliberate concealment, even repudiation, of cultural identity by the people of Northern Ireland. The insistence by militant groups of both sides in dividing the Irish people along sectarian and cultural lines may, ironically and ultimately, result in a land where no one wishes to be known by his or her cultural or sectarian affiliations—or to fight for them.

Such an outcome could bring the stories of the Troubles—that began more than eighty years ago with the celebration of Irish identity—to an ironic end. A more welcome end, of course, would result from a peaceful conclusion to the Troubles, an excellent—if uncertain—possibility now that the Good Friday Agreement is under implementation. Borne out of political and historical realities, Troubles stories, though richly nourished by literary modes from romanticism and naturalism to comedy, satire, irony, and realism, ultimately live off those realities that they represent. When the realities end, so will the stories of the Troubles.

I

Romantic Nationalism

The Quest for an Irish Nation

In that moment life became one with the emotion of Ireland.

—Sean O'Faolain, *Vive Moi!*

I

Many of the stories written by Daniel Corkery, Frank O'Connor, and Sean O'Faolain that portray Irish revolutionary events, especially the Easter Rising and the War of Independence, were written in the mode of romantic nationalism. This literary mode was designed to be the exact counterpart—an "objective correlative"—for the emotions of excitement, hope, idealism, romance, and thrilling danger that these writers felt as young men during their participation in Ireland's struggle for independence. The romantic stories were thus intended to recreate in the reader, particularly the Irish reader, the intense emotions associated with revolution and nationalism. A second intended effect for Corkery, who fashioned the mode of romantic nationalism and wrote all of his revolutionary stories in this mode, was to engage the Irish reader's enthusiastic support for the revolution. Corkery's collection of stories, *The Hounds of Banba*, appeared in 1920 in the midst of the War of Independence, and thus it had the potential of creating this effect. O'Connor's stories (collected in *Guests of the Nation*, 1931) and O'Faolain's (*Midsummer Night Madness and Other Stories*, 1932), on the other hand, were written and published after the Civil War, and by then the two writers were interested only in recording their experience of republican idealism, not in reviving it.

All three writers were nationalists and republicans, and all three were idealists—Corkery throughout his life, O'Connor and O'Faolain until the Civil War disillusioned them. Corkery, born in 1878, was the oldest of the three and in many ways the most ardent, though he apparently never joined the Irish Volunteers, as O'Connor and O'Faolain did. Aside from his writings, his efforts to further the republican cause mostly took the form of encouraging and supporting others. His enthusiasm for Irish language, culture, and nationalism was by all accounts intense and infectious. Mentor to both O'Connor and O'Faolain, he encouraged their literary efforts, their interest in the Gaelic language and culture, and their revolutionary endeavors. O'Connor says in *An Only Child*, the first volume of his autobiography, that in the Civil War he "took the Republican side because it was Corkery's" (OC 211) and that, when he and a friend fled Cork after the Free State soldiers invaded the city, they sought refuge and advice from Corkery in his Inniscarra cottage (OC 228).

O'Faolain was born John Whelan in 1900 to a pro-British father who served in the RIC. In spite of his father's British leanings, he converted to Irish nationalism for the same reasons that so many others did—the sweeping infectiousness of the Gaelic revival. At first antipathetic to the 1916 rebels, he was disturbed by the British executions of the rebel leaders and at about the same time became enthused with Gaelic culture. His cultural interests were sparked, he says in his autobiography, *Vive Moi!*, by Padraig O'Domhnaill, a young teacher who spoke Irish and served in the Irish Volunteers (VM 129–32). Corkery was also his mentor, encouraging O'Faolain in both his writing and his Irish interests. In 1918 O'Faolain studied Gaelic in the west of Ireland, changed his name from John Whelan to Sean O'Faolain, and joined the Volunteers. His participation in the War of Independence, however, consisted of "safe" activities, such as carrying dispatches. After the Treaty and the outbreak of the Civil War, he joined the republican side, at first making bombs and then serving as a director of publicity. Even as the Free State forces were overpowering the rebels, O'Faolain retained his idealism, only gradually losing it in the aftermath of the Civil War. Indeed, a sense of romantic nationalism was integral to his life as a young rebel, as he notes in this comment from *Vive Moi!*: "In that moment [the revolutionary years] life became one with the emotion of Ireland" (VM 172). His later remark about this period of revolution, "It was one of the most ecstatic periods of my life,"[1] reveals how completely he was invested in romantic idealism.

Born Michael Francis O'Donovan[2] in 1903, O'Connor embraced republican idealism in much the same way as O'Faolain. Like O'Faolain, O'Connor had a father with British affinities (his father was a Munster Fusilier who had fought in South Africa). O'Connor also reacted negatively at first toward the 1916 rebels but changed his mind when the British executed the leaders. He says in *An Only Child* that he was especially upset when he heard that the British had executed a poet (i.e., Patrick Pearse) who wrote in Irish (OC 155). By this time, O'Connor, too, was under the enchantment of Gaelic language and culture, primarily through the influence of Corkery, his teacher at St. Patrick's National School. Like O'Faolain, O'Connor studied Gaelic and joined the Irish Volunteers. His participation in the War of Independence was also limited to "safe" activities, but in the Civil War, in which he also served in publicity for the republicans, he experienced gunfire, violence, and eventually imprisonment. O'Connor's statements about this period of his life are not as effusive as O'Faolain's (his later disillusionment colors his accounts of it in *An Only Child*), but he does speak of the "magical improvisation" (OC 270) of the revolution and admits to his romantic idealism, mentioning, for instance, that during this time he "saw life through a veil of literature" (OC 211).

It was in this context of personal feelings about, and experiences of, revolution that Corkery, O'Connor, and O'Faolain developed the story of romantic nationalism.

1. Sean O'Faolain, "A Portrait of the Artist as an Old Man," *Irish University Review* 6 (spring 1976): 16.

2. O'Connor began using the pen name Frank O'Connor (his middle name combined with his mother's maiden name) in the mid-1920s.

II

Romantic nationalism, a cultural and political phenomenon with roots in nineteenth-century Europe, was fashioned to instill in a people a strong emotional, even spiritual sense of their own cultural identity for the purpose of inspiring a movement toward nationhood. It attempts to do so by making people aware and proud of their heritage, especially as it is revealed in various cultural forms—literature, myth, art, music, sports, and the like—many of which need to be recovered from the past. In Ireland, romantic nationalism meant the recovery of the eclipsed Gaelic culture and its elevation above that of the dominant Anglo-Irish tradition. In the nineteenth century, romantic nationalism came to play an important role in the pursuit of an Irish nation, serving as an alternative to the more pragmatic constitutional nationalism and ultimately as a handmaiden to the more violent revolutionary nationalism.[3]

Constitutional nationalism, under the successive leadership of Daniel O'Connell, Isaac Butt, Charles Stewart Parnell, and John Redmond, pursued—over the nineteenth and early twentieth centuries—the goals of Catholic emancipation, repeal of the 1800 Act of Union, land reform, and home rule through the mostly peaceful and gradualist means of constitutional reform. The expressed goal of constitutional nationalism was home rule, a form of self-government, not full Irish independence. Nevertheless, at times constitutional nationalists allied themselves with violent revolutionaries more interested in complete independence, such as in 1879 when Parnell joined with the Fenian Michael Davitt to form the Land League. Constitutional nationalism did not, however, openly endorse violence, nor did it embrace an exclusively Irish cultural identity, at least partially because some constitutional nationalists, such as Butt and Parnell, came from the Anglo-Irish tradition. By the outbreak of world war in 1914, constitutional nationalism had failed to achieve its

3. For a discussion of romantic, revolutionary, and constitutional forms of Irish nationalism, see Alan J. Ward, *The Easter Rising: Revolution and Irish Nationalism* (Arlington Heights, Ill.: Harlan Davidson, 1980), chapters 3 and 4.

goal of home rule, prompting more violent efforts by others toward independence.

Revolutionary nationalism, committed to complete independence through "physical force" and thus the antithesis of constitutional nationalism, also began in the spirit of dual cultural identity, embracing both Anglo-Irish and Gaelic traditions. The United Irishmen, a secret society intent initially on constitutional reform, was founded in 1791 in Belfast by Anglo-Irish Protestants who advocated an independence that would embrace both cultures. It eventually turned revolutionary, and its Protestant leaders—Wolfe Tone, Lord Edward Fitzgerald, and Robert Emmet—became the hero-martyrs of the 1798 and 1803 rebellions. Young Ireland, a group of cultural nationalists that also eventually turned to violent means, was founded in the 1840s by both Catholics and Protestants who were nonsectarian in their nationalist aspirations. John Mitchel, perhaps the Young Ireland member most often associated with the failed rebellion of 1848, was an Anglo-Irish Protestant. In the latter half of the nineteenth century, membership of the major violent revolutionary organizations—the IRB in Ireland and the Fenian Brotherhood and its successor, Clan na Gael (Family of the Gaels), in America—came from both the Catholic and Protestant communities, but in their absolute commitment to Irish independence, these organizations emphasized the Gaelic tradition. A major sign of their emphasis on Gaelic identity is the fact that members of both organizations became generally known as Fenians, a name drawn from the Fianna, the warrior band of the ancient Celtic hero Fionn MacCumhaill. Sinn Féin, the political organization founded in 1907 that became—and still remains—most closely associated with Irish revolutionary nationalism, also embraced a distinctly Gaelic heritage. The organization's name, Gaelic for "ourselves," suggests a cultural exclusivity. By the time of the Easter Rising in 1916, revolutionary nationalism under the charismatic leadership of Patrick Pearse embraced the concept of an exclusive Irish identity, vigorously promoted by romantic nationalism, as the cultural foundation of a future Irish republic.

Irish romantic nationalism (also called cultural nationalism and the

Irish Ireland movement) had its roots in the first half of the nineteenth century when similar movements were taking hold in Germany and Italy. The movement began in Ireland with the founding in 1842 of the Young Ireland group, led by Thomas Davis and Charles Gavan Duffy. In the group's weekly newspaper, *Nation*, which reached a significant portion of the Irish population, Davis, Duffy, and others, as Alan J. Ward notes, "expound[ed] their view that Ireland was both a geographical and a spiritual entity." Through essays, poems, and ballads Young Ireland promoted a Gaelic vision of Ireland, "extoll[ing] the heroic image of ancient Ireland and urg[ing] the preservation of the Irish language. . . ." Although the group, made up of both Catholics and Protestants, urged a nonsectarian nationalism, arguing "that Irish nationality transcended religion and race," their intense promotion of a Gaelic cultural identity implicitly excluded the Anglo-Irish tradition.[4]

Young Ireland eventually allied itself with revolutionary nationalism, taking a militant stand against English rule and ultimately becoming involved in the failed rebellion of 1848. From the beginning, a revolutionary tenor pervaded the cultural offerings of Young Ireland, particularly the ballads[5] published in the *Nation*. Reprinted in 1843 in a separate edition entitled *The Spirit of the Nation*, these ballads often recounted the past heroic attempts of the Gael to forcibly expel the Saxon oppressor, thereby infusing the cultural awareness of romantic nationalism with the suggestion of violent rebellion characteristic of revolutionary nationalism. As Thompson remarks, "[t]hrough countless battle poems the new ideology of physical force galloped anapestically until an entire generation knew *The Nation* by heart."[6]

Romantic nationalism gathered greater momentum in the late nineteenth and early twentieth centuries, though with a far less militant

4. Ibid., 57.

5. For a selection of Davis's ballads, see the Appendix in Helen F. Mulvey, *Thomas Davis and Ireland: A Biographical Study* (Washington, D.C.: The Catholic University of America Press, 2003), 243–53.

6. William Irwin Thompson, *The Imagination of an Insurrection: Dublin, Easter 1916* (Oxford: Oxford University Press, 1967; reprint, West Stockbridge, Mass.: The Lindisfarne Press, 1982), 14 (page citations are to the reprint edition).

tenor, through concerted efforts to revive Irish history, literature, myth, folklore, sports, music, and dancing and, especially, the Gaelic language. This revival and promotion of Irish culture was the specific goal of such newly founded Irish institutions as the Gaelic Athletic Association (1884), the Irish Literary Society (1892), the National Literary Society (1892), the Gaelic League (1893), the Irish Literary Theatre (1899), the Irish Texts Society (1899), the Irish National Theatre Society (1902), and—the most famous symbol of Irish cultural identity—the Abbey Theatre (1904).

The Irish literary renaissance, begun in the last decade of the nineteenth century, was in its initial stages indistinguishable from the romantic nationalist movement. The early contributions of W. B. Yeats, Lady Augusta Gregory, J. M. Synge, and others in the form of poetry, drama, and new editions of Irish folklore, fairy tales, and myth were intended, in the spirit of romantic nationalism, to make the people of Ireland conscious of their Irish heritage. Yeats was especially taken by the Irish heroic sagas, myths, and folktales which had been revived in such texts as Standish O'Grady's books on heroic Ireland (1878–1882) and Lady Wilde's collections of Irish folktales (1887 and 1890). His interest in Gaelic culture led Yeats to publish his own collections of Irish fairy tales and folk tales, to work the Irish myths into his poems and plays, and to help found such organizations as the Irish Literary Society, the National Literary Society, and the Irish Literary Theatre in the 1890s, as well as to become one of the founders of the Abbey Theatre.

Ultimately, however, the aims and ideals of the literary renaissance and romantic nationalism diverged, and a severe rift developed between the renaissance writers and the proponents of romantic nationalism, especially those proponents intent on merging romantic and revolutionary nationalism. David Krause articulates the division between the more politically minded nationalists and the writers of the renaissance:

> [T]hey were sharply divided by the common goal of seeking to reassert the country's heritage and pride. On the nationalist side, the political spokesmen tried to establish a public cult to idealize and purify the national life; and on the literary side, the creative artists tried to express their personal views of the ideals and ironies of the national life. It was

> therefore inevitable that the artists would question and even mock many of the nationalist dogmas ... [including] the proposition that every Irishman is a courageous patriot, every Irishwomen is a paragon of virtue, and an unquestioning love of country is the greatest glory.[7]

This split between writers who sought a truer portrayal of Irish life and nationalists, both romantic and revolutionary, who preferred an idealized version to serve the cause of nationalism achieved its most divisive manifestation in the Abbey Theatre riots over Synge's *The Playboy of the Western World* (1909) and Sean O'Casey's *The Plough and the Stars* (1926). The latter play, especially, is instructive in highlighting the great gap between the writers of the literary renaissance and the revolutionary nationalists who had carried out the Easter Rising. O'Casey's play, set during the Rising, deals with two essential elements of revolutionary nationalism—violence and the myth of blood sacrifice—that the renaissance writers could not ignore but found difficult to fully endorse.

The long history of heroic but failed rebellions in Ireland led ultimately to the myth of blood sacrifice espoused by revolutionary nationalists. According to this myth, the Irish republic would ultimately be born out of the self-immolation of its hero-martyrs. Pearse especially, through the soteriological language of his speeches and writings in the years leading up to the Easter Rising, was responsible for making the myth central to revolutionary nationalism. Seán Farrell Moran says that Pearse's "ideas about blood sacrifice, redemptive violence, chiliastic expectation, and Irish national identity constitute the ideological heart of the physical-force republican tradition." Pearse fused Irish nationalism with religious aspiration, "argu[ing] that death in service to Ireland could bring personal and national redemption that would ultimately liberate the Irish people."[8] Such a seemingly irrational strategy was necessary, as Moran points out, because, as Pearse and the other leaders well

7. David Krause, *The Profane Book of Irish Comedy* (Ithaca: Cornell University Press, 1982), 106–7.

8. Seán Farrell Moran, *Patrick Pearse and the Politics of Redemption: The Mind of the Easter Rising, 1916* (Washington, D.C.: The Catholic University of America Press, 1994), 2.

knew, the Easter Rising held no potential for military success. Its only chance for achieving the goal of an independent republic was to become, as it ultimately did, a powerful symbol of revolutionary nationalism, the Irish nation rising from the blood sacrifice of its heroes.[9]

Needless to say, writers treating the theme of violence in the revolution, especially the myth of blood sacrifice, are forced to examine, and reveal, their attitude toward violence and sacrifice, and ultimately—if they are nationalists—their commitment to revolutionary nationalism. Consequently, treatments of these themes in the literature of the renaissance range widely: from Yeats's early (1902), romantic—and perhaps thoughtless[10]—treatment in his play about the rising of 1798, *Cathleen Ni Houlihan*, to O'Casey's satire of Pearse's ideas in *The Plough and the Stars*. In between lies Yeats's great poem "Easter 1916," which takes an ambivalent attitude toward the sacrifice of the hero-martyrs, expressing awe over their transformative act ("A terrible beauty is born") while questioning its wisdom ("Was it needless death after all?").

The most intense literary expressions of faith in the myth of blood sacrifice are found in the works of Pearse and Joseph Mary Plunkett. MacDara, the hero of Pearse's play *The Singer*, is "the rebel [as] the perfect imitation of Christ"[11]: he willingly gives his life for Ireland. The final couplet of Plunkett's poem "The Little Black Rose Shall be Red at Last," which uses the symbol of the rose as Ireland, is perhaps the most succinct expression of the myth: "Praise God if this my blood fulfils the doom / When you, dark rose, shall redden into bloom."[12] But the principal commitment of Pearse, Plunkett, and Thomas MacDonagh, the other poet to be executed after the Rising, was unquestionably to revolution and their own self-immolation, not to poetry. Poetry, insofar as it fer-

9. Ibid., 14–15.

10. In a late poem, "The Man and the Echo," Yeats seems to express regret over the effect *Cathleen ni Houlihan* might have had on nationalists: "Did that play of mine send out / Certain men the English shot?"

11. Thompson, *Insurrection*, 118.

12. See Thompson, *Insurrection*, especially chapters 4, 5, and 7, for commentary on the treatment of the myth in the works of Pearse, Plunkett, Thomas MacDonagh, Yeats, and O'Casey.

vently expressed the ideals of the revolution, was a means to the republic, not an end in itself. Costello says of these three poets: "They gave themselves to the great theme of their poetry, the cause of Ireland, and made the Rising not merely a political event but also a poetic creation."[13]

The three writers of the romantic stories examined in this chapter—Corkery, O'Connor, and O'Faolain—present a different case than those mentioned above. Unlike Yeats and O'Casey, all three were fully committed to the revolution; and unlike Pearse, Plunkett, and MacDonagh, who were once referred to as "the three Bad Poets of the Rising,"[14] their works that treat the revolution are valued more for the literary qualities than for ideological impact. All three were ardent romantic nationalists *and* aspiring artists who sought to capture Ireland in their literature. In 1908, Corkery had helped found the Cork Dramatic Society, which produced plays, some in Gaelic, about Irish historic and mythic themes. By the time of the Easter Rising, Corkery had also published *King and Hermit* (1909), a play written in Irish English (sometimes referred to as Hiberno-English), and *A Munster Twilight* (1916), a collection of stories about Gaelic peasants. O'Faolain and O'Connor, still in their teens when the rebellion occurred, aspired to be writers in the romantic nationalist tradition, having become infatuated with Gaelic culture. The stories of all three illustrate the literary merger of romantic and revolutionary nationalism, as well as provide insightful perspectives on the issue of violence as a means of achieving the goal of an independent Ireland. Interestingly, and perhaps revealingly, none of the three—not even Corkery, the most ardent nationalist of the three—touches the theme of blood sacrifice in the short story.[15]

13. Peter Costello, *The Heart Grown Brutal: The Irish Revolution in Literature from Parnell to the Death of Yeats, 1891–1939* (Dublin: Gill and Macmillan, 1977), 83.

14. Ibid., 77.

15. Of the short-story writers discussed in this and the next chapter, only Liam O'Flaherty treated the theme of blood sacrifice. He did so, however, not in his short stories, but in two of his novels: *The Martyr* (1933), set during the Civil War, and *Insurrection* (1950), set during the Easter Rising. Each depicts the blood sacrifice of its hero, Commandant Crosbie and Bartly Madden, respectively, the latter in a more sympathetic light than the former.

III

The fictional mode of romantic nationalism consists of a complex of thematic, structural, and stylistic elements that can be grouped under the two categories of "romantic aspects" and "nationalism." The category of romantic aspects links these stories to the Romantic Age of literature, particularly to the idealistic "spirit of the age" and to the romance genre favored by the Romantic writers as the best vehicle for that spirit. Nationalism, which in this case must be seen in the context of colonial or post-colonial theory, involves the pursuit of an independent Irish nation, to be achieved through an armed, violent struggle against the colonial power, the British Empire. This struggle is encouraged among the Irish people through the recognition and advocacy of an Irish cultural identity distinct from that of the English colonizers. The merger of these two categories in various thematic, structural, and stylistic ways results in the story of romantic nationalism.

These stories are romantic, then, in that they resemble the literature of the Romantic Age in several important aspects. The most significant resemblance is that both Romantic literature and these Irish stories express a belief in the attainment of the Ideal through revolution. In his essay "English Romanticism: The Spirit of the Age," M. H. Abrams identifies the prevailing spirit or emotion of the Romantic Age as the idealistic belief that the world might be changed for the better through revolution—"[t]he intoxicating sense that now everything was possible."[16] This spirit was inspired in the Romantics by the advent of the French Revolution with its republican vision of social and political equality. Corkery, O'Connor, and O'Faolain were similarly inspired by the Easter Rising and the War of Independence, events that gave rise to the very real possibility of attaining the ideal of an independent Irish Republic. No doubt they had the French Revolution in mind. O'Faolain later wrote: "During those heavenly years [1918–1924] I dreamed of lib-

16. M. H. Abrams, "English Romanticism: The Spirit of the Age," in *The Correspondent Breeze: Essays in English Romanticism* (New York: Norton, 1984), 49.

erty, equality, fraternity"[17]—evoking the slogan of the French revolutionaries. As the Romantic poets had hoped to spread their idealistic feelings and revolutionary ideals among their English readers, so Corkery wrote his stories of romantic nationalism in order to infect the Irish people with feelings of revolutionary ardor and idealism, while O'Connor and O'Faolain wrote theirs to pay tribute to those feelings that they and others had once experienced.

Bald expressions of revolutionary exaltation are found throughout these stories. The narrator of "The Patriarch," one of O'Connor's stories, says, "One is glad to have been young in such a time" (GN 215), echoing Wordsworth's famous lines in *The Prelude* about the Romantics' feelings for the French Revolution ("Bliss was it in that dawn to be alive, / But to be young was very Heaven!"). Another of O'Connor's characters is exhilarated by "a world of youth and comradeship and adventure" (GN 182) that awaits her as a participant in the rebellion. The narrator of "Seumas," a story by Corkery, exclaims: "After the Rising there was in Ireland, as everyone knows, a sense of spiritual exaltation . . ." (HB 95). Although these overt statements make clear the writers' feelings, the feelings are even more forcefully conveyed through the structure and style of the stories.

Northrop Frye states that the social and intellectual leaders of an age often "project [their] ideals in some form of romance," which he says is "nearest of all literary forms to the wish-fulfillment dream."[18] The Romantics made the romance the pre-eminent genre of their age. Corkery, who saw himself as a leading advocate of Irish nationalism, also turned to the romance genre, though he developed it in the form of the short story rather than poetry, the favored form of the Romantics. O'Connor and O'Faolain followed their mentor's lead.

The essential element of the romance genre, whether embodied in fiction, poetry, or drama, is a sequence of exciting, often dangerous adventures undertaken by a hero, usually for the love or benefit of a lady.

17. O'Faolain, "Portrait," 16.

18. Northrop Frye, *The Anatomy of Criticism: Four Essays* (Princeton: Princeton University Press, 1957), 186.

Some romances—Frye calls them "naïve"—are simply a seemingly endless series of adventures without a shaping principle or a structured ending.[19] More "sophisticated"—and famous—romances, such as Spenser's *The Faerie Queen,* Keats's *The Eve of St. Agnes,* and various versions of the Arthurian legend, are structured by the hero's quest for a goal or prize, such as the lady herself or a buried treasure, or a grander goal, such as the liberation of a people or the regeneration of a wasteland. When the adventures are patterned after this quest archetype, the hero's success, or failure, in the quest brings the story to an end.[20]

The quest, of course, belongs not just to the hero but to the hero's community, to the writer of the romance and to his or her readers—in short, to humanity. Moreover, the quest goes beyond the literal goal of the hero: it symbolizes the larger ideal of the human community. That ideal is, as Frye has argued, the earthly paradise: the perfect human community—fertile, abundant, socially harmonious, and free of pain, suffering, evil, old age, and even death. It is "a world in which the inner desire and the outward circumstance coincide," "the innocent world of fulfilled desires, the free human society."[21]

This is the purpose to which the Romantics put the romance genre. While the goal of the French Revolution for a just and equal society was the initial ideal of the Romantics, their eventual vision was, as Abrams says, far greater: "a new man on a new earth which is a restored paradise."[22] The goal of the Irish revolutionaries—rebels and writers—was perhaps less grand than that of the Romantics in the sense that it was limited to the creation of a new Irish nation, or the recovery of an imaginary lost one. It was, nevertheless, envisioned in idealistic terms—a society in which justice, equality, social harmony, and, especially, economic prosperity would prevail because oppressive English rule would cease. Pearse expressed the ideal in this way:

19. Ibid.

20. Ibid., 187.

21. Northrop Frye, "The Archetypes of Literature," in *Fables of Identity: Studies in Poetic Mythology* (New York: Harcourt, Brace, 1963), 18.

22. Abrams, "Romanticism," 57.

> A free Ireland would not, and could not, have hunger in her fertile vales and squalor in her cities. Ireland has resources to feed five times her population; a free Ireland would make those resources available. A free Ireland would drain the bogs, would harness the rivers, would plant the wastes, would nationalize the railways and waterways, would improve agriculture, would protect fisheries, would foster industries, would promote commerce, would diminish extravagant expenditures . . . , would beautify the cities, would educate the workers . . . , would, in short, govern herself as no external power—nay, not even a government of angels and archangels could govern her.[23]

Structurally, the Irish stories of romantic nationalism represent the first of the three stages of the quest romance, that is, "the stage of the perilous journey and the preliminary minor adventures."[24] The typical plot presents a rebel hero engaged in risky revolutionary adventures, such as attacking colonial forces, holding secret meetings, or fleeing the enemy while under fire. Corkery's "A Bye-Product" and O'Connor's "Attack," for instance, feature assaults on the enemy. Corkery's "An Unfinished Symphony," O'Connor's "September Dawn," and O'Faolain's "Fugue" all depict exciting flights of their rebel heroes. The immediate, limited goal of the rebel is to attack, or escape from, the enemy, and the story ends when the rebel either succeeds or fails in his endeavor. But there is never a sense of full closure in these stories because the promise of another revolutionary adventure looms ahead for the rebel, and because the ultimate goal of an Irish nation remains unfulfilled. The limited adventures of these individual stories, however, point to the greater quest for an Irish nation, and while no individual story completes that quest (as a traditional romance would), each one is to be imagined as a small step toward its fulfillment. No single story of romantic nationalism shows the completed quest, nor even the final stage of completion, because in actuality an Irish republic was not achieved during the historical period in which the stories are set. Corkery's stories, published in

23. Patrick H. Pearse, "From a Hermitage," in *Political Writings and Speeches* (Dublin: Talbot Press, 1952), 180, quoted in Terence Brown, *Ireland: A Social and Cultural History, 1922 to the Present* (Ithaca: Cornell University Press, 1985), 13.

24. Frye, *Anatomy,* 187.

the midst of the War of Independence, were intended to encourage the quest, whereas those of O'Connor and O'Faolain, written in the years after the failed quest (failed in the sense that the Free State was not the ideal the rebels envisioned), were written to record the spirit of the quest.

The Irish stories are also structured like the quest romance in the way that they arrange the conflict. Frye says that in the romance "everything is focussed on a conflict between the hero and his enemy, and all the reader's values are bound up with the hero."[25] Thus, in the Irish stories the conflict is most often either an outright physical struggle between Irish rebels and imperial forces or a disagreement between the rebels and Irish civilians who are initially reluctant, but finally willing, to support the rebels in their cause. In both cases, the conflict is developed in such a way as to ensure the reader's identification with the hero and his fellow rebels.

True to the nature of romance, most of these stories do not develop any serious moral qualms in the rebel hero regarding the validity of the revolutionary cause or the often violent means used to pursue it. O'Faolain says that during the revolution "all moral problems vanished in the fire of patriotism,"[26] and these stories are proof of that. Corkery does not build his stories on moral conflict, for he sees no troubling moral questions about the motives, methods, or ideals of the rebels. As Benedict Kiely says, in Corkery's stories "there is no evident internal division, no heartscalding contradiction. . . ."[27] None of Corkery's characters is ready to give up the revolutionary ideal because of moral qualms, although several of his stories are built on the question of whether the young rebels have the necessary courage and resolve to carry on the struggle. In the end, Corkery always shows his rebels capable of heroism and thus removes any doubt. For instance, Muirish, an old Fenian in "On the Heights," at first scoffs at the Irish Volunteers who are secretly training

25. Ibid.

26. O'Faolain, "Portrait," 16.

27. Benedict Kiely, *Modern Irish Fiction—A Critique* (Dublin: Golden Eagle Books, 1950), 9.

for rebellion in the mountains, but the 1916 Rising convinces him of their heroism and so he contributes to their cause with a bag of Fenian gold he has held in trust for fifty years. In several of O'Connor's and O'Faolain's romantic stories, the rebel protagonists express a temporary weariness over the revolution, but only in O'Faolain's "The Patriot" is the issue of doubt treated as the major theme.

In addition to using the romance genre with its quest structure and clear-cut conflict to create a spirit of revolution, Corkery and the others use the language and imagery associated with Romantic literature, especially romantic pastoral literature. The countryside settings of these stories—most are set in Munster, particularly in the hills, mountains, and vales of western Cork—provide the opportunity for descriptive romantic passages filled with nouns like *mist, dew, dusk, glow, moonlight*, and *dawn;* color adjectives such as *silver, golden, green, grey,* and *rosy;* and verbals such as *darkened, brightened, glowing, rustling,* and *flashing.* A typical sentence in these stories is this one from O'Connor's "September Dawn": "The sunlight swam in a rosy mist before his darkened eyes" (GN 81). Romantic abstractions—*youth, beauty, passion, joy, emotion, danger,* and the like—recur frequently, as in this sentence from O'Faolain's "Fugue": "Excited by danger, and by the beauty of this calm place, the falling stream beside me, the trees moving all around, I began to think again of the young woman in the black cloak . . ." (CSO 55); or this one from Corkery's "An Unfinished Symphony": "I was drinking a cup full of joy in a night of serene and stately beauty" (HB 165).

There is one other resemblance between the literature of the Romantic Age and these Irish stories. The best of these Irish stories may be said to have been written, as Abrams says of the great Romantic poems, "not in the mood of revolutionary exaltation but in the later mood of revolutionary disillusionment or despair."[28] Two of the best stories to be written about the revolution, O'Faolain's "The Patriot" and O'Connor's "Guests of the Nation," were created out of their authors' disillusionment and despair over the direction events had taken.

28. Abrams, "Romanticism," 62.

IV

If an understanding of key elements of Romantic literature helps in an analysis of the romantic aspects of the stories of romantic nationalism, then post-colonial literary theory illuminates the aspects of nationalism. Post-colonial theory identifies the themes and stylistic features that writers develop in order to portray the quest for nationalism in a colonial situation. Most of these themes and stylistic features are present in the Irish stories of romantic nationalism.

The central post-colonial themes, according to the authors of *The Empire Writes Back,* a major post-colonial theoretical text, are oppression, exile, displacement, and "cultural denigration," the last defined as "the conscious and unconscious oppression of the indigenous personality and culture by a supposedly superior racial or cultural model."[29] To balance these negative themes, the post-colonial text offers "the celebration of the struggle towards independence,"[30] national independence being, of course, the goal toward which colonized people quest. This struggle for nationhood is signaled in post-colonial texts through a variety of supporting themes, including the creation of a "sentimental connection," Antonio Gramsci's term for the emotional tie between the leaders of the revolution and the people whose emotional, moral, and economic support is indispensable to the attainment of the goal.[31] Another important means of supporting the struggle for nationhood in post-colonial texts is the theme of "identity-thinking," the re-establishment of cultural identity among the oppressed people whose culture has been denigrated and replaced by that of the colonizer.[32]

Violence is also a pervasive theme in post-colonial literature, sanctioned as requisite for the attainment of the new nation. As David

29. Bill Ashcroft, Garth Griffiths, and Helen Tiffin, *The Empire Writes Back: Theory and Practice in Post-Colonial Literatures* (New York: Routledge, 1989), 8–9.

30. Ibid., 27.

31. Antonio Gramsci, *Selections from the Prison Notebooks* (London: Lawrence and Wishart, 1971), cited in David Cairns and Shaun Richards, *Writing Ireland: Colonialism, Nationalism and Culture* (Manchester, England: Manchester University Press, 1988), 14.

32. Ashcroft, Griffiths, and Tiffin, *Empire,* 9.

Lloyd, invoking the concepts of Walter Benjamin, explains in *Anomalous States: Irish Writing and the Post-Colonial Moment,* "bloodshed is subordinated to the founding of the state."[33] The violence, however, is often muted or otherwise presented in a palatable form since, if too vivid, there is the danger that the reader will be repulsed and the bond between writer and reader will be broken. One palatable form of violence, for example, depicted in post-colonial literature is the destruction of colonial buildings, the metonymic representations of colonial power.[34] The brutal killing or maiming of the enemy, of informers, or of innocent civilians, while certainly a reality in revolutions, is a less common occurrence in post-colonial literature because, again, it may very well counteract the intended effect of the literature.

Post-colonial themes, particularly those of identity-thinking and the sentimental connection, are effected in post-colonial texts through a set of stylistic features. These features include cultural allusions, allegory, descriptions of the landscape, references to places important to the oppressed people, a sprinkling of the native language (words, names, phrases, and idioms), and the use of "syntactic fusion" in which the vocabulary of the oppressor's language is phrased in the syntax of the native language.[35] Allusions to the oppressed people's cultural heritage—ethnic traits and customs, myths and legends, religion, historical events and heroes, songs, sports, and poetry—serve to promote identity-thinking among readers and create a sentimental connection between them and the writers of the texts, who represent the leaders of the struggle for nationhood. Allegory, either taken from the cultural heritage or newly created to convey messages related to the nationalist struggle, also furthers these ends. Description or mention of the landscape and places dear to the oppressed people helps to reconnect them to the land, thus overcoming the sense of displacement that the colonial power has created in them.[36]

33. David Lloyd, *Anomalous States: Irish Writing and the Post-Colonial Moment* (Durham: Duke University Press, 1993), 126.

34. Ashcroft, Griffiths, and Tiffin, *Empire,* 28.

35. Ibid., 8–10, 28, 56–59, 68–72.

36. Ibid., 8–9.

The use of linguistic elements in post-colonial texts to promote identity-thinking, a sentimental connection, and, ultimately, a desire for nationalism is more complex. In many colonial situations, the native language has been suppressed to the point that its recovery among the people is deemed by the leaders of the nationalist movement as too difficult to achieve, despite its importance to a sense of cultural identity. The alternative, then, is to appropriate the colonizer's language and reconstitute it in such a way that it becomes distinct from the oppressor's language and part of the oppressed people's cultural identity. The authors of *The Empire Writes Back* refer to this, among British colonies, as transforming "English" (with a capital E) to "english" (with a small e).[37]

The Irish stories of romantic nationalism contain all of these post-colonial themes and stylistic features. The themes of oppression, violence, exile, and displacement are evoked through the recurrent narrative element of the rebel on the run from the forces of oppression—English troops, Black and Tans, the RIC, or, in stories of the Civil War, Free State soldiers. The rebels are exiles in their own land, displaced and forced to hide and conduct their meetings and drills in secrecy. At the same time, they are carrying out the struggle for nationhood, at times through violent attacks but more often by spreading their fervent nationalism among the people. When violence does occur in these stories, it is most often reported, rather than dramatized, so as not to convey any brutal, gruesome, or otherwise repulsive quality to it, and it is often associated with the romantic aspects of revolution. For instance, in "Attack," one of O'Connor's stories, Volunteers are planning an attack on a police barracks, but the story's main focus is on the relationship of the Volunteers to the people who are harboring them, and the story ends before the actual attack begins. Furthermore, O'Connor gives the attack a romantic, unreal quality by having children sing in the street: "Do you want your old barracks blown down, blown down? / Do you want your old barracks blown down?" (GN 21). The primary focus of these stories is the spirit of Irish nationalism, which is intensified through the two

37. Ibid., chapter 2.

most important post-colonial themes of identity-thinking and the sentimental connection.

A sentimental connection occurs both within the story of romantic nationalism, between the rebels and the Irish characters who sympathize with them, and in the reading process, between the writers who advocate revolution and the readers who come to imaginatively believe in it. The typical plot of the romantic story includes an encounter, in an isolated cottage, inn or barn, between one or more rebels on the run and Irish sympathizers—old people, families, young women, nuns, innkeepers—who hide, shelter, and feed the rebels and offer them moral support. The physical support of shelter and food is, of course, important, but the emotional and moral support—at the core of the sentimental connection—is paramount. O'Faolain remarks in *Vive Moi!* on the importance of the sentimental connection in the War of Independence: "They [the rebels] could not, it must always be said, have done anything without the silence, patience, and loyal help of the whole people" (VM 181). This sentimental connection between the Irish people and the rebels had been secured when, after the Easter Rising, the British executed Pearse, Connolly, and other leaders and thereby turned civilian hostility toward the rebels into sympathy and support for them and their cause.

In most of these stories, such as O'Connor's "September Dawn" and "Laughter," O'Faolain's "Fugue," and Corkery's "The Ember," "The Aherns," and "On the Heights," the rebels are welcomed and encouraged by the Irish people, thus bolstering the rebels' spirits and giving them the courage to continue the fight. The narrator of "The Ember" exalts in the support that he feels: "How their Irish welcome went round my heart! Gaels of the Gael, they received me, spoke to me, welcomed me, slaved for me in the true Gaelic spirit . . . " (HB 25). In some stories the importance of the people's support is signaled to the reader by the effect on the rebels when it is withheld. In O'Connor's "Nightpiece with Figures," set during the Civil War when support for the republicans was not pervasive, one of the rebels hiding in a barn bitterly tells his sympathizer, a nun, that the people are "against" them. In other stories rebels must win the sympathy and support of the people by demonstrating their courage and determination.

A sentimental connection is also effected between writer and reader in many of these stories through the use of allegory, a kind of code understood by those with ties to each other but not by outsiders. The central allegory of the Irish nationalist movement is, of course, that Ireland is a woman (Cathleen ni Houlihan, Dark Rosaleen, the Shan van Vocht, the Aisling figure) whose lands have been seized by strangers. This allegory appears in somewhat veiled form (far less obvious, say, than in Yeats's play *Cathleen ni Houlihan)* in Corkery's "An Unfinished Symphony," O'Connor's "September Dawn," and O'Faolain's "Fugue." In all of these stories the protagonist is a young rebel on the run, and in each case he meets or seeks union with a beautiful young woman somehow linked to the nationalist movement. In each story the rebel hero is denied permanent union with the young woman and is forced to continue his struggle against imperial forces. In O'Faolain's "Fugue," the lovers are interrupted by a girl who has come to warn the protagonist that his fellow rebel has been taken by the Black and Tans, who are now coming for him. In Corkery's "An Unfinished Symphony," the hero is a Volunteer organizer who hears that his lover is nearby and decides to "dare all and go to her" (HB 155), but he is caught at the train station by the police and spends the night in Cork jail. O'Connor's "September Dawn" ends at dawn with the rebel amorously embracing the daughter of the family harboring him and his companion, but there is no doubt that the rebels will have to move on as the day begins. In all three stories the allegorical meaning is clear: consummation and permanent union with the woman, the symbol of Ireland, will be achieved only when the Irish nation is established.

The theme of sentimental connection is closely bound in these stories to the re-establishment of Irish cultural identity: sympathizers help rebels because they share a cultural identity and a desire for their culture to be the basis of an Irish nation. The theme of cultural identity in Irish literature, including these stories, raises, however, an essential question: What exactly are the essential elements of Irish identity? In answering that question, some Irish nationalists have claimed that Irish identity is rooted in Celtic ethnicity, the Gaelic language, the Catholic religion, and the peasant class. But this answer, as scholars have shown, is simplistic.

The authors of *Writing Ireland: Colonialism, Nationalism and Culture* trace the issue of Irish identity as it is created by writers throughout Ireland's history. David Cairns and Shaun Richards show that the key cultural elements of ethnicity, language, religion, and class are formulated and reformulated in various ways over time in the effort to portray the "true" Irish identity. Claims for the authenticity of Gaelic language and ethnicity, Catholicism, and the peasantry are established and then challenged, though never completely overturned, by counter-claims for the authenticity of Anglo-Irish ethnicity (with its English language), Protestantism, and the bourgeoisie. The result is a succession of shifting Irish identities, revolving on the axes of Gaelic and Anglo-Irish, Catholic and Protestant, and peasant and bourgeoisie.[38]

Of all these elements, that of Celtic ethnicity has made the strongest claim as an element of Irish identity. Indeed, by the twentieth century, ethnicity as a component of Irish identity quite clearly meant Celtic, or Gaelic. The Celts had settled in Ireland several centuries before Christ and therefore had the longest historical claim of any recorded people to Irish identity. By contrast, the first group of invaders from England, the Anglo-Normans, who in many ways assimilated Irish culture and therefore made claim to being "Irish," did not arrive until the twelfth century. Even nationalists who came from the Anglo-Irish branch of the population promoted Gaelic identity. Douglas Hyde, for example, co-founded the Gaelic League and urged the "de-anglicising" of Ireland. As noted above, writers such as Yeats, Synge, and Lady Gregory, all descendants of Anglo-Irish families, promoted Celtic and Gaelic identity through the re-creation of Celtic myths, the recounting of Irish folklore, and the portrayal of Gaelic peasants. In their famous statement announcing the Irish Literary Theatre, Yeats and Lady Gregory proposed "a Celtic and Irish

38. Cairns and Richards, *Writing Ireland*, see especially chapters 4, 5, and 6.

school of dramatic literature" that would "bring upon the stage the deeper thoughts and emotions of Ireland."[39] Whereas in previous centuries some nationalists had sought to include aspects of English culture in Irish identity, or even claim Anglo-Irish as the true Irish identity, by the twentieth century any serious attempt to do so was moribund.

Regarding the issue of Celtic ethnicity (or "Celticism," as it was sometimes called), Cairns and Richards point out that the English and Anglo-Irish people often accepted without question the analysis Matthew Arnold advanced in "On the Study of Celtic Literature." Arnold attributed to the Celtic nature such attractive traits as sensitivity, love of natural beauty and color, spirituality, and otherworldliness. Against these virtues, he balanced such flaws as emotionalism, willfulness, and ineffectuality in politics and other practical matters—flaws that justified in the eyes of the Anglo-Irish their own superior position.[40] Writers of Gaelic heritage or sympathy promoted the positive and ignored or rejected the negative Celtic qualities described by Arnold. Defining Irish identity by personality traits, however, is a questionable practice, given the extensive intermixture of Celtic people with others who came to Ireland, for example, the Norse and the Normans. As Richard J. Loftus points out, it is more convincing to characterize the Irish by reference to their history: hence, writers of the literary renaissance portrayed the Irish as possessing "tragic heroism" and "a spirit of perseverance," developed over the long centuries of suffering from foreign invasions of the Vikings, Normans, and Elizabethans, as well as the crushing effects of Cromwell's massacre, the penal laws, famine, and emigration.[41]

Regarding the component of social class, by the turn of the twentieth century the peasantry (i.e., the tenant farmer) was the class most closely associated with Irish identity. Historically, Irish peasants traced their lin-

39. Lady Augusta Gregory, "Our Irish Theatre," in *Modern Irish Drama,* ed. John P. Harrington (New York: Norton, 1991), 378.

40. Cairns and Richards, *Writing Ireland*, 47–50.

41. Richard J. Loftus, *Nationalism in Modern Anglo-Irish Poetry* (Madison: The University of Wisconsin Press, 1964), 23–24.

eage back to the Gaels, so as a class the peasantry was nearly synonymous with Gaelic, or Celtic, ethnicity. Moreover, many Irish peasants spoke Gaelic and embraced Catholicism, the other elements thought to characterize Irish identity. In many of the literary works of the Irish renaissance, especially drama, the peasant was idealized as the true Gael (so much so that the term "Peasant Quality" came into use to refer—often cynically—to this practice). As for a Gaelic ruling class, it had disappeared. The Gaelic chieftains, such as Red Hugh O'Donnell and Hugh O'Neill, had been eradicated or driven out of Ireland in the sixteenth and seventeenth centuries.

In contrast, members of Ireland's ruling and middle classes were often of English heritage: descendants of the Anglo-Norman invaders, the Elizabethan settlers of the sixteenth and seventeenth centuries, and the Protestant Ascendancy of the eighteenth century. In previous centuries some Anglo-Norman nobles, like the Fitzgeralds of Munster, had become as the saying goes "more Irish than the Irish themselves," and many from the Anglo-Irish middle and upper classes had proven their Irishness by leading rebellions against England (Tone, Fitzgerald, and Emmet, to cite the most famous). In the twentieth century, however, literary depictions of Ireland's ruling class (landowners, government officials, politicians, etc.) were often characterized as less than Irish or even hostile to the Irish, thereby reinforcing the idea that the divide between ruler and ruled, bourgeois and peasant, was identical to the ethnic divide between Anglo-Irish and Gaelic. In this formulation, the peasantry was truly Irish; the bourgeoisie was not.

Religion as a component of Irish cultural identity has not always been as clear-cut as it seems today when, in the much publicized Northern Troubles, most nationalists are Catholic (or from a Catholic heritage) and most unionists, Protestant. Historically, the situation is more complex. While those of Gaelic heritage have for the most part retained their Catholic identity, many of the Anglo-Norman families, who settled in Ireland as Catholics, also refused to embrace the Protestant religion after Henry VIII's break from Rome. Furthermore, as mentioned above, not all of the English Protestant families who settled in Ireland remained loyal to the crown. Tone, Fitzgerald, Emmet, Mitchel, Davis, and Parnell, to name some of the more prominent nationalists, came from Protestant backgrounds. Among writers and scholars who supported the nationalist movement in the late nineteenth and early twentieth century, Yeats, Lady Gregory, Hyde, and Synge were all from Protestant families. In other words, historically in Ireland—even in the first part of the twentieth century—one could be both Protestant and nationalist. Adding to the complexity is the fact that the Catholic Church has not always supported the nationalist cause, particularly the physical force movement. The Catholic clergy often condemned the Fenian movement of the mid-nineteenth century, and some of its members were instrumental in Parnell's downfall, thus delaying the progress toward nationhood. One result of this complex situation is that religion does not appear as a particularly important element of Irish identity in much of the literature of the renaissance.

Language is universally recognized as an essential component of cultural identity, and it is no different with regard to Irish identity. Many, though not all, of the Irish nationalists believed in the importance of the Gaelic language (the great Catholic statesman Daniel O'Connell did not) and, thus, worked to make it a key part of the nationalist movement despite formidable obstacles. By the nineteenth century, English was commonplace in the east and northeast of Ireland, and the British introduction in 1831 of the national school system, which taught children in English, furthered the decline of Gaelic. By the end of the century, the Gaelic-speaking population in the west had been dramatically reduced through famine and emigration. The few remaining pockets of Gaelic speakers in the west became known as the Gaeltacht areas.

The most systematic attempt to recover the Gaelic language and make it a cornerstone of the romantic nationalist movement was the creation of the Gaelic League in 1893 by Hyde, Eoin MacNeill, and others. Mostly social in function, the League had an extensive branch system that offered Irish language classes and social gatherings that featured Gaelic music, songs, poetry, and dances. Gaelic was also employed for political and literary uses but less extensively. According to Moran,

Pearse "equated the language movement with the national movement"[42] and argued that "[w]hen Ireland's language is established, her own distinctive culture is assured."[43] Interestingly, Pearse did not use Gaelic (except for the title: *Poblacht na hEireann*) in writing the most important of republican political documents, the 1916 Proclamation. He did, however, write short stories in Gaelic, publishing two collections: *Íosagán agus Sgéalta Eile* (1907) and *An Mháthair agus Sgéalta Eile* (1916). There were other efforts in the early twentieth century to make Gaelic common in literature. Hyde's play *Casadh-an-tSúgáin* was performed in Gaelic by the Irish Literary Theatre in 1901. In 1902, George Moore had several of his stories translated into Gaelic (he was not proficient in the language) and published in a collection entitled *An tÚrGhort*. (In 1903 he published those stories, and others, in English as *The Untilled Field*, the first collection of modern Irish stories.) Despite these accomplishments, the greater part of the literature of the renaissance was written in English, the language of the colonizer.

These four components of cultural identity—ethnicity, language, religion, and class—are found in the stories of romantic nationalism in varying degrees, from the pervasive presence of Gaelic ethnicity to the relative scarcity of Catholicism. The peasant class is frequently portrayed in the stories and is obviously intended to represent the "true" Irish, though class is not emphasized as extensively as ethnicity. The Irish language is also represented in the stories through occasional Gaelic words, names, phrases, and sentences. All three writers—Corkery, O'Connor, and O'Faolain—were proficient in Gaelic but chose not to write their stories in Gaelic, most likely in order to reach a wider audience. Instead, they employ the post-colonial strategy of appropriating and reconstituting English, the language of the oppressor, into a language that suits their purpose of creating a national or cultural identity.

Gaelic, or Celtic, ethnicity is advocated in these stories through post-colonial stylistic features. Allusions to Celtic and Gaelic culture are per-

42. Moran, *Pearse*, 114.

43. Patrick H. Pearse, *An Claidheamh Soluis*, 27 August 1904, quoted in Moran, *Pearse*, 115.

vasive. Corkery frequently refers to "the Gael" and to "Eirinn," the Old Irish name for Ireland, and he alludes to Celtic mythical heroes and heroines, such as Oisin, Cuchulain, Emer, Deirdre, and Naisi. In "The Ember" he refers to old Fenians, who once took part in rebellion but are now too old for the struggle, as "Oisins dreaming of the heroic dead they have so long outlived" (HB 16). His allusion reminds the Irish reader that the current rebels are related back through the Fenians of the nineteenth century to Oisin and his father Fionn, the eponymic founder of the heroic warriors. Celtic fables are also alluded to: the narrator of O'Faolain's "Fugue," wearied by his flight from the Black and Tans and hearing in the woods the cry of an owl, recalls a Celtic fable of an owl watching the slow passing of time.

Popular Irish songs, poems, and ballads, such as "Wrap the Green Flag round me, Boys" and "The Felons of Our Land," are also frequently alluded to, or quoted in part or full, in these stories. In the nineteenth century Young Irelanders Davis and Duffy advocated the use of ballads, which could easily reach the great masses of Irish, to instill a sense of Irish nationalism in the people. These stories incorporate that concept. Some of the quoted lines are designed to evoke the Celtic sensitivity for, and love of, the natural beauty of the land: "O-o-oh! / Will anybody tell me where the Blarney roses grow? / Is it over in Kilmurry South, or yonder in Cloghroe?" (CSO 45); but more often the lyrics express a strong anti-colonial sentiment: "No more our ancient sireland / Shall shelter the despot or the slave" (HB 84). Sometimes they combine elements of both:

'Tis Ireland, 'tis beautiful Ireland
Ireland, the gem of the sea,
Oh, my heart is at home in old Ireland,
And I wish that old Ireland was free. (HB 144)

Historical and heroic allusions are also plentiful in these stories, but they do not promote Gaelic identity exclusively over Anglo-Irish. Anglo-Irish nationalist heroes, such as Tone, Emmet, and Parnell, are as readily evoked and honored as are the Gaelic heroes, such as the O'Neills, O'Donnells, and O'Sullivans. In O'Connor's "September Dawn," the peasant family that gives shelter to the two fleeing rebels has pictures of Emmet and Parnell on the wall. Allusions to historical events such as the flight of the Earls (the Gaelic chieftains), Cromwell's massacre of the Irish Catholics, the Battle of the Boyne in which the Catholic James was defeated by the English forces, and—in stories set after 1916—the Easter Rising, as well as to such historical revolutionary groups as Fenians, rapparees (Gaelic *rapaire*), and Cumann na mBan help, however, to portray the national movement in Gaelic terms.

Descriptions of landscape and references to Gaelic place names, particularly in western areas, are also very effective ways to create a sense of cultural identity and nationalism; they also help counter the feelings of displacement and dislocation felt by colonized people. The authors of *The Empire Writes Back* argue that "the special post-colonial crisis of identity comes into being" when the displacement that colonized people feel destroys "an effective identifying relationship between self and place." This feeling of displacement, they note, need not result from a literal displacement from one's native country; it may result as well from the cultural denigration that the colonizer undertakes.[44] For example, the British project in the early 1800s to map Ireland and, in the process, Anglicize the Gaelic place names served to dislocate and psychologically displace the Irish. Invoking the Gaelic names helps to overcome those effects.

The republicans understood the importance of evoking a sense of Gaelic place in their drive toward nationalism. In *Vive Moi!* O'Faolain writes of their intention to preserve the aspects of western Ireland that held great symbolic import: "the Gaelic-speaking West, its hard ancestral memories, its ancient ways, its trackless mountains, small cottages, lonely lakes, ruined hermit chapels, [and] wild rocky seas" (VM 188–89). Hence, these stories of romantic nationalism attempt to re-establish the "identifying relationship" between the Irish people and the land by evoking the natural beauty of the land and its traditional Gaelic identity. They are all set in the Gaelic province of Munster, mostly in the rural ar-

44. Ashcroft, Griffiths, and Tiffin, *Empire,* 8–9.

eas—the mountains, hills, and vales—of western Cork, though also at times in the city of Cork. Narrators and characters refer frequently to Gaelic place names in Munster: Inchigeela, Glenmanus, Rossbuidhe, Kilsheelan, Rossadoon, Knockacashlawn, and Gougane Barra, among many others. They also use Gaelic-derived words for landscape features: bog, glen, coom, cairn, and bohereen (or boreen). All three writers also dwell at length on the natural beauty of western Ireland, a trait associated with the Celtic character. The following passage from O'Connor's "September Dawn" describing the rebels' approach to a safe house is typical:

> It was darkening when they reached her house, and having stowed their rifles away in a dry wall, they made their way up the long winding boreen to the top of the hill. A sombre maternal peace enveloped the whole countryside; the fields were a rich green that merged into grey and farther off into a deep, shining purple. A stream flashed like a trail of white fire across the landscape. The beeches along the lane nodded down a withered leaf or two upon their heads, and the glossy trunks glowed a faint silver under the darkness of their boughs. A dog ran to meet them barking noisily. (GN 86)

Such passages illustrate the ways in which the romantic style was used to instill nationalistic feelings in the people.

In keeping with the idea that real Irish identity means the peasant class, peasants dominate the cast of supporting characters in these stories, especially Corkery's. Tenant farmers and their families, rural laborers, carters, "mountainers," old cottagers, and such, make up the "Irish people" in these stories. They are usually portrayed, in romantic fashion, as good country people, noble and loyal to the goal of nationalism—though never leaders in the cause. Those in remote areas may at first be wary of the rebel seeking refuge, but ultimately they prove themselves supportive. Corkery labels his peasants "awkward" and "slow by nature," but he does not mean this to be condescending, and he is never scornful in speaking of them.

Many of the rebels also come from the peasant class, but almost invariably the rebel leaders are a cut above the others, usually by virtue of intelligence or education rather than economic status. For instance, one of Corkery's rebels has written a book of verse and articles about the revolution. Several rebel characters in Corkery's and O'Connor's stories are poor university students or graduates who carry novels or books of poetry in their pockets; their interest in music, opera, and literature is almost as strong as their interest in revolution. If there is somewhat of a contradiction here—that the real Irish people are uneducated but their leaders in the revolution must come from an intellectual, if not economic, elite—the authors do not acknowledge it.

Religion as an element of Irish cultural identity does not figure as prominently as Gaelic and peasant elements in the literature of the renaissance; and that fact holds true for these stories. Of course it is implicit that most of the characters, being of the peasant class, are Catholic, but there are very few signs of Catholicism in the stories and fewer still that Catholicism is essential to Irish identity. Occasionally allusions are made to Irish saints, such as Ciaran, Finnbarr, and Brendan, or there is an occasional prayer by a peasant, but for the most part, Catholicism is not portrayed as a significant cultural element. This fact can perhaps be partially attributed to the recognition by these writers, all of whom were Catholic, that many nationalists were Protestants. But another reason is pointed out by Cairns and Richards. They note that, while Catholicism had become "a fundamental tenet of the political movement of the people-nation in its move towards national self-determination, it simultaneously became for many writers the cause of an even more profound enslavement than that of Union with England—the enslavement of the self."[45] O'Connor and O'Faolain might certainly be included among these "many writers" taking the latter view of Catholicism, though the evidence is largely found in their stories of Irish domestic life published in later collections.

O'Connor and O'Faolain say nothing in their autobiographies about the relationship of Catholicism to nationalism, and their stories include very little of Catholicism as an influential national element. O'Connor presents only one major Catholic figure, a Gaelic-speaking nun who

45. Cairns and Richards, *Writing Ireland*, 71.

shelters rebels in "Nightpiece with Figures," but her religious beliefs are not emphasized. Two of O'Faolain's stories contain extensive Catholic references, but neither makes a strong connection between Catholicism and nationalism. The case of Corkery is more problematic. In *Synge and Anglo-Irish Literature*, his polemic on the essential elements of the "Irish national being," Corkery included "The Religious Consciousness of the People," by which he meant Catholicism, as one of the essential elements.[46] But his revolutionary stories do not reflect this concept. His characters occasionally say prayers, but only one of the nine stories in *The Hounds of Banba* presents a strong Catholic element, and it does so in an ambivalent manner. In "The Price," the heroine, Nan Twohig, fuses a Catholic piety with nationalist fervor, sheltering, nursing, and praying for a wounded rebel and otherwise devoutly supporting the local volunteers. But Nan's fusion of Catholicism and nationalism is countered by the local priest. He speaks out against the rebels and takes offense when, during mass, Nan requests that the people pray for the soul of Roger Casement, a republican executed for his role in the Easter Rising. Cairns and Richards say that the Church hierarchy was not officially against rebel activities during the War of Independence, sometimes in fact "offering tacit endorsement of the I.R.A.,"[47] but Corkery's depiction of the priest suggests otherwise.

Like the Catholic religion, the Gaelic language plays less of a role in these stories than one might have expected, given the notions of Irish identity at the time and the precedence of publishing stories in Gaelic set by Moore and Pearse. All three writers chose to write their stories in English, despite having a knowledge of and some skill in the composition of Gaelic. In a brief autobiographical piece written in 1932 for *Now and Then*, O'Faolain says that he originally wrote "Fugue" in Gaelic but changed the story into English because he "did not have absolute control of the [Gaelic] language. . . ."[48] The same may have been true of

46. Daniel Corkery, *Synge and Anglo-Irish Literature* (Cork: Cork University Press, 1931), 19.

47. Cairns and Richards, *Writing Ireland*, 116.

48. Sean O'Faolain, "About Myself," *Now and Then* 41 (spring 1932): 35.

Corkery. A biographer of Corkery says that "he did not attain high personal fluency in writing Irish."[49] As a young man, O'Connor wrote an award-winning essay in Gaelic on the Russian writer Turgenev, and then made a name for himself in translating old Irish poetry into English, but there is no indication that he considered writing his stories of romantic nationalism in Gaelic.

Nevertheless, whatever misgivings these writers may have had about their talent for writing in Gaelic, the fact that they wrote the stories of romantic nationalism in English, with only occasional bits of Gaelic, gainsays the notion that Irish identity must be rooted in the Gaelic language. Even Corkery, who worked tirelessly to spread proficiency in the Gaelic language and in other respects had a narrower definition of Irish identity than O'Connor or O'Faolain, allowed for, even admitted the necessity of, English as the language of Irish culture by not listing the Gaelic language in *Synge and Anglo-Irish Literature* among his essential elements of the "Irish national being."[50]

Any thought by these writers about writing in Gaelic may, of course, have been abandoned simply out of their awareness of an insurmountable practical obstacle: most of their readers were unlikely to be fluent in Gaelic.[51] A clear indication of this awareness is revealed in the fact that, when their narrators mention that the characters speak in Gaelic, what the characters say is either recorded in English or, if given in Gaelic, followed by an English translation.

That these writers chose not to make the Gaelic language an essential component of Irish identity is understandable for another reason: the immense success of the Irish literary renaissance had been effected in English by Anglo-Irish writers. The very success of the literary renaissance, as Seamus Deane suggests, may have actually worked against the revival of Gaelic, producing a "hesitant relationship" between the liter-

49. George Saul, *Daniel Corkery* (Lewisburg: Bucknell University Press, 1973), 21.

50. Corkery, *Synge*, 19.

51. O'Faolain makes a related point when he says that he was deterred from writing in Irish because "to write in Irish accentuates the great difficulty confronting all Irish writers—lack of criticism." O'Faolain, "About Myself," 35.

ary movement and the Gaelic revival movement. Early modern Irish writing, as Deane says, created its own language: "The recovery from the lost Irish language [took] the form of an almost vengeful virtuosity in the English language, an attempt to make Irish English a language in its own right rather than an adjunct to English itself."[52]

Thus, the abandonment of the goal of re-establishing Gaelic as an essential cultural component did not mean an acquiescence to English. The alternative, which the writers of the Irish literary renaissance pursued, was to appropriate English and reconstitute it as Irish English, a process that post-colonial critics argue is effective in establishing a national identity by distancing the post-colonial text from the imperial culture.[53] The process is carried out through the use of names, words, phrases, and idioms (translated or not) from the native language and the syntactic fusion of the Gaelic with English, that is, by phrasing the English words of characters in Gaelic syntax, as Irish speakers actually do.

These Irish stories are littered with Gaelic names, words, phrases and sentences, as well as lyrics from Gaelic songs and ballads, translated whenever the writer thinks it necessary. Corkery sometimes uses the Gaelic spelling of a character's name, such as Tomas O'Miodhachain (called Tom Mehigan by an Anglo-Irish character) or Eibhlin ni Charta ("or Eileen MacCarthy, if you find it easier to remember that form of her name" [HB 153–54]), and the Gaelic for place names, such as *Cnoc na gCaorach,* glossed as "the Hill of the Sheep" (HB 132). There are frequent references to towns and areas with Gaelic names like Inchigeela and Knockacashlawn. Gaelic exclamations ("wisha!": "well!" or "indeed!"; "whisht!": "hush!"), greetings ("*Dia bhur mbeatha, a dhaoine maithe*": "God be your life"[GN 62]), and phrases of affection ("my *gradh geal*": "my bright love"[HB 159]; "*a ghile*": "O Brightness" [GN 133]), as well as brief conversations, also frequently appear in the stories.

Irish pronunciations, particularly in character dialogue, are also used

52. Seamus Deane, Introduction to *Nationalism, Colonialism, and Literature*, by Terry Eagleton, Frederic Jameson, and Edward W. Said (Minneapolis: University of Minnesota Press, 1990), 10.

53. Ashcroft, Griffiths, and Tiffin, *Empire,* 38.

to give the English an Irish quality. Characters say "ould" for old, "wan" for one, "dacent" for decent, "aisy" for easy, "lave" for leave, "tink" for think, "ye" for you, "meself" for myself, and "'tis" for it is. Syntactic fusion, a common feature of post-colonial literature, also frequently occurs in the stories; Gaelic syntax fuses with the English vocabulary to give the speech a distinctively Irish quality. A pervasive Gaelic construction found in Irish English is the use of the verb "to be," especially in the form of "it is" at the beginning of the sentence, followed by the word or phrase that the speaker wishes to emphasize:[54] "'Tis there he lives" (HB 20); "'Tis late ye're stopping from yeer homes" (GN 25). The progressive form of the verb, in place of simple present tense, is another readily recognizable Irish construction:[55] "I do be deceiving myself, I do be fancying I hear voices" (HB 29); "Ach, sure, I do be only taking a rise out of her, boys" (GN 63). Another common feature is the preference for participles, especially in "after" and "and" constructions:[56] "[O]nly that 'tis how a tourist is after losing his way in the fogs" (HB 47); "He don't know is it on his head or his feet he is, with the column in on him and he keeping it quiet from the abbot" (CSO 79). Other linguistic features of Irish English include the use of "sure" or "surely" to preface a remark ("Sure God knows it's dry. . . . sure you can see for yourself . . ." [CSO 71]) and the aspiration of consonants ("sthream," "shcattered," "dhrinkin," "shtop").

V

Corkery deserves credit for fashioning the story of romantic nationalism: all nine stories in *The Hounds of Banba* are in that mode, so that the entire collection is a testament to the romantic idealism of the nationalists. O'Connor and O'Faolain imitated—and then surpassed—their teacher. "September Dawn" is O'Connor's finest example of the mode, though the best story in his collection of revolutionary stories is

54. Alan Price, *Synge and Anglo-Irish Drama* (London: Methuen, 1961), 44–45.

55. Nicholas Grene, *Synge: A Critical Study of the Plays* (London: Macmillan, 1975), 66.

56. Ibid., 66, 68.

the title story, "Guests of the Nation," written in the tragic mode. The best example of romantic nationalism—that is, the story that most artistically incorporates the elements of romance and nationalism—is O'Faolain's "Fugue."

In "Fugue," an unnamed narrator relates how he and his rebel companion, Rory, flee Black and Tans, from Inchigeela to Ballyvourney in the mountains. The path of their flight provides O'Faolain with ample opportunity to describe the Cork landscape romantically—everything from fields and bogs to rivers, mountains, and woods—and to incorporate fog, rain, wind, night, and dawn in his setting. The following passage is typical: "The damp of the dawn was everywhere that I might look. It softened the lime gable of the out-house beneath me, it hung over the sodden hay in the barn and, like the fog and mist last night under the blazing moon, it floated over the rumbling river to my right" (CSO 49).

As the story opens, the two rebels have stopped for the night at the house of some sympathizers. One of the sympathizers—a young woman with black hair and bare feet—keeps the rebels informed of the Tans' movements. During their dangerous escape the next day the narrator has recurrent thoughts about the woman. In the evening the rebels stop at a mountain cottage, where a carter and his family give shelter to Rory and take the narrator to another house of refuge. There, to his surprise, the narrator finds the young woman with black hair. After dinner they embrace, but the carter's daughter rushes in with the news that the Tans have killed Rory and are coming for the narrator. He must abandon the woman and the warm house and spend the rainy night alone in the mountain woods. The story ends at dawn with the rebel-narrator feeling "life begin once more its ancient, ceaseless gyre" (CSO 64).

"Fugue" is the quintessential story of romantic nationalism because, better than any other story written in this mode, it fuses the elements of the romance genre and the romantic spirit of idealism with an ardent sense of Irish nationalism. It does so—in imitation of the fugue musical structure—by counter-pointing experiences and emotions associated with both revolution and romance: danger and beauty, excitement and calm, flight and dalliance, fear and sexual attraction, and death and love. At the same time, it incorporates post-colonial themes and supporting stylistic features. The flight of Rory and the narrator evokes the theme of the Irish struggle for independence, while the three houses of refuge and the rebels' brief relationship with the carter's family represent the theme of sentimental connection. Stylistic features include descriptions of Munster landscape and references to Gaelic place names, such as Inchigeela and Ballyvourney, the allegory of Ireland as a woman, and aspects of Irish culture, including a ballad, a Celtic fable, and a Celtic-style poem about the bleak but beautiful Irish countryside: "Keen wind and cold ice / Have burst upon the little world of birds. / The blackbird cannot shelter its side / In the wood of Cuan" (CSO 63).

The fusion of romance and revolution is further achieved by O'Faolain's handling of the black-haired woman. She is both the lady of the knight's romantic quest and the symbol of Ireland. In the musical structure she becomes, as critics have pointed out, the dominant recurring image. The narrator sees her in person at night, at dawn, and again at night; and he dreams of her intermittently throughout the day and when he awakes at dawn at the story's end. Critics have made much of the suggestion in the text that the narrator's romantic feelings for the woman cause his dissatisfaction with his "vagabond life" as a rebel and create a conflict between romance and revolution. While it is true that she is literally a romantic and sexual distraction for the narrator, she is also an allegorical figure of Irish nationalism and, therefore, an inspiration to the narrator. She is a rebel sympathizer, providing the rebels with shelter, food, moral support, and information about the Black and Tans. It is her image that the narrator takes with him at the end of the story as he faces the "ceaseless" revolutionary struggle. In a subtle way she is Ireland—Dark Rosaleen, Cathleen ni Houlihan, the Aisling—because the rebel-narrator lives for her image, for union with her. When Irish independence is achieved, romantic and sexual consummation with her may also be achieved. The interruption of their love-making at the climax of the story is to be seen as temporary, just as the delay in national independence is considered temporary.

O'Faolain's stories of romantic nationalism reveal an obvious debt to Corkery. The musical structure of "Fugue," for instance, was most likely prompted, as Deborah Averill says, by Corkery's musical structure in "An Unfinished Symphony."[57] But despite the strong structural and stylistic resemblances in the stories of Corkery and O'Faolain, there are differences in the two collections. The most significant one is O'Faolain's inclusion of doubt and disillusionment about the revolution. Doubt begins in O'Faolain's stories of romantic nationalism in a small way with the brief weariness expressed by the rebel-narrator in "Fugue" and grows through several other stories until it culminates in the protagonist's full-blown disillusionment in "The Patriot," the last story in the collection.[58]

O'Faolain explained his break from Corkery's mode of romantic nationalism in a *Dublin Magazine* article: "We loved *The Hounds of Banba* . . . as long as we were elated by being young revolutionaries ourselves: but the more we saw of revolution the less we liked Corkery's lyric, romantic idea of revolution and revolutionaries."[59] Whereas Corkery's idealistic feelings about the revolution never wavered, O'Faolain's and O'Connor's turned to doubt and then disillusionment. The effect of these painful feelings on both writers was, however, salutary. As Abrams says that the best romantic works were not born of "revolutionary exaltation" but of "disillusionment or despair," the same may be said of these two Irish writers. Each wrote his best story of the revolution out of disillusionment: O'Connor produced the tragic "Guests of the Nation," and O'Faolain wrote "The Patriot," a story having many of the elements of the mode of romantic nationalism but without the absolute exuberance and optimism of that mode.

Set during the Civil War, "The Patriot" traces the development of two relationships. One is the love affair between Bernie, the rebel pro-

57. Deborah Averill, *The Irish Short Story from George Moore to Frank O'Connor* (Washington, D.C.: University Press of America, 1982), 170.

58. Maurice Harmon, *Sean O'Faolain: A Critical Introduction* (South Bend: University of Notre Dame Press, 1966), 65–66.

59. Sean O'Faolain, "Daniel Corkery," *Dublin Magazine* 11 (April–June 1936): 52.

tagonist, and Norah, a dark-haired beauty; the other is the friendship between Bernie and Edward Bradley, a fierce nationalist who has inspired Bernie and the other rebels with his passionate oratory. Much of the story is in the mode of romantic nationalism: it has the beautiful descriptions of Munster landscapes, romantic diction, a song, the motif of the rebel on the run, the house of refuge, and a love affair between rebel and beautiful woman. But within this mode O'Faolain develops a theme of disillusionment and withdrawal, thus creating the only story of romantic nationalism that seriously questions the ideals of the revolution.

The disillusionment begins when Bernie, after months of guerrilla life in the mountains, goes to division headquarters in hope of getting enough money to visit Norah. He also hopes to see Bradley there and receive from him reassurance that republican goals are still within reach. What he finds there, however, is a republican force in disarray. Officers and men are drinking and quarreling. There is no discipline, no organization, no plans for maneuvers. Bradley speaks at a meeting, but he has no effect. The approach of Free State soldiers forces the rebels into the mountains where eventually Bernie is captured. More than a year in prison leaves him in poor health and disenchanted with republican idealism.

When Bernie is released from prison, he marries Norah, and for their honeymoon they go to the seaside town where they first met. By coincidence, Bradley is there to give a nationalist speech. The newlyweds go to hear him, but, though Bradley is as fiery as ever, he has no effect on Bernie. It is not that Bradley has lost his revolutionary eloquence or the ability to hold his audience. O'Faolain's description makes clear that Bradley still has both: "The years between that night and the day in the market-square [when Bradley had aroused Bernie and other rebels with his oratory] had not dulled his eloquence, and though his temples were gone quite white now—premature for his years—the terrible passion of the man blazed like the fire of burning youth. Yet as he talked the lovers did not join in the cheers of the audience" (CSO 161). Rather, Bradley's rhetoric fails to revive Bernie's patriotism because his experiences in the field have irrevocably dispelled his idealism. Experience has given the lie to rhetoric. Later that night from their hotel window Bernie sees Bradley ride out of town. Then Bernie turns to make love to Norah—a real woman, not a symbol of Ireland. His withdrawal from Bradley and all that he represents is complete.

O'Faolain's placement of "The Patriot" as the last story in *Midsummer Night Madness* is significant. Maurice Harmon says that "[t]he whole collection moves toward that final decision" of the young rebel to choose a personal, human relationship and reject the abstract nationalist cause.[60] Unlike Corkery, who in writing stories about the revolution never put feelings of patriotism and idealism into question, and unlike O'Connor, who turned to other modes to record his disillusionment and doubt about the revolution, O'Faolain poignantly used the romantic mode to express his disillusionment in, and withdrawal from, Irish nationalism.

The story of romantic nationalism was the perfect vehicle for conveying the romance and ideals of the young republicans, and even, as O'Faolain's "The Patriot" demonstrates, for evoking the sense of loss when the "magical improvisation" (to use O'Connor's phrase) ended and those ideals seemed out of reach. It was not, however, suited to expressing the profound despair and disillusionment that the brutality, violence, and betrayal of the Civil War occasioned. For that, the naturalistic story of violence and betrayal was required.

60. Harmon, 65.

2

Violence, Betrayal, Disillusionment

The Naturalistic Story

The romantic improvisation was tearing right down the middle, and on both sides the real killers were emerging.
—Frank O'Connor, *An Only Child*

I

The literary reaction against the stories of romantic nationalism came not from writers with opposing political stances, but rather from two of the writers of the stories of romantic nationalism, O'Connor and O'Faolain, and from Liam O'Flaherty. All three of these writers chose to fight with the republicans in the Civil War—only to become deeply disillusioned with the republican endeavor. Corkery, on the other hand, never lost his republican ideals, perhaps because he did not experience the violence at first hand. It is also true, however, that he wrote no more stories about the revolution after *The Hounds of Banba.*

The Civil War disappointed and disillusioned almost all concerned, so it is no surprise that the ideals of these writers suffered. The rebels ("diehards") who refused to accept the Treaty that created the Free State were bitterly disappointed that so many of their fellow nationalists would give up their demands for an immediate independent Ireland—a disappointment that deepened when it became apparent that the republicans could not win the Civil War. Those who did accept the conditions of the Treaty and joined or supported the Free State forces were just as bitterly disappointed that the republicans would not give up the gun and turn to politics in their pursuit of an independent nation. The fact that the war was waged, not against the traditional English enemy, but among Irish—brother against brother, father against son, neighbor against neighbor—was particularly disheartening. The wide-scale executions of rebels by the victorious Free State government ensured that the bitterness and disillusionment would last a long time into the future. Romance had gone out of the nationalist endeavor.

Several factors account for the change in O'Connor's feelings from romantic idealism to disillusionment in the revolution. For one, as he notes in his autobiography, his idealism had not been based on close observation of the reality around him, but rather on notions that he developed from reading romantic literature. He says several times in *An Only Child* that, at the same time he was engaged in the revolution, he was also reading the romantic novels and poetry of European and American writers, such as Tolstoy's *Sebastopol* and *The Cossacks,* Goethe's *Hermann und Dorothea*, and Whitman's *Leaves of Grass*. His own accounts of his character portray him as a dreamer, someone who was unable to see the harsher aspects of people and life or to recognize many of the events of the rebellion for what they really were—acts of brutality and violence. Furthermore, he was able to sustain this romantic view of the revolution for a time because in his early experiences as an Irish Volunteer he saw little of the brutality and bloodshed that was going on.

All that changed several months after the Civil War began. For the first time, he saw bloodshed and violence, particularly the gratuitous brutality practiced by both Free State soldiers and republicans. Although he did not have many of these experiences, those that he did have had a profound effect on the young O'Connor. They demonstrated for him what Corkery had told him about the Russian Revolution, that "control of a revolutionary movement passes from the original dreamers to men who are professional revolutionaries" (OC 239–40). He counted himself as one of the former, not the latter. At one point O'Connor was told that he was needed for a "job": "to shoot unarmed soldiers courting their girls in deserted laneways, and the girls as well if there was any danger of [the rebels] being recognized." He was horrified by such a prospect. Fortunately, the order was rescinded before he was called upon to carry it out. This experience was an epiphany; it made him realize that "the real killers were emerging" (OC 240).

A more gruesome and shocking experience occurred later, after he had been captured by Free State soldiers (the capture, he says, "came as a relief because it took all responsibility out of my hands"). While imprisoned in Women's Gaol in Sunday's Well he saw an IRA prisoner who had been brutally beaten and "[s]kewered" with bayonets by his Free State captors; the face of the prisoner was "like a lump of dough." But the brutality was not one-sided. The "boy," who was executed a few days later, had apparently been caught attempting "to burn a widow's home and [pour] petrol over the sleeping children" (OC 242–43). Of his experience in witnessing the boy's condition, O'Connor says:

> I had been able to think of the Killmallock skirmish [in which he had also been captured but then rescued by other republicans; one Free State soldier was killed in the skirmish] as though it was something I had read of in a book, but the battered face of that boy was something that wasn't in any book, and even ten years later, when I was sitting reading in my flat in Dublin, the door would suddenly open and he would walk in and the book would fall from my hands. Certainly, that night changed something for ever in me. (OC 244)

The image here of violence disrupting romance, the vision of the battered boy causing the book to fall from O'Connor's hands, is an apt symbol of O'Connor's disillusionment. By the time he was freed from prison in 1924, O'Connor had been completely disabused of his dreamy, romantic attitude toward revolution. He now saw republican idealism as "sentimental high-mindedness" accompanied by "an extraordinary inhumanity" (OC 255).

O'Faolain's disillusionment with republican idealism did not come as a sudden epiphany as O'Connor's had, perhaps because he had less actual involvement in the fighting of the Civil War than O'Connor had and because he apparently did not witness acts of gratuitous brutality. He began his involvement in the Civil War making bombs in various secret places in and outside of the city of Cork and then was appointed Director of Publicity for the First Southern Division when the Director, Erskine Childers, was executed by the Free State government. O'Faolain apparently did not contemplate the ultimate effects of the bombs he made, nor the possibility that he might encounter Childers' fate. He says that during his time in the IRA he "shot nobody" and "was briefly under fire once" (VM 174)—as he and other republicans were retreating from government troops in the mountains of western Cork. This experience, which became the basis of "Fugue," the best of the stories of romantic nationalism, indicates that his "sole experience of warfare" was not one of disillusionment.

Apparently O'Faolain was able to sustain his idealism through the Civil War, though the seeds of disillusion were certainly planted during that experience. In the chapter in *Vive Moi!* that recounts his Civil War experiences, O'Faolain says, "I took pride in our idealism" (VM 215), and he speaks of the republicans as being "the side of pride and honor" and of the Free State side as "letting material things get in the way of principles" (VM 189–90). One measure of his sustained idealism was his willingness to follow orders to go to Dublin and continue to put out republican propaganda after de Valera's ceasefire order.

Even as he held on to his idealism, however, O'Faolain recognized the "folly" of the republicans' enterprise, engaged as they were in "the impossible task of holding to their ideals in a pragmatical world" (VM 190). The republican women, he says, were "ruthless, abstract in discussion, and full of a terrifying sentimentality" (VM 214–15). As time wore on, he could see the effect on himself: "Like all idealists," he says, "I was fast becoming heartless, humorless and pitiless" (VM 208). By the time he returned to Cork in 1924, O'Faolain's idealism was at the breaking point: he was, he says, "a more than disillusioned and embittered young man" (VM 217).

O'Faolain's disillusionment with republican idealism was sealed by the political compromises that came in the years just after the Civil War, compromises that seemingly forsook republican ideals. For example, de Valera instructed those in his Fianna Fáil party to take the oath of allegiance that they had so bitterly opposed. If O'Faolain was not fully aware of his disillusionment during the Civil War, in retrospect he felt that his experiences in the war nevertheless contributed to his transformation from idealist to realist. In the autobiographical piece "About Myself," O'Faolain speaks of the causes of his "bitter disillusionment following the Irish Civil War": "men unwilling to fight and without the character to throw in their guns, much cruelty and brutality, politicians maneuvering for position while young boys and young men were being executed or murdered for murdering one another by the score."[1] The fact that he professed to be an idealist throughout the war while he unconsciously understood the folly of being so is perhaps best explained by his statement that the whole experience of revolution had left him "dazed."[2]

Their disillusionment with republicanism, and to some extent with nationalism, necessitated that O'Connor and O'Faolain break away from their mentor Corkery, whose ardent republicanism had not waned and whose concept of Irish nationalism was too narrow for them to endorse. The break was both marked and facilitated by their departure from the provincial town of Cork, where both had grown up under the tutelage of Corkery. O'Faolain went to Boston to study and then teach from 1926 to 1929; O'Connor left for Dublin in 1929 to take up a library post. Both were exposed to liberating ideas that enlarged their views of Irish nationalism. James Matthews, O'Connor's biographer, says that O'Connor found Dublin to be "about as chaotic culturally as it was politically": he was exposed to intellectuals who had strong and diverse views on everything from partition, censorship, and the puritanical attitudes of the Catholic Church to the importance of the Gaelic language and the nature of Irish literature.[3]

Meanwhile, in 1931, Corkery published *Synge and Anglo-Irish Literature,* his tract on the failure of Anglo-Irish literature to reflect the "Irish national being." In the following years, both O'Connor and O'Faolain attacked Corkery's ideas, thereby publicizing their break from him. In articles in *Dublin Magazine* and *The Bell*, O'Faolain rejected Corkery's narrow view of Irishness. Corkery, he said in one article, "began to ide-

1. Sean O'Faolain, "About Myself," *Now and Then* 41 (spring 1932), 35.

2. Sean O'Faolain, "Forward" to *The Finest Stories of Sean O'Faolain* (Boston: Little, Brown, 1949), viii.

3. James Matthews, *Voices: A Life of Frank O'Connor* (New York: Atheneum, 1983), 57.

alise what he had observed from a distance, and worst of all, to idealise it according to a certain set of a priori ideas about life and literature which were wandering around Ireland at the time. . . ."[4] O'Connor assailed his former mentor in a lecture on Synge at the Abbey Theatre Fesitival in 1938. In that lecture, he called Corkery's concept of an Irish national being, with its three categories of religion, nationalism, and land, another of the "middle-class formulas"[5] and contrasted it unfavorably to the ascetic philosophy of art held by Yeats, Lady Gregory, and Synge. By attacking Corkery, Matthews says, O'Connor was "[i]n a personal sense . . . rejecting a father": "O'Connor believed that Corkery once wrote from the ascetic impulse himself, that he once stripped Irish life and language bare, and that he once triggered a revolution in the soul of two Cork boys, fathered them into literary life, and then orphaned them by selling out to the tyranny of middle-class abstractions. . . ."[6]

O'Flaherty's involvement with republicanism proved to be ambivalent, to say the least, and so his eventual disillusionment with the movement is not as much a surprise as O'Connor's or O'Faolain's. That his commitment was less than complete, however, is rather strange since his background would seem to mark him as a natural for the republican movement. He "was born into extreme poverty" (SD 9) on the Aran Islands to a family of Gaelic, Catholic farmers. Thus, he had all of the cultural markers—Gaelic ethnicity and language, peasant-class status, and Catholicism—that republicanism claimed as the true Irish identity. There was also a tradition of nationalism in his family: his father was a member of the Fenians, the Land League, and Sinn Féin—"[a]n incurable rebel."[7]

All of these elements, however, were mitigated in O'Flaherty by opposing forces. His Gaelic language and heritage were balanced by an education in English. His Catholic upbringing, which included several

4. Sean O'Faolain, "Daniel Corkery," *Dublin Magazine* 11 (April–June 1936): 53.

5. Frank O'Connor, "Synge," in *The Irish Theatre*, ed. Lennox Robinson (London: Macmillan, 1939), 40.

6. Matthews, *Voices*, 143 and 144.

7. James H. O'Brien, *Liam O'Flaherty* (Lewisburg: Bucknell University Press, 1973), 16.

years in a seminary studying for the priesthood, was countered by bouts of anti-clericalism and at least temporary atheism. His republicanism (he is said to have joined the Irish Volunteers near the end of his seminary days)[8] was countered first by a stint in the British Army and then by a strong, though temporary, fling with communism. Finally, his peasant-class status was erased by his education, travels, and writing career. The result was that O'Flaherty's attraction to republicanism turned out to be fleeting.

After leaving the seminary, O'Flaherty joined the Irish Guards in 1915 under the assumed name of Bill Ganly (his mother's maiden name) and served in France, where he was shell-shocked. He was invalided out of the British Army in 1918 and spent several years travelling, during which time he became a communist. In early 1922, he says in *Shame the Devil*, one of his autobiographical works, he "seized the Rotunda in Dublin with a small army of unemployed men . . . [and] hoisted the red flag over the building" (SD 22), thus acting on his socialist principles. He left after a few days, rather than provoke a violent response. A few months later he joined the republican force that seized the Four Courts in Dublin and set up headquarters in defiance of the Free State Army, the event that launched the Civil War. O'Flaherty, however, was one of those who left the seized buildings before the Free State troops blasted the republicans out. He recalls in *Shame the Devil* that, standing in the crowd that was cheering for the Free State forces to drive out the rebels, he heard an old woman rejoicing in his rumored "death" and defaming him as a "bloody murderer" and anti-Catholic. Dismayed by these rumors and disillusioned by republicanism, he left for England, his short stint as an Irish idealist finished. "I had," he says, "abandoned hope in the coming of the revolution" (SD 35–36).

It was out of this deep disillusionment that these three writers created stories that had effects diametrically opposed to the stories of romantic nationalism. The mode of romantic nationalism, while aptly suited

8. John Hildebidle, *Five Irish Writers: The Errand of Keeping Alive* (Cambridge: Harvard University Press, 1989), 2.

for portraying the early idealism of the Irish writers, excluded other valid perspectives on the revolution. In particular, it did not allow them to depict realistically those violent and brutal incidents that they personally encountered or to express the repulsion and disillusionment that resulted from those experiences. Thus, they turned to another mode to express these negative, ironic attitudes about the revolution. The result was the naturalistic story.

II

Just as the stories of romantic nationalism borrowed themes and stylistic traits from the romantic movement that took place at the beginning of the nineteenth century, the stories written in reaction to romantic nationalism borrowed heavily from naturalism, the literary movement that came in the latter half of that century as a pessimistic counter to the ideals of romanticism. Whereas romanticism had helped the Irish writers to express the idealism that had motivated and, for a period, sustained the revolution, literary naturalism enabled them to convey the disillusion, pessimism, and sense of irony that resulted from their experiences in the Civil War.

Literary naturalism had turned for its basic philosophical tenets to the natural and social sciences, specifically to the mechanistic determinism of Newton, the evolutionary biology of Darwin, Marx's ideas of class struggle, and Freud's notions of the unconscious forces in the human psyche.[9] In all of these, literary naturalism found evidence for its essentially pessimistic view that human life was entirely physical, not ultimately spiritual as the romantics believed, and highly determined. It professed that human action and behavior result, not from the operation of free will or from the pursuit of ideals as the romantics would have it, but from the forces of heredity and environment. Strong and often violent passions, brutish instincts, biological drives for sex and survival, as well as economic and social pressures—rather than the ideals and good will of institutions and the human character—shape human life.

9. *A Handbook to Literature*, 3d ed., ed. C. Hugh Holman (New York: Odyssey, 1972), s.v. "naturalism."

With this view of human life in mind, literary naturalists, such as Émile Zola in France, Thomas Hardy in England, and Frank Norris in America, sought to portray their characters' lives with scientific accuracy and objectivity. They focused not on ideals, heroic actions, and moral choices of characters, as the Romantics had, for they admitted to none of these, but on the ordinary, mundane, and even sordid physical details of their characters' lives—details that revealed these passions, instincts, drives, forces, and pressures. Zola, the father of literary naturalism, said that he chose characters "completely dominated by their nerves and blood, without free will, drawn into each action of their lives by the inexorable laws of their physical nature."[10]

Denied free will and, therefore, moral choices, the characters in naturalistic fiction are depicted as amoral; the author or narrator refuses to make moral judgments about them in the interest of scientific objectivity. Life, especially human life, is presented as a Darwinian struggle to survive, so whatever violence occurs in the struggle is a natural result, rather than an immoral choice. Naturalistic fiction often ends in tragedy, but it is not tragic in the classical sense. That is, the protagonist is not a tragic hero who valiantly and freely exercises his individual character in a losing struggle against superior forces but is rather "a pawn to multiple compulsions" who "disintegrates, or is wiped out."[11]

The resulting style of literary naturalism, which stands in sharp contrast to the colorful, inspiring style of the Romantics, is plain, analytical, scrutinizing, and "realistic" (in the sense of mundane), often displaying the mean, dreary, sordid detail rather than the beautiful, inspiring, or pleasant one. When the language is metaphorical and not just plain and literal, it is often characterized by animal imagery to suggest the bestial aspects of human existence.

Irony is a chief effect of naturalistic fiction, a result of the characters' failure to attain their expectations and dreams, particularly for love, hap-

10. Émile Zola, Preface to the Second Edition of *Thérèse Raquin*, trans. L. W. Tancock (Baltimore: Penguin, 1962), 20.

11. *A Glossary of Literary Terms*, 5th ed., ed. M. H. Abrams (New York: Holt, Rinehart and Winston, 1985), s.v. "realism and naturalism."

piness, beauty, or goodness. In Frye's scheme, irony is the diametrical opposite of romance, "a parody of romance,"[12] confirming the failure of the quest for the ideal that romance had promised. Romance opens up the possibilities of life, irony closes them. But there is also something ironic about this pessimistic view of naturalistic fiction, that while it "presume[s] the reality of evolution, [it] often work[s] in terms of devolution: degeneration and personal decline are embedded in most naturalistic fiction."[13] In other words, while focusing on the negative aspects of life, it ignores what is positive in the natural and social sciences. Both the evolutionary biology of Darwin and Marx's notion of class struggle, for example, point to the possibility of a brighter future for human life. Zola, in fact, predicted that mankind would "make use of nature and . . . utilize its laws to produce upon the earth the greatest possible amount of justice and freedom."[14] Hence it is ironic, as Richard Lehan notes, that literary naturalists pay "far more attention to evolutionary throwbacks than to the forward progress of the species. . . ."[15]

The choice of literary naturalism as the thematic and stylistic basis for stories intended to convey disillusionment in the Irish revolution was particularly apt because, as David Weir says, "the scientific dictates of naturalism run counter to the aims of revolutionary politics. [Literary naturalism] usually assumes that the machinery of environment and heredity is sufficiently powerful to cancel out the kind of human intervention in individual and social destiny that politics involves: evolution, not revolution, forms individuals and shapes society."[16]

According to this view, republican ideals had no chance against the

12. Northrop Frye, *The Anatomy of Criticism: Four Essays* (Princeton: Princeton University Press, 1957), 223.

13. Richard Lehan, *The City in Literature: An Intellectual and Cultural History* (Berkeley and Los Angeles: University of California Press, 1998), 52.

14. Émile Zola, "Naturalism on the Stage," trans. Belle M. Sherman, in *Modernism: An Anthology of Sources and Documents*, ed. Vassiliki Kolocotroni, Jane Goldman, and Olga Taxidou (Chicago: The University of Chicago Press, 1998), 170.

15. Lehan, *City*, 51.

16. David Weir, *Anarchy & Culture: The Aesthetic Politics of Modernism* (Amherst: University of Massachusetts Press, 1997), 63.

natural instincts and social forces at work in the revolution. To use O'Connor's terms, the "dreamers" would inevitably be replaced by "professional revolutionaries," "the real killers." In post-colonial theoretical terms, counter-hegemony is at work: in the post-colonial moment, Lloyd says, the hegemony of the imperial power is replaced by the counter-hegemony of the emerging nation, thereby "drowning out other social and cultural possibilities" for its people.[17] For those writers who came to believe that the revolution had degenerated into a violent power struggle between equally ruthless forces, thus excluding "other social and cultural possibilities," the mode of literary naturalism was the appropriate choice to convey such a view.

III

O'Connor, O'Faolain, and O'Flaherty use the naturalistic mode to convey their deep disillusionment with the Irish revolution, and they do so through two pervasive and powerful themes appropriate to that mode: violence and betrayal. They show that violence and betrayal, in various forms, have compromised the ideals and the goals of the republicans. Their stories are strongly naturalistic in theme and style; that is to say, they depict a world that is governed by violence, brutality, betrayal, animal instincts, and irrational behavior, rather than by reason and humane ideals, and they are written in a plain, analytical style that reflects the world they depict. Their protagonists are no longer heroic, romantic revolutionaries engaged in establishing an ideal Irish nation. They are primitive, ignorant, violent, and morally reprehensible men motivated by bloodlust, revenge, and fear. (Kiely calls O'Flaherty's characters "troglodytes."[18]) They are more interested in satisfying their own brute cravings than in achieving the ideals of the revolution. Their lives and the lives of their victims are sordid, ugly, and morally depraved.

17. David Lloyd, *Anomalous States: Irish Writing and the Post-Colonial Moment* (Durham: Duke University Press, 1993), 3.

18. Benedict Kiely, *Modern Irish Fiction—A Critique* (Dublin: Golden Eagle Books, 1950), 18.

All three of the stories that O'Flaherty wrote about the Irish revolution—"The Sniper," "Civil War," and "The Mountain Tavern"—are written in the naturalistic mode. O'Connor included three stories written strictly in this mode in *Guests of the Nation* ("Jo," "Alec," and "Jumbo's Wife"), but he also transcended the naturalistic mode by using the themes of violence and betrayal to create a story of truly tragic proportions—"Guests of the Nation." O'Faolain produced one thoroughly naturalistic story of the revolution, "The Death of Stevey Long," but naturalistic elements, particularly violence and betrayal, can be found in other stories in *Midsummer Night Madness and Other Stories*, including the title story, "The Small Lady," and "The Bombshop." Most of the naturalistic stories are set during the Civil War, which can be viewed either as a struggle for hegemony between two anti-imperialist forces, republicans and Free State troops, or—if the Free State government is seen as having capitulated to the British—as another stage of the nationalist (i.e., republican) struggle against imperial forces.

Violence portrayed in graphic and gory detail is a pervasive theme in these stories. In O'Connor's "Jo," the narrator and Jo Kiely, republican irregulars, go on a "little [violent] spree." The narrator "split[s] one man's head with the butt of [his] revolver" (GN 140), and Jo kills a man who has switched sides from the republicans to the Free State forces, relishing the way he shoots him down from a railway bridge: "He went bash between the rails, his cap sailed one way and his rifle another, and when I looked at him, I seen his head twisted skew-ways; he cracked his neck in the fall. But two of the shots had got him, brother, two out of three!" (GN 144–45). In "Jumbo's Wife," Jumbo, an informer responsible for the death of an Irish Volunteer, regularly beats his wife, who in turn beats their child. Jumbo is eventually hunted down and killed by the brothers of the man he has betrayed. "Alec" is the most brutal of O'Connor's stories. Larry, the narrator of the story, relates how he and two other rebels, Alec Gorman and Peter Keary, are betrayed to Free State soldiers, imprisoned, and brutally treated. Alec is punched in the face, struck with a revolver butt, and kicked in the stomach. Larry is throttled and banged against the wall. Peter is wounded by a bullet in the head. Still another prisoner is flung down a flight of stairs, kicked, and jabbed with a bayonet. The Free Staters' violence is extremely brutal and gratuitous, but it is not one-sided. Alec engages in similar violence. He throws a tub of water on the head of an old woman rumored to be a Free State spy, burns down the home of a Free State sympathizer, and fatally beats the caretaker who has betrayed him and the other two rebels to Free State soldiers.

O'Flaherty, the most dedicated literary naturalist of the three,[19] also portrays much violence in his stories, doing so in the clinical, matter-of-fact manner of the naturalist. In "Civil War," he depicts a gun battle on the rooftops of Dublin. Bodies are everywhere: two rebels lie dead of a bomb explosion on the steps; three Free State soldiers are dead in the street. On the roof, two rebels, Dolan and Murphy, are being attacked by Free State forces. Fearing death, Dolan wishes to surrender, but Murphy threatens to kill him if he does; in the ensuing struggle between the two, Murphy is killed by the attackers. When Dolan tries to surrender, the soldiers shoot him in cold blood. In "The Sniper," the protagonist, a rebel in a death-struggle with a Free State sniper, shoots another Free State soldier and a woman who has given his position away to the soldier. Then, after being wounded, he tricks the Free State sniper into revealing himself and kills him—only to discover that he has killed his own brother.

O'Faolain also shows how violence has overtaken the revolution. Stevey Long, a violent character who appears in two of O'Faolain's stories ("Midsummer Night Madness" and "The Death of Stevey Long") is responsible for much mayhem and killing. In the latter story, he escapes

19. O'Faolain calls O'Flaherty an "inverted Romantic" because "he sets out in the most self-conscious and deliberate way to attack with violence the things that hurt the inarticulated dream of his romantic soul." Sean O'Faolain, "Don Quixote O'Flaherty," *London Mercury* 37 (December 1937): 173–74, reprinted in James M. Cahalan, *Liam O'Flaherty: A Study of the Short Fiction* (Boston: Twayne, 1991), 137. Cahalan elaborates on O'Faolain's remark: "Following naturalism, O'Flaherty emphasized the entrapped, tragic fate of both animals and people, but solace and beauty were always to be found in primitive, passionate Nature, the romantically unifying principle beyond innocence and despair" (56).

from prison in Macroom Castle with the help of his Black and Tan guard. Long has promised to help the guard return to his wife in London; instead, he betrays him to a fellow rebel, who shoots the guard in cold blood.

The fictional representation of violence as a component of revolution is problematic. On the one hand, writers supporting the revolution cannot ignore the indispensable role of violence in achieving the goals of revolution, and readers, to the extent that they are potential sympathizers to be engaged in the sentimental connection, need to acknowledge the role of violence and to see it represented in fiction. On the other hand, the graphic representation of violence is likely to repulse readers and thereby possibly sever the sentimental connection. Hence, if the stories are to sustain faith in the revolution, it is important that the violence be represented in an acceptable manner. This is what the stories of romantic nationalism do: they give violence a remote, sanitized quality by reporting it in a general way, rather than dramatizing or graphically describing the brutal and gory details. In this way, "what was violence," as Lloyd says, "ceases to be violence."[20]

Because violence is portrayed so graphically and repulsively in the naturalistic stories, it is obviously a deliberate attempt by the authors to expose the real nature and effects of violence and to sever the sentimental connection between reader and fictional revolutionaries. The foregrounding of violence makes it real for readers and serves to bring about their disillusion with the revolution. Violence, especially barbaric acts against innocent civilians and gratuitous acts against combatants or prisoners, can no longer be seen as legitimate acts of revolution necessary for the establishment of the nation. Violence is seen for what it is, an expression of the brutish side of human nature and the destroyer of civilization, not the means to a better world.

Betrayal is the other pervasive theme in these naturalistic stories. In O'Connor's "Jo," a man named Marshall betrays the rebels by switching to the Free State side. In "Alec," a caretaker gives up Alec, Peter, and the

20. Lloyd, *States*, 126.

narrator to Free State soldiers. Jumbo, a paid informer in "Jumbo's Wife," has betrayed Michael Kenefick, a rebel, to the English; Jumbo's wife then betrays her husband to the Kenefícks. O'Flaherty's stories also prominently feature betrayal. In "The Sniper," an old woman reveals the sniper's hidden position to a Free State soldier. In "Civil War" Dolan betrays Murphy, his fellow rebel. O'Faolain's Stevey Long in "The Death of Stevey Long," deceives the Black and Tan guard, who has betrayed his duty by helping Stevey escape from prison. An English woman, the title character in O'Faolain's "The Small Lady," has betrayed six rebels to the English.

Although betrayal in these stories is sometimes a spontaneous and open act, such as the old woman's disclosure of the sniper's position in O'Flaherty's story, it is at other times committed through the secret and deliberate act of an informer, such as O'Connor's Jumbo. The informer is abhorrent in any political organization, but he is particularly so in an emerging nation state, and this is especially true in the history of Irish nationalism. The informer is anathema not only because he has rejected his own nationalist allegiance and betrayed members of the nationalist cause, but also because he has done so in secrecy and remains a threat to others. The informer in Ireland seems to be particularly hated because throughout the centuries the English have actively recruited and employed Irish informers to spy on and testify against Irish rebels, thereby thwarting revolution.

Betrayals by combatants, such as Marshall's switch to the Free State side in O'Connor's "Jo" or Dolan's attempt to give himself and Murphy up to Free State soldiers in O'Flaherty's "Civil War," reveal the cracks in republican idealism. But a more damaging kind of betrayal is that which severs the sentimental connection between rebels and the Irish people. The story of romantic nationalism emphasizes the great importance of the sentimental connection to the republican cause by focusing the narrative on the encounter between rebels and supportive sympathizers. It shows how the rebels were nourished after the Easter Rising and during the War of Independence by the emotional and moral support of the people. In contrast, the naturalistic story shows how this relationship deteriorated during the Civil War. Because the Civil War pitted Irish against Irish, even brother against brother, the people often had no clear choice of allegiance. Some supported the rebels, but many turned against them and backed the Free State government. This point is vividly illustrated by O'Flaherty's account in *Shame the Devil*, in which he describes the crowd that gathered outside the Four Courts to cheer the Free State army and jeer the rebels. More importantly, many Irish became weary of the fighting and the violence and, as a result, supported neither side.

In some naturalistic stories the breakdown in the sentimental connection between rebels and people plays a minor role. In "The Sniper," for instance, the old woman, representative of the people, betrays the sniper's position, and in "The Death of Stevey Long," Stevey wanders through Cork unable to find a safe house. In two stories, "The Mountain Tavern" and "Alec," such breakdown is the major theme. In O'Flaherty's "The Mountain Tavern," three republican soldiers, one of them severely wounded, have staggered over the snow-covered mountain terrain in hope of finding shelter and food at a tavern. When they arrive at the place where the tavern should be, all that they find is "a smoking ruin" (WC 114). They learn that Free State soldiers have bombed the tavern to drive out republicans taking refuge in it. Worse yet, the rebels receive no welcome or encouragement from the owners of the tavern who, bitter over their loss, are trying to salvage what they can from the burned-out building. Even as the wounded soldier bleeds to death in front of them, the civilians are not moved to support, or even sympathize with, the rebels. Instead, the wife of the owner calls them robbers and castigates them for leaving her "homeless and penniless" (WC 117). When one of the rebels suggests that she "might respect the dead that died for [her]," she retorts, "Let them die. They didn't die for me" (WC 117). In a passage that is particularly revealing of how much the sentimental connection has disintegrated, O'Flaherty describes the civilians looking at the defeated men: "[They] looked at the soldiers sitting in the snow. The others had a curious malign look in their eyes. They looked at the dazed, exhausted soldiers and at the corpse with a curious apathy.

They looked with hatred. There was no pity in their eyes. They looked steadily without speech or movement, with the serene cruelty of children watching an insect being tortured. They looked patiently, as if calmly watching a monster in its death agony" (WC 119). When the Free State soldiers come, the rebels make no effort to defend themselves or escape. The end of the sentimental connection with the people signals the end of the revolution.

O'Connor's "Alec" is an ironic treatment of the theme of the sentimental connection as it is developed in the story of romantic nationalism—a perfect example of Frye's point that irony parodies romance. In the typical story of romantic nationalism, rebels engaged in some purposeful, heroic action are forced to go into hiding. They seek—and find—refuge in the home of rebel sympathizers and are thus safe to fight another day. In "Alec," on the other hand, the three rebels spend most of their time drinking and lounging about in pubs. Then one night on a whim they decide to go out with their guns, despite the protests of Alec's parents, who feel that the young men are up to no good. They wander for hours on the road without engaging in any meaningful action. Finally, they seek refuge for the night at a suburban home, but instead of being invited in by willing sympathizers, they have to force their way in because the caretaker is reluctant to admit them. The next morning they awake to find themselves surrounded by Free State soldiers summoned by the caretaker. The romantic story of the heroic rebel on the run, sheltered by sympathetic civilians, becomes a story stripped of all romantic quality, about shiftless, violent men looking for trouble and forcing themselves on unwilling civilians, who in turn betray them to the authorities. Both "Alec" and "The Mountain Tavern" suggest that revulsion to violence, even violence committed in the name of nationalism, has caused the people to sever the sentimental connection with the rebels.

In addition to being the right vehicle for conveying the themes of violence and betrayal, the naturalistic mode was well suited to portray the amorality of rebels whom O'Connor referred to as "the real killers" of the revolution. It was, in fact, O'Connor's recognition that the revolution had been taken over by such men that largely brought about his disillusion with republican ideals, and the same is probably true of the other two writers, judging from the damning portraits of such men in their stories. Thus, it was important in their stories to expose these killers. But by implicitly condemning the amorality of their characters, these writers diverged significantly from the philosophical position of literary naturalism. Whereas naturalism excused amoral behavior on the grounds that it was determined by external forces or inner drives beyond the control of the individual, O'Connor and the others suggest that the amoral behavior of their characters cannot be excused on the grounds of lack of control or ignorance of communal moral standards.

None of the major characters in these stories—Alec, Jo, Jumbo, Stevey Long, Dolan, Murphy, O'Flaherty's sniper—and for that matter none of the minor characters, such as the Kenefick family in "Jumbo's Wife" or the Free State soldiers in "Civil War," considers the moral implications of his or others' actions. These men do not realize that the ideals of the revolution are compromised by their violence. They betray people or inflict violence without any moral awareness of what they are doing. They all act out of brutish or selfish instincts: Dolan betrays Murphy out of fear for his own life; Jumbo informs on Michael Kenefick for money; the Kenefick kill Jumbo out of revenge; Alec and Jo inflict their violence out of revenge and bloodlust; Stevey Long and O'Flaherty's sniper act out of the instinct for self-preservation.

Nor do the narrators of these stories pronounce moral judgments on the characters. The final statements of the third-person narrators in O'Flaherty's "Civil War" and "The Sniper" demonstrate this restraint. As "Civil War" ends with Dolan attempting to surrender to two Free State soldiers, the narrator simply records the action: "They both fired point-blank into his head" (TT 62). At the end of "The Sniper," the title character approaches his victim out of curiosity: "Then the sniper turned over the dead body and looked into his brother's face" (SS 161). In neither case does the narrator add moral commentary. Only the first-person narrator of O'Connor's "Jo" shows so much as an inkling of a moral response. Despite his great affection for Jo and his aversion for the man Jo kills, the narrator gradually becomes appalled by Jo's behavior, and in the end he says, in an understatement that reveals how weak his moral recognition is, "I could never bring myself to be pally with Jo again" (GN 146). Even as he is recounting the events, he calls Jo "a real, nice, good-natured fellow" (GN 136) and attributes Jo's behavior to "a terrible wild streak" (GN 146). Although he seems a bit repulsed by Jo's behavior, the narrator is completely oblivious to the fact that the revolution has permitted, or even fostered, such violence in the name of idealism.

The absence of moral awareness in characters or explicit moral judgments by narrators does not mean, however, that the authors subscribe to the amoral world of the literary naturalists or excuse the behavior of their characters. On the contrary, it is clear that they bemoan the lack of moral awareness in these characters. They do so by evoking from readers, through the sheer repulsiveness of their characters' behavior, a moral response condemning the characters, and they thereby raise significant moral questions about the use of violence and brutality in the name of idealism. The reader of "Civil War" and "The Sniper" may be temporarily stunned by the sheer factual nature of the concluding sentences, but those sentences are designed to provoke moral reflection about the action that has taken place.

IV

To fit the themes of violence, betrayal, revenge, and amorality of the rebels, these naturalistic stories use a style of "scrupulous meanness," to borrow Joyce's phrase. The poetic language and the beautiful landscape imagery of romantic nationalism are largely abandoned for a flat or plain prose that records the ugly, sordid details and suggests the squalid lives of the characters. Also forsaken are the post-colonial stylistic features used to promote Irish cultural identity. These stories are almost entirely devoid of cultural allusions to Irish mythical and historical figures; they present few quotations of Irish ballads, songs, and poems; they contain few expressions of Gaelic words, phrases, or sentences. In a rare instance of Gaelic allusion, O'Connor calls Alec "a solitary Cuchulain at the ford" (GN 147). Given the context, however, the allusion is most likely meant ironically, drawing attention to Alec's Cuchulain-like blood-spilling rather than to any heroic defense of the nation.

The following passage from O'Connor's "Alec" is representative of the naturalistic style:

> Her kitchen was bare and dirty; there was a ladder leading up to the loft; a strip of old curtain half hid the bedroom, in which a sacred lamp was burning before a picture of Our Lady of Perpetual Succour and casting a greasy light upon the pillows of the bed. Over the mantelpiece under which we sat was a picture of the Sacred Heart. The tiny window was covered by an old red petticoat, and in the light of an oil lamp bracketed to the wall the white room, with its deal table and bath, its handful of plain chairs, looked hateful and bleak and sordid. (GN 156)

Animal imagery and descriptive language associated with animals are often used to convey the brutish, amoral traits of characters. O'Connor's Jumbo is called "a brute of a man," a "hunted thing," and a "wild quarry" (GN 46–48). Jo is said to be "very wild" (GN 141). O'Faolain's Stevey Long is "cunning" and "fearless" (CSO 127) with the "instinct of a trapped man" (CSO 138). The Free State soldiers who shoot Dolan in cold blood in O'Flaherty's "Civil War" are described as having "lips curling into a snarl and . . . eyes narrowing" (TT 62). The wounded rebel in "The Mountain Tavern" "bare[s]" his teeth and breathes "with a hissing sound" (WC 112).

Of the three writers, O'Faolain was the least like a literary naturalist in style. He was more often, especially in his early stories, a romantic in style, even when he was treating subject matter associated with the naturalists. But the following lengthy passage from "The Death of Stevey Long," in which Long is being hunted by Free State soldiers, illustrates well the various aspects of the naturalistic style: the penetrating analysis of the physical scene, the attention to sordid detail, and the depiction of the character as sub-human and buffeted by controlling forces:

> He wiped the sweat of fear from his forehead and peeped cautiously out of his alley-way, thanking his good-fortune that he did so, for the next instant the heavens seemed to open with light and every cranny and crevice of the lane was flooded by a powerful searchlight. At the same moment

> he heard the soft whirring of a car and low voices. He was taut and trembling like a string that has been made vibrate by a blow. He thought he heard steps approaching and he slunk backwards down the alley, halting in doors and watching the flooded light of the lane, beyond the tunnel of the arch. He came to the alley-end and his feet crunched on the head of a dead fish, the guts oozing under his heels. He glanced about the great pitch-dark square—he was in the markets. In the limelight of the arch far down the alley he saw two khaki figures who turned towards him and entered the arch and faced the wall. It was enough for Stevey—he turned and crouched his way along the markets, slipping on the rotting vegetables and the slime of fishgut, resting in door after door with something of the feeling that he had walked into the wrong region. . . . (CSO 138)

O'Flaherty's stories, written in a simple, flat, and direct prose restricted almost exclusively to the observable facts, exemplify well the style of literary naturalism. They convey his "naturalist intentions," as James Kilroy remarks, through "unambiguous endings, the generally direct narrative techniques, and his rejection of stylistic elaboration." They "tend to begin abruptly, with no historical background or topical commentary, and to end sharply, often with accounts of death or separation. . . ."[21] The closing sentences of "Civil War" and "The Sniper," quoted above, illustrate his sharp endings; the opening of the former illustrates his abrupt beginnings and pared-down sentences. It begins, "Day had dawned. It was the fourth day. Now everything was lost, but they would not surrender" (TT 51). Clued only by the title and these brief details, the reader is left to figure out that the story takes place during the Free State government's siege of the Four Courts that opened the Civil War. O'Flaherty also emphasizes more than the others the hostile influence of nature, a hallmark of literary naturalism, and the corresponding naturalist concept that man is a "small and insignificant . . . creature in a cruel and indifferent universe. . . ."[22] O'Flaherty's refusal to name his characters, such as the rebels in "The Sniper" and "The Mountain Tavern," is a stylistic device meant to emphasize their insignificance. The

21. James F. Kilroy, "Setting the Standards: Writers of the 1920s and 1930s," in *The Irish Short Story: A Critical History*, ed. James F. Kilroy (Boston: Twayne, 1984), 98–99.

22. Ibid., 98.

closing of "The Mountain Tavern" is written in a style that conveys both the power of nature and the insignificance of human life: "There was nothing in the whole universe again but the black ruin and the black spot where the corpse had lain. Night fell and snow fell, fell like soft soothing white flower petals on the black ruin and on the black spot where the corpse had lain" (WC 120). That image of the "soft soothing white flower petals" might at first seem romantic—until we remember that the snow flakes are cold and obliterating. It should also be noted that the closed endings of the naturalistic stories contrast noticeably with the open endings of the stories of romantic nationalism. Whereas the endings of the romantic stories suggest that the quest for the ideal nation will continue, the naturalistic stories suggest that the quest has ended—in failure and death.

Irony is another stylistic feature of these naturalistic stories. All three of O'Flaherty's stories are built on situational irony in which there is a discrepancy between appearance and reality or expectation and outcome. "The Sniper" is the most blatantly ironic, using as it does the surprise-ending formula made popular by O. Henry and Maupassant to reveal that the protagonist, who thinks he has killed a hostile stranger, has in reality killed his own brother. (The fact that such an outcome was well within the realm of possibility during the Civil War lends power to what would otherwise be just a trick ending.) Perhaps the more subtle irony of the story is that political allegiance, the act of choosing a side in order to achieve a nationalist ideal, has destroyed family allegiance, without which the nation cannot exist. The other two stories contain less blatant ironies: in "Civil War," Dolan expects to live by surrendering to Free State soldiers but instead is killed by them; the rebels in "The Mountain Tavern" trudge through harsh terrain expecting to find refuge and support but instead meet with indifference and capture. The latter story also reflects, particularly in its final sentence quoted above, the cosmic irony, often utilized by naturalistic writers, that the universe is indifferent to the hopes and ideals of human beings.

The reader's understanding of the importance of the sentimental connection—and therefore the significance of its absence—creates an additional sense of situational irony in "The Mountain Tavern" and in O'Connor's "Alec." There is a particularly sharp irony evoked in this regard when the rebels in "Alec" wake up in what they thought was a sympathizer's home only to discover that they are surrounded by Free State soldiers. O'Faolain also uses situational irony in "The Death of Stevey Long." Once caught, Stevey is tried, convicted, and executed for a crime he did not commit, while his real crimes of escaping prison and bringing about the guard's death go undetected. He is then buried with honors by fellow republicans, despite being, as Paul Doyle says, "one of the most unscrupulous, dishonorable, and thoroughly unprincipled members" of the rebels.[23]

The theme of betrayal in these stories reflects another irony: betrayal is the ironic converse of the theme of cultural identity promoted in the stories of romantic nationalism. Cultural-political identity bonds people together to achieve the nationalist cause; betrayal, especially through the act of informing, exploits that identity in order to destroy the nationalist cause. Hence, cultural-political identity, one of the primary means by which the nation-state is to be established, becomes the greatest liability for the members of the aspiring nation.

Finally, the overriding irony of all of the naturalistic stories results from the great discrepancy in them between the ideal sought through revolutionary war and the reality that it brings. What Maurice Wohlgelernter says about the theme of O'Connor's war stories is true of all of these naturalistic stories: "Not only does war reveal to man the 'unreality' of his fascination with violence, but also . . . war shows man how removed the real is from the ideal; however widening is the gap between what actually is happening or has happened to his hopes and plans and what he thought he was fighting for."[24]

The naturalistic story was successful in conveying the deep disillusion that many of the idealists came to feel in the revolution. It exposed, with telling irony, the violence, brutality, and betrayal that characterized the

23. Paul Doyle, *Sean O'Faolain* (New York: Twayne, 1968), 34.

24. Maurice Wohlgelernter, *Frank O'Connor: An Introduction* (New York: Columbia University Press, 1977), 33–34.

Civil War and the republicans' relentless pursuit of an independent Ireland. In doing this, it also exposed the shortcomings of the story of romantic nationalism, particularly its blindness to the more repulsive aspects of revolution. But the naturalistic story had faults of its own. Most importantly, it was incapable of expressing the deep sense of tragedy experienced during the Civil War by the more sensitive idealists, particularly O'Connor. Although, as Abrams says, it often has a tragic end, naturalistic fiction is incapable of conveying great tragedy, because it deprives its characters of free will and, therefore, of moral choices and heroic actions. In order to convey a sense of the profound tragedy of war and revolution, O'Connor created the one truly great tragic story of the Irish revolution: "Guests of the Nation."

V

In "Guests of the Nation,"[25] set in the War of Independence,[26] two Irish soldiers, Bonaparte (the narrator) and Noble, are charged with guarding two English prisoners, Hawkins and Belcher. All four are quartered in a boardinghouse run by an old woman. There, the four men spend their time playing cards and arguing good-naturedly about politics and religion, and soon their hostile relationship of guards and prisoners evolves into a friendly relationship of hosts and guests. Then Jeremiah Donovan, another Irish soldier with a particularly zeal-

25. O'Connor revised the story for inclusion in *More Stories by Frank O'Connor* (New York: Knopf, 1954), a version that most anthologists prefer. (The changes are mostly in the speech patterns and dialects of the narrator and characters.) I use the original version here because of my focus on chronological development of the Irish stories of revolution and because the changes do not significantly affect my interpretation.

26. In setting "Guests of the Nation" during the War of Independence (rather than the Civil War which brought about his disillusion), O'Connor is remaining faithful to the details of the incident that he said was the source of the story: two English soldiers "who had been held as hostages and who soon got to know the countryside better than their guards" were executed in response to the English execution of Irish prisoners. However, O'Connor *heard* the story while imprisoned in Gormanstown Internment Camp at the end of the Civil War, so in that sense it is a reflection of his disillusion with the Civil War, as well as with the entire revolution. See Matthews, *Voices*, 72 and 392, n. 9.

ous notion of duty, brings orders that he, Bonaparte, and Noble are to execute Belcher and Hawkins in retaliation for the English execution of Irish prisoners. Bonaparte and Noble are morally sickened by this demand that duty places on them. Bonaparte in particular sees, and feels, the conflict between exercising his duty and behaving humanely toward the prisoners. The thought of executing the prisoners makes him feel "sad" and "miserable" (GN 8), yet the alternative—refusing to carry out the orders—is unthinkable: "disunion between brothers seemed to me an awful crime" (GN 9). On the way to the bog where the prisoners are to be shot and buried, Bonaparte desperately hopes that the English prisoners will escape, thus dissolving the moral conflict. But they do not attempt to do so, thereby heightening his anguish, and in the end, Bonaparte acquiesces in the executions. Returning to the boarding-house, he is left feeling "very small and very lonely" (GN 19).

"Guests of the Nation" is generally regarded as the finest short story—by any writer—treating the Irish revolution. It deserves this appraisal for several reasons aside from its superb construction and characterization. First of all, it incorporates the two powerful themes of the naturalistic story, violence and betrayal, and thus reflects the darker truths of the revolution, while at the same time transcending the limitations of naturalistic fiction, especially its philosophical position that human beings are essentially amoral. The betrayal in this case is a betrayal of friendship, which, because the story convincingly elevates the friendship of the four men above the political conflict, is worse than political betrayal. The violence—the cold-blooded executions of Hawkins and Belcher—is excruciatingly painful to Bonaparte and to the reader. Donovan shoots Hawkins in the back of the neck, but when his body continues to move Bonaparte has to shoot him again. Then Donovan shoots Belcher in the same manner.

Still another element of the naturalistic story is the presence of the revolutionary killer in the character of Jeremiah Donovan, whose fanatical devotion to duty ensures the executions of the prisoners. Donovan transcends the typical naturalistic character, however, in that his devotion to violence is indistinguishable from his devotion to republican idealism. He is more repugnant than Jo Kiely, Alec, Stevey Long, or any of O'Flaherty's characters precisely because he lacks their wildness and insists that his actions are required by patriotic duty: "You understand," he says to Belcher after shooting Hawkins, "it's not so much our doing. It's our duty, so to speak" (GN 17–18).

Another reason that the story deserves high praise, and the chief reason that it transcends the naturalistic story, is that its protagonist admits to a moral dimension in revolutionary war: Bonaparte is faced with an overwhelming moral crisis. "Guests of the Nation," in fact, is the only story about the 1916–1923 Irish revolutionary period in which the protagonist must make an immediate and painful moral choice. Even though Bernie, in O'Faolain's "The Patriot," must choose between the revolution and his personal life with Norah, he seems to make his choice without much anguish or regret, perhaps because it comes after a very gradual and complete disappointment with the republican movement. He does not have to choose at a time when his love for Norah and his faith in the revolution are equally strong. Bonaparte, on the other hand, is faced with an immediate and intense moral crisis. His anguish in having to choose is enormous because the two conflicting forces—his sense of duty toward the revolution and his feelings of brotherhood toward the Englishmen—are both very strong. So strong and equally balanced are the two conflicting forces that Bonaparte at first regrets that he and Noble have become friends with the prisoners, and then he desperately hopes that the prisoners will escape, thus dissolving the conflict. What he does not want to do—but ultimately must—is to choose between his duty and his new friends.

When Bernie chooses Norah and love over Bradley and the revolution in "The Patriot," we feel that, given his circumstances and the state of the revolution, he has made the right choice. In this sense, his choice is romantic, i.e., hopeful. He has replaced a lost ideal with a new one, and the melancholy felt over the loss is balanced by the hope in the new ideal. But Bonaparte is faced with an ironic and tragic situation: he must choose, but there is no "right" choice. In choosing duty by participating in the executions of the English prisoners, he betrays his friends; but had he stood by them, perhaps by helping them to escape or by refusing to participate in their executions, he would have betrayed his duty to the Irish cause. Either way he loses. The choice of duty over friendship leaves him feeling alone and insignificant. The irony is that had he chosen friendship over duty his feeling of anguish would have been just as strong. The great tragic power of the story comes from the way that it makes the reader understand Bonaparte's moral dilemma and experience the pain that Bonaparte feels in making his choice.

A final reason that "Guests of the Nation" stands out so clearly from the other stories of the Irish revolution is that it, more than any of the others, has a distinctly modern temper. The romantic and naturalistic stories have a nineteenth-century quality to them, whereas "Guests of the Nation," written in the tragic mode, has the ironic and tragic tones that are so often adopted in modern literature. O'Connor's focus in "Guests of the Nation" is not on the romantic ideals of the revolutionaries, as is the case in the stories of romantic nationalism, nor on the revelation that many of the rebels are really ignorant, violent men, as it is in the naturalistic stories. Rather his focus is on the essential human condition as represented in Bonaparte's moral dilemma, and he views that condition as ironic and tragic. Bonaparte's moral dilemma and tragedy are symbolic of the lives of modern human beings. We admire, or perhaps even envy, the idealists in the romantic stories, and we scorn the brutal men of the naturalistic stories, but we sympathize, even empathize, with Bonaparte in his anguish.

To say that "Guests of the Nation" is written in the tragic mode is not, however, to say that it is a tragedy in the Aristotelian sense of having a tragic hero who falls from a position of renown and fortune. Bonaparte does not have the stature of a classical tragic hero, and for this reason the "ironic component of tragedy predominates over the heroic one."[27] But the story does share some of the essential elements of classical tragedy. There is "the theme of isolation" in which the protagonist

27. *The Harper Handbook to Literature*, ed. Northrop Frye, Sheridan Baker, and George Perkins (New York: Harper & Row, 1985), s.v. "tragedy."

"becomes isolated from the community."[28] Bonaparte's sense of isolation ("I was somehow very small and very lonely" [GN 19]) is the direct result of the execution of the prisoners, "an act of aggression" that disturbs the "contract of order and stability in which gods, human society, and nature all [participate]."[29] The old woman who runs the boardinghouse has warned the others of the consequences of such acts when she says early in the story, "nothing but sorrow and want follows them that disturbs the hidden powers!" (GN 5). And, in the fashion of the Greek chorus, she is there at the end to prick the consciences of Bonaparte and Noble: "'What did ye do with them?' she said in a sort of whisper. . . . 'I heard ye. Do you think I wasn't listening to ye putting the things back in the houseen?' . . . 'Was that what ye did with them?' she said, and Noble said nothing—after all, what could he say?" (GN 19).

The final paragraph of the story—written in an understated and at times ungrammatical style designed to evoke irony—powerfully conveys both the feeling of Bonaparte's isolation and, in the references to shrieking birds, distant stars, and the incongruous perceptions of size and distance, a sense that the tragic event has thrown the "cosmic machinery out of gear"[30]:

> So then, by God, she fell on her two knees by the door, and began telling her beads, and after a minute or two Noble went on his knees by the fireplace, so I pushed my way out past her, and stood at the door, watching the stars and listening to the damned shrieking of the birds. It is so strange what you feel at such moments, and not to be written afterwards. Noble says he felt he seen everything ten times as big, perceiving nothing around him but the little patch of black bog with the two Englishmen stiffening into it; but with me it was the other way, as though the patch of bog where the two Englishmen were was a thousand miles away from me, and even Noble mumbling just behind me and the old woman and the birds and bloody stars were all far away, and I was somehow very small and very lonely. And anything that ever happened me after I never felt the same about again. (GN 19)

28. Ibid.

29. Ibid.

30. Ibid.

Frye says that "[t]he discovery or *anagnorisis* which comes at the end of the tragic plot is not simply the knowledge by the hero of what has happened to him . . . but the recognition of the determined shape of the life he has created for himself, with an implicit comparison with the uncreated potential life he has forsaken."[31] In this final, poignant paragraph of "Guests of the Nation," Bonaparte recognizes that the tragic event has forever changed his life. But his words also bring the reader to the realization that the "uncreated potential life" of the ideal Irish republic, promised by the revolution and dreamed of in the story of romantic nationalism, has been forever lost. Once O'Connor and the others introduced the violence and tragedy of the revolution into their stories, the idealism and hope of the romantic story was destroyed. After the tragic fall, the ideal can no longer be envisioned: the tragic story makes the story of romantic nationalism obsolete.

31. Frye, *Anatomy*, 212.

3

Gaining Distance

Humor and Satire

The [National] *Foresthers' is a gorgeous dhress! I don't think I've seen nicer, mind you, in a pantomime. . . . Th' loveliest part of th' dhress, I think, is th' osthrichess plume. . . . When yous are goin' along, an' I see them wavin' an' noddin' an' waggin', I seem to be lookin' at each of yous hangin' at th' end of a rope, your eyes bulgin' an' your legs twistin' an' jerkin', gaspin' an' gaspin' for breath while yous are thryin' to die for Ireland!*
—Mrs. Gogan, *The Plough and the Stars* by Sean O'Casey

I

The Civil War was just ending as the playwright Sean O'Casey turned his comic and satiric gaze on the Troubles of 1916–1923. In rapid fashion, O'Casey wrote, and the Abbey Theatre produced, the three plays that make up his Dublin Trilogy, *The Shadow of a Gunman, Juno and the Paycock*, and *The Plough and the Stars*—works that ensured that humor, wit, and satire would not be absent in dramatic and literary treatments of the Troubles. Not that such was even a remote possibility: as Vivian Mercier says, "no aspect of life is too sacred to escape the mockery of Irish laughter."[1] Short-story writers soon followed O'Casey's lead.

After the Civil War, Ireland was particularly conducive to humor and satire. In a study of Irish Menippean satire, José Lanters argues that the frustrations caused by the presence of political, economic, and cultural turmoil in Ireland in the years following the Treaty and the Civil War

1. Vivian Mercier, *The Irish Comic Tradition* (Oxford: Oxford University Press, 1962), 248.

created a "climate [that] was right for satire." The result was a flourish of works by such writers as Austin Clarke, Flann O'Brien, and Mervyn Wall that satirically addressed "the new country's lack of political daring and imagination . . . [and] the more serious side effects of national insecurity, censorship, and repression."[2] It might also be argued that the decades following the tumultuous events of 1916–1923 fostered a climate that was right for a humorous and satiric treatment of the Troubles—though in this case it was the distance from, rather than a proximity to, the subjects of humor and ridicule that created the right climate.

The decades between the end of the Civil War and the renewal of the Troubles in the north in the late 1960s were marked by both a respite from persistent and extensive violence *and* continued antagonism surrounding those issues over which the Civil War had been fought: British dominion, partition, and the reunification of north and south. The absence of open rebellion and warfare provided the Irish with some sense of distance from the immediacy and the intensity of revolution. On the other hand, the presence of the issues mentioned above, as well as sporadic violence by the IRA, served to remind them that the Troubles might return at any time.

Regarding the issues of partition and reunification, neither William T. Cosgrave's Cumann na nGaedheal government, in power from the Civil War until 1932, nor de Valera's Fianna Fáil government that took the reins in 1932, made any headway. In some ways, in fact, partition was solidified. For instance, custom houses set up along the border resulted in "giving [partition] a permanence and physical appearance it had not had previously."[3] Later, the IRA would attack these custom houses as symbols of partition. Furthermore, the Boundary Commission, established by the Treaty and promoted to nationalists as a means of reducing the size of Northern Ireland, failed to effect any changes.[4]

2. José Lanters, *Unauthorized Versions: Irish Menippean Satire, 1919–1952* (Washington, D.C.: The Catholic University of America Press, 2000), 2.

3. Ronan Fanning, *Independent Ireland* (Dublin: n.p., 1983), 86, quoted in Alvin Jackson, *Ireland 1798–1998: Politics and War* (Malden, Mass.: Blackwell, 1999), 280.

4. Jackson, *Ireland 1798–1998*, 259, 280–81.

On the issues of British dominion and Irish sovereignty, greater progress was made by both the Cosgrave and de Valera governments. The Irish government, for example, influenced the passage of the Statute of Westminster in 1931, by which the British parliament relinquished legislative authority over the Free State and the other British dominions. In 1933 shortly after Fianna Fáil was elected to power, the oath of allegiance, a major symbol of British dominion, was removed from the Free State constitution. In 1937 de Valera introduced a new constitution that changed the name of the Free State to Éire; in December 1948, the Dáil passed the Republic of Ireland Act; and the following year Ireland left the British Commonwealth to become a republic. As a further repudiation of British dominion, the 1937 constitution declared sovereignty over the six counties of Northern Ireland, a provision that was not rescinded until recently as part of the 1998 Agreement. British rule in the north, however, meant that the dominion issue remained.

As for militant activity in the period after the Civil War,[5] the IRA, though greatly weakened in membership and organization, carried out sporadic attacks on British soldiers, Irish police, informers, and others deemed inimical to republicanism. The most infamous case was the assassination of Kevin O'Higgins, a Cosgrave minister, in July, 1927. Also during these years, the IRA bombed and raided Garda barracks and custom stations, and they clashed with organizations opposed to their goals, such as the National Guard (the "Blueshirts"), a fascist-minded organization loosely aligned with Cumann na nGaedheal. The violence escalated in the period of 1929–1931 to the point that, in October 1931, the Cosgrave government declared the IRA an illegal organization. The 1932 election of Fianna Fáil, the so-called "Republican Party," brought with it the possibility of a resurgence in the IRA. In fact, the de Valera government repealed the order banning the IRA. But the IRA's continued violent activities provoked the public's antipathy and challenged the government's authority, ultimately forcing Fianna Fáil to distance itself

5. For an account of IRA activity during the 1920s and 1930s, see Tim Pat Coogan, *The IRA*, rev. ed. (New York: Palgrave, 2002), chapters 2 and 3.

from violent republicanism. In June 1936, the de Valera government outlawed the IRA. Through the 1940s and 1950s the IRA, though not an exceptionally formidable force, continued to be both a nagging problem to Irish governments and a reminder of Ireland's failure to achieve complete independence.

In the years between 1923 and 1969, this combination of the absence of full-scale Troubles and the presence of the conditions which had fostered, and would eventually renew, the Troubles created a climate conducive to the composition of humorous and satiric stories about the revolution. It allowed writers to view the revolution from a distance of years, a kind of comic recollection in tranquility. The humorous and satiric stories of the Troubles, with few exceptions, did not arise out of frustration over the immediate situation or climate in Ireland, in the way that—as Lanters shows—Menippean satire sprung from frustration over the political and cultural turmoil in post-Civil War Ireland. Instead, most of these humorous and satiric stories seem to be the result of the writers being able to view their disaffection with the events and ideology of 1916–1923 from a distance. In looking back to the revolution, short-story writers found much to laugh about and satirize.

Only a few of these stories take place in post-Civil War Ireland; most are set in the past during the Troubles. Several stories, however, relate the main action that takes place during the Troubles from the perspective of a contemporary, post-Troubles setting, which creates a more explicit sense of distance. The narrator or a character recalls an incident from the Troubles and presents it in a comic or satiric light, usually in contrast to the more serious perspective with which it was viewed when it originally took place. Furthermore, several of the stories are set in a pub, the quintessential Irish place of reminiscence, storytelling, and joking. The resulting comic and satiric stories are amusing and relaxed and have less intensity and immediacy than the romantic and naturalistic stories, yet nevertheless offer insightful views of the Troubles.

Of the writers who wrote romantic and/or naturalistic stories about the 1916–1923 events, only O'Connor also wrote comic and satiric stories. It is not surprising, of course, that neither Corkery nor O'Flaherty wrote humorous stories of the Troubles. Corkery's unremitting and undiluted idealism must have precluded any humorous response to revolution. Similarly, O'Flaherty's predominant tendency toward naturalistic bleakness may have made him constitutionally incapable of viewing revolution with humor, though he did write comic and satiric stories on other, less intense topics.[6] On the other hand, one might have expected O'Faolain, who later employed so much humor and satire to depict various aspects of Irish life, to write humorous stories about the Troubles, but only "Lilliput," a story set in Cork during the War of Independence, has as much as a hint of humor.[7]

Nor is it surprising that O'Connor, the superb satirist and comic writer, would ultimately turn to comedy and satire to finish off his impressions of the Irish revolution. In the story of romantic nationalism, he had fervently expressed his youthful idealism for the revolution, and the naturalistic story had enabled him to convey his profound sense of disillusion with the outcome of that enterprise. In the wake of his disillusion, he turned to comedy and satire. These modes allowed him to distance himself once and for all from the revolution.

The sources of many of O'Connor's comic and satiric stories are to be found in his experiences in the revolution, recorded in *An Only Child*. Once he looked back at those experiences and the people involved—and reexamined his attitudes toward them—he was able to see the absurdity and folly oftentimes inherently present. One of the first things O'Connor noticed in retrospect about the revolution was the *lack* of a humorous perspective by the participants. In their autobiographies, both O'Connor and O'Faolain remark about the absence of humor among the republicans they worked with during the Civil War. O'Faolain became aware of it near the end of the Civil War, just before he became disillusioned. He says that he suddenly realized that, "[l]ike all idealists, I

6. See the chapter entitled "Satire and Comedy" in James Cahalan, *Liam O'Flaherty: A Study of the Short Fiction* (Boston: Twayne, 1991).

7. Pierce Butler says that "Lilliput" "is reminiscent of some of Chekhov's early humorous pieces." *Sean O'Faolain: A Study of the Short Fiction* (New York: Twayne, 1993), 40.

was fast becoming heartless, humorless and pitiless" (VM 208). O'Connor similarly remarks about "the lack of humour that seems to accompany every imaginative improvisation," to which he adds: "I must have been as humourless as everybody else" (OC 255). It was, perhaps, out of this recognition that he turned to humorous modes.

Short-story writers of the next generation, those who were either born after the Troubles of 1916–1923 or were too young to participate, also skillfully employed humor and satire to treat the Troubles. Denis Johnston,[8] Flann O'Brien, James Plunkett, Tom MacIntyre, Helen Lucy Burke, David Marcus, and John Morrow all wrote at least one humorous story of the Troubles. Most of these writers, like O'Connor, looked back to the revolutionary events of 1916–1923 for their material, though without benefit of personal experience. They often frame the past incident in a contemporary setting, which serves to emphasize the distance between the past and the present. Although most of these writers lived to see the renewal of hostilities in the north, only Morrow has written with humor or satire about the Northern Troubles. His stories, written during and about the Northern Troubles, are, in fact, the only exception to the notion that humorous treatments of revolution and violence require a sense of distance.

II

In treating the Troubles with comedy and satire, O'Connor and those who followed him turned to the various literary devices and techniques for which the Irish are famous: comic by-play and absurdities, exaggeration, farce, wit, pub jokes, invective, mockery, irony, black humor, and the portrayal of comic figures such as the *omadhawn* or clown, the rogue, the stage Irishman, and other Irish stereotypes and

8. Born in 1901, Johnston is actually O'Connor's contemporary, but I mention him with those in the next generation because he did not take part in the Troubles of 1916–1923 and because his comic story, "A Call to Arms," set in a pub years after the main action, resembles more the stories of the writers who followed O'Connor than those of O'Connor. "A Call to Arms" appeared in *Tears of the Shamrock*, ed. David Marcus (London: Wolfe Publishing, 1972). Johnston, of course, is best known for his plays, some of which examine the Troubles, often with humor and satire.

caricatures. Satire, as might be expected, predominates in these stories because of its implicit critical stance. Its presence links the Troubles stories to what Mercier calls "the great antiquity and unbroken continuity of the Irish satiric tradition."[9]

The extensive use of humor and satire in these stories confirms that these modes play just as important a role in our understanding of the revolutionary events as do the modes of romantic nationalism and naturalism. In fact, humor and satire provide multiple perspectives on the revolution, whereas the other two modes are more narrowly focused. Romantic nationalism is largely restricted to expressing the spirit of idealism and romance that characterized the early stages of the revolution, and naturalism concentrates on the disillusionment and despair that followed. The perspectives in the comic and satiric stories, on the other hand, create effects ranging more widely, from hope to despair, and from the comic impulse toward liberation and survival, to the dark, sardonic laugh of capitulation in a dystopian world of terror and violence. Underlying all is the implicit criticism of life that comedy and satire convey.

Comedy, humor, and satire in their various manifestations have traditionally been viewed as capable of offering optimistic perspectives on life, even though their prime subject matter of human folly, stupidity, and absurdity would lead one to think otherwise. Comedy may present an absurd situation in which the characters are in a state of repression or bondage, but then it typically moves toward "a more sensible order of things,"[10] thereby offering a hopeful view of life. On the other hand, some comedy (Frye terms it ironic comedy)[11] does not get beyond the condition of absurdity, repression, or bondage, and so ends in frustration and despair. Nevertheless, because such comedy addresses the sources of our frustrations, the effect can still be psychologically, if not

9. Mercier, *Comic Tradition*, 105.

10. *The Harper Handbook to Literature*, ed. Northrop Frye, Sheridan Baker, and George Perkins (New York: Harper & Row, 1985), s.v. "comedy."

11. Northrop Frye, *The Anatomy of Criticism: Four Essays* (Princeton: Princeton University Press, 1957), 178.

actually, liberating. In *The Profane Book of Irish Comedy*, Krause says, "[t]he comic impulse [has] . . . the fictive power of reconstructing and releasing our unconscious aspirations, our private desires that are frustrated in the conscious or public world. These submerged or repressed emotions find a liberating outlet in . . . laughter. . . ."[12] In other words, in the face of bondage or repression, comedy may express a deep desire for, without actually realizing, a state of freedom and harmony. Obviously, humor and laughter in themselves can not actually liberate people from repression, but they help by expressing the desire to be so liberated. Irony, mockery, even invective—all found in the comic stories of the Troubles—convey in various ways the desire for a better state of affairs.

Satire also may have an optimistic effect, if only by exposing the failure of humans and their institutions to live up to their ideals or by revealing the pretense that they have lived up to them. Maureen Waters remarks that in Irish literature "[s]atire is used to achieve perspective against contemporary pressure to romanticize and sentimentalize history and tradition."[13] Certainly, this might be said of the satiric stories of the Troubles. In looking back at the revolution, the stories shed critical light on romanticized or sentimentalized views of revolutionaries and patriotic noncombatants and thus suggest a need for a revisionist view of the Troubles.

Black humor, with its macabre and grotesque elements and its sardonic tone, stands alone among humorous modes in the unrelenting dark view it takes and, consequently, seems not to require a sense of distance but perhaps even thrives when none exists. It evokes laughter, but rarely of a hopeful kind. It is not surprising, therefore, that it first appears in the Troubles stories in the 1970s when Northern Ireland was plunged into the nightmare of sectarian violence and terrorism. At the same time, the lighter and more amusing forms of comedy disappear from the Troubles stories.

12. David Krause, *The Profane Book of Irish Comedy* (Ithaca: Cornell University Press, 1982), 18.

13. Maureen Waters, *The Comic Irishman* (Albany: State University of New York Press, 1984), 90.

The fifteen or so stories of the Troubles that employ comic and/or satiric modes do so in varying and complex mixtures of techniques and themes. The following analyses present four categories of stories that illustrate the ways writers have used humor and satire to offer perspectives on the Troubles: 1) comic absurdities: themes of repression and liberation; 2) satiric attacks on revolutionary types and their sympathizers; 3) farce, mockery, and the myths of revolution; and 4) black humor and sectarian violence.

III

Comic theorists point out that the sense of absurdity found in much comedy ultimately springs from the awareness we human beings have of our condition of bondage: that is, we are trapped in a world that we neither understand nor have the power to control. We can imagine a world of liberation, but we can not actualize it. Our response to this awareness of the absurd can take different forms, including indifference, despair, resolve, and laughter. Consequently, literary treatments of the absurd range from the tragic and the heroic to the comic. In writing about Brendan Behan's literary treatment of absurdity, Ted E. Boyle explains the significance of responding with laughter: "Perceiving the disparity between the world as it is and the world as he can imagine it, the man aware of the absurd laughs; and in this laugh he protests that he is superior to the world because he possesses the power to imagine it as something better than it is. The laugh also asserts man's vitality, his refusal to accept the sentence which the world passes on him. . . ."[14]

Revolution offers the writer with a sense of the absurd plenty of material from which to draw. Because revolution fundamentally has to do with resistance to repression and bondage and the pursuit of liberation and freedom, it contains the essential elements of absurdity and, therefore, great potential for humor. O'Connor, especially, had a keen eye for the absurdities of revolution. He records in *An Only Child* several comically absurd incidents that he observed, some of which he worked into

14. Ted E. Boyle, *Brendan Behan* (New York: Twayne, 1969), 61.

his Troubles stories. In one incident during the Civil War, for example, rebels planned to attack the barracks in Inchigeela by having one of their members "disguised as a tinker and carrying a baby . . . drive on an ass-cart to the barrack door, shoot the sentry, and hold the way open for his men." The plan fell through, however, partly because the man responsible for it, "going from door to door, trying to borrow a baby," was unsuccessful, which led him to bemoan "the lack of patriotism in Irish mothers" (OC 234). O'Connor was particularly interested in how absurdity is often inherent in matters of repression and liberation. He treated the theme in two stories, "Machine-Gun Corps in Action" and "Freedom."

In writing "Freedom," O'Connor drew from an incident he experienced while he was imprisoned at Gormanstown during the last months of the Civil War. The incident, related in *An Only Child* (255–57), was the logical, yet absurd consequence of the republicans' "lack of humour" and their insistence "that the Irish Republic was still in existence and would remain so." O'Connor says that Republican prisoners at Gormanstown "had a complete military organization that duplicated and superseded that of [their] gaolers." Consequently, when one of the republican prisoners, Frank Murphy, refused to do the fatigues assigned to him by his republican superiors, they "court-martialed" and "imprisoned" him in "a small time-keeper's hut with barred windows" borrowed from *their* captors. He was "guarded" by two republican prisoners "wearing tricolour armlets," who of course were, themselves, being monitored by Free State guards. Murphy retaliated by going on a hunger strike, thus using the republicans' own resistance strategy against them. His captors then countered by releasing him from their prison and boycotting him. This solution was proposed and voted on at a meeting of all the republican prisoners. Out of some nine hundred votes, only O'Connor's was cast against the proposal. Apparently only O'Connor was able to see the absurdity of "people who were in prison for refusing to recognize majority rule" becoming so exercised over someone who was simply doing the same.

In recreating this incident in "Freedom," O'Connor changes a few details but keeps the essential, absurd one of a prison within a prison containing a prisoner held captive by other prisoners. He shifts the setting from the Civil War to the War of Independence and, thus, has the internment camp run by the British rather than the Free State forces. Like the republican prisoners in the Free State camp, the Irish prisoners in the story have duplicated the organization of their captors: "[W]e recognized only our own officers. The Quartermaster drew the stores from the British and we received them from him and signed for them to him. The mail was sorted and delivered by our own post-office staff. We had our cooks, our doctors, our teachers and actors—even our police. Because, if one of our fellows was caught pinching another man's stuff, we had our own police to arrest him and our own military court to try him" (SFO 99).

When Mick Stewart, a character modeled on Frank Murphy, refuses to do fatigues assigned to him by the republican hierarchy, he is arrested by two men "wearing tricolour armlets" (SFO 99), tried, and imprisoned in "a timekeeper's hut" (SFO 103) with bars on the window. Like Murphy, Mick retaliates by going on a hunger strike. At the meeting held by the rebels to discuss the crisis, there is a general discussion, rather than a vote, for a proposal to boycott Mick. The narrator (obviously O'Connor's alter ego) is the only one to speak out against the boycott, but he is ineffectual, unable to convince the assembly that the whole matter is absurd, that (as he has remarked earlier) "You would think that men who were rebels themselves and suffering for their views would have some sympathy for [Mick]" (SFO 100–101), a comment that resembles the one O'Connor recorded in *An Only Child* about the actual incident.

"Freedom" is a comic response to the absurdity of human behavior, and the humor is of a light, amusing variety, evoking laughter at the irrationality of the republicans' "logic." But the story is also serious in its insight about the issue of human bondage and liberation because it reflects the universal human plight through the particular situation of the story. The narrator's final comment alludes to the absurdity of the human condition as it is revealed in the prison camp experience: "Seeing that a man can never really get out of jail, the great thing is to ensure that he gets into the biggest possible one with the largest possible range of modern amenities" (SFO 109).

"Machine-Gun Corps in Action" also treats the theme of repression and liberation, and it does so, like "Freedom," in an amusing way. The light tone is due in large part to O'Connor's development of the protagonist in the tradition of Irish comic figures. Set during the Civil War, the story relates the adventures of a tramp who refuses to turn over his machine gun, bought from a British soldier for two pounds, to a republican brigade much in need of its fire-power in its struggle with Free State forces. In the course of the story the tramp eludes attempts to corral him and put his gun in service to the republican cause.

The central character of the tramp is drawn from two traditional Irish comic figures, the *omadhawn*, or rustic clown, and the rogue, both described in detail by Waters in *The Comic Irishman*. O'Connor's protagonist is a "little ragged figure . . . dressed in an outworn check suit, a pair of musical-comedy tramp's brogues, and a cap which did no more than half conceal his shock of dirty yellow hair" (GN 100). His appearance thus associates him with the *omadhawn* who, as Waters says in describing one of her examples of the type, is often "[d]ressed in ill fitting and oddly assorted garments. . . ."[15] Interestingly, despite wearing brogues, the shoes after which the comic Irishman's speech is named, O'Connor's clown does not speak in brogue.

The tramp may look like a clown, but he acts the part of the rogue, whom Waters links to the *rapparee* and the highwayman, figures who roamed and plundered but also gave to the poor and defenseless.[16] Like the rogue, O'Connor's character is wild and reckless, roaming where he will, but in "his career as knight-errant," he also takes up with "quixotic enthusiasm" (GN 116) the defense of a widow besieged by her dead husband's family. He also resembles the rogue in his ability to elude pursuers. In eluding the republicans on several occasions, the tramp, like

15. Waters, *Comic Irishman*, 19.
16. Ibid., 30.

the traditional rogue, relies on shrewdness, trickery, boldness, and verbal skill.[17] At one point, for instance, he asks the narrator for directions to the republican brigade, feigning an intention to join the unit, but then makes off elsewhere. In the end, the tramp's fate, like that of the traditional rogue, is sealed by women.[18] He is caught by the republicans while defending the widow, and then he is "rescued" by his domineering wife who has come looking for him and is certain to keep him under wraps.

The clown and the rogue, according to Waters, share other traits that are also developed in O'Connor's character. Both have an appealing vitality and "live by their wits." Most importantly, both resist domination by others, a trait that points up the theme of repression and liberation. Waters says that the rogue is motivated by "a desire for freedom and autonomy" and that the clown eventually becomes "his own master."[19] In that vein, O'Connor's character declares to the republicans who have captured him: "I refuse to return with you. I'm a free citizen of this country and nobody has any rights over me. I warn you I'll resist" (GN 118).

O'Connor also incorporates an element of comic absurdity into the story from an incident he experienced in the Civil War and recorded in *An Only Child*. The incident involved a big gun expropriated by O'Connor from the owner, who, like the tramp in the story, had a proprietary attitude toward it. Republicans then used it to bombard a parsonage inhabited by Free State troops. The absurdity developed when the men firing the gun did not notice that, after the first shot, "the enemy rushed out of the parsonage with their hands in the air." When the republicans continued to fire, the Free State soldiers ran off, again unobserved by the rebels who proceeded to waste the rest of the shells on the empty parsonage (OC 225–26). In "Machine-Gun Corps in Action," the rebels, using an armored car with the tramp and his machine gun perched on top, attack a town which they think is being held by Free State forces but in actuality has been abandoned. The narrator, driving the vehicle,

17. Ibid., 36, 40.

18. Ibid., 30.

19. Ibid., 21, 40, 13.

cannot see what is going on outside and has to rely on the tramp for directions. The tramp shoots up the town and in the process wounds some of the republican soldiers. He then escapes while the narrator is attempting to restart the stalled armored car.

The tramp's resistance of the republicans, comic as it is, offers a model of liberation: a refusal to submit to forces professing a goal of liberation but pursuing it through means of repression. In fact, the story sketches a larger pattern of repression and liberation that threatens to dissolve into absurdity: the Free State soldiers, having won some measure of liberation from the British, are in the act of repressing the republicans, who are themselves attempting to repress the tramp. But while the tramp has managed to maintain his independence from the republicans, he eventually is brought under control by his wife. In a story about the forces of repression—English, Free State, and republican—the tramp's submission to his wife may be O'Connor's ultimate joke.

IV

If the absurdities of the revolution were apparent to O'Connor, so were the many aspects of it susceptible to satiric attack, especially the cant, hypocrisy, and pretensions of the participants and their sympathizers. The Troubles provided O'Connor and other Irish writers with plenty to satirize, including the romantic notions and outfits of the revolutionaries; the sentimental, patriotic blather of civilians; the fanatical proclamations of those who asked young men to die for Ireland; the hypocrisy that disguised a propensity for violence or material gain with a veneer of idealism; and the simple failure of many to live up to the ideals of the revolution. The result is an array of satiric stories, employing a variety of techniques ranging from light, amusing irony at one end, to bitter, sardonic criticism and sheer invective at the other end. They all, however, have the same intent: to expose the failings of the revolution and its participants. O'Connor was particularly interested in satirizing Irish types that embraced without question, or sentimentally blathered about, the revolutionary cause: the romantic, the idealist, the drunken patriot, and so on. In "Lofty," "Eternal Triangle," and "Private

Property," he skewers those types, though in his characteristically light manner.

In "Lofty," O'Connor satirizes the Irishman whose interest in revolution is purely romantic—the romance of the slouch hat, the trench coat, and the gun. There is a touch of self-mockery in O'Connor's satire: he writes in *An Only Child* of his early days as a Volunteer, walking "the country roads on summer evenings, slouching along in knee breeches and gaiters, hands in the pockets of one's trench-coat and hat pulled over one's right eye" (OC 202). The title character of "Lofty," a middle-aged owner of a successful plumbing business, has nurtured his romantic notions of soldiering through a life-long fascination with playing soldier and an interest in, ironically, the British army: "Soldiering was Lofty's secret delight and sorrow. He began with toy soldiers and went on to gangs and wooden swords and water pistols, but by the time he was fifteen he could recognize almost any regiment by its uniform, and every symbol of the intricate craft had significance for him" (BC 118).

When the Civil War breaks out, Lofty chooses to join the republican forces rather than the Free State army, though not out of any ideological agreement. He is more concerned with his image as a romantic revolutionary: "For months it was uncertain which way he would jump, but on the day the fighting broke out, Lofty drove off in his brand-new car, wearing a bandolier and Sam Browne belt and a sombrero pinned up at one side by a tri-coloured rosette. He had turned up the two ends of his moustache at right angles" (BC 128).

Despite his choice of the republican side, Lofty "refuse[s] to be associated with the irregulars," so he and two of his plumbers drive up into the "Wicklow mountains, twenty miles from anywhere" (BC 128–29). There he establishes his own headquarters, where he can remain safely removed from the war, observing the dust raised by cattle on distant roads and mistaking it for troop skirmishes. When he is finally noticed by Free State troops, he is summoned by a General who turns out to be his Free State double: both tweak their moustaches, glare at the other, boast of their military prowess, and trade Michael Collins stories. But whatever revolutionary fervor Lofty might have possessed deserts him.

When pressed by the General to explain himself, he invents an excuse that he and his plumbers were on their way to repair the drains at a convent and disguised themselves as rebels in order to make their way out of the city. Nevertheless, he is able to get through the war—at some distance from the fighting—with his lofty notions of himself relatively intact.

O'Connor's satiric gaze broadens to include other revolutionaries and associated types in "Eternal Triangle," a story that in character, setting, incident, and tone recalls O'Casey's satiric treatment of the Easter Rising in *The Plough and the Stars*. Originally entitled "The Rising" when first published in *Cornhill Magazine* (Autumn, 1951), the story takes place in Dublin during the Easter Rising of 1916. The narrator, a watchman for the tramway company, has been assigned to "keep an eye" on a disabled tram until a repair crew can get to it. When he arrives at the tram, he finds a revolution in progress. Irish Volunteers are in the streets firing guns, and the tram is in the middle of the action, its windows smashed and its upholstery torn. Nevertheless, the narrator dutifully takes possession of the tram, and as he waits out the fighting he is joined by a prostitute, a Volunteer, and a drunk.

Like O'Casey in his Dublin Trilogy and Behan in his play *The Hostage*, O'Connor exploits these traditional Irish stereotypes in order to satirize their romantic and sentimental attitudes toward Ireland and the revolution. The prostitute is by turns scornful and sentimental about Ireland. Angry that the combatants are "banging their bloody bullets all round [her]," she notes with scorn that the police haven't arrived to stop the fighting and then remarks: "Damn soon them fellows would be along if it was only me talking to a fellow!" (MS 31–32). But a moment later with "a tear in her eye" she tells the watchman: "Still and all . . . if 'twas for Ireland, you wouldn't mind so much" (MS 32). With satiric thrust, the narrator sums up her type: "That is the kind of women they are. They'll steal the false teeth from a corpse, but let them lay eyes on a green flag or a child in his First Communion suit, and you'd think patriotism and religion were the only two things ever in their minds" (MS 32).

The drunk exhibits the traits of the stage Irishman: he is garrulous, bellicose, full of patriotic blather, and cowardly. He is so inebriated that the effects of the shooting, explosions, and fires all around him make him think he has the D.T.s. He "surrenders" to the tram watchman, but once he enters the car and manages a drink of whisky he becomes belligerent and a false courage surfaces: "I'd cut the throat of any bloody Englishman," he says; "I'm not afraid of anyone" (MS 38). At the sound of gunfire, however, he throws up his hands and falls over as if shot. When the watchman, at the prostitute's prompting, attempts to say an act of contrition in the "dying" man's ear, he confuses it with the Apostle's Creed, provoking an argument between him and the prostitute. At that point, the drunk revives, resumes his threats against the English troops, and then falls asleep and begins to snore.

The source of the drunk's "shooting" is in an incident O'Connor experienced in the Civil War, still another instance of his perception of humor in the revolution. Captured by Free State forces, O'Connor was being escorted by three soldiers to a farmhouse when one of the soldiers, annoyed by O'Connor's verbal abuse, fired his revolver at his heels. Immediately, a "little soldier on [O'Connor's] left dropped his rifle, threw up his hands, and fell," believing himself to have been struck by the bullet. When the other Free State soldiers panicked, one "shout[ing] into the prostrate man's ear what he thought was an Act of Contrition but was really the Creed," O'Connor opened the man's tunic to examine him. The soldier, having simply fainted, woke up and cursed everyone: "Then he rose with great dignity, dusted himself, buttoned his tunic, shouldered his rifle, and resumed his march" (OC 219–20).

The Volunteer in "Eternal Triangle" is also an object of O'Connor's satire. Shortly after entering the tram, he smashes out all of the windows, heedless of the "[m]illions of pounds' worth of property burning" (MS 36) caused by the Rising. The watchman scorns the Volunteer's behavior, saying that, but for the gunfire, he would "have taken him and wrung his neck" (MS 33). It is, in fact, this disgust for the destruction caused by the combatants that provokes the narrator's most incensed comment, the story's opening paragraph:

> Revolutions? I never had any interest in them. A man in my position have to mind his job and not bother about what other people are doing. . . . All I ever seen out of things like that was the damage. And who pays for the damage? You and me and people like us, so that one set of jackeens can get in instead of another set of jackeens. What is it to me who's in or out? All I know is that I have to pay for the damage they do. (MS 29)

The watchman ends the story by telling the reader that he went home to bed, where he stayed for a week until the Rising was over. "Eternal Triangle" is O'Connor's most hilarious account of the revolution, but it is also one of his strongest denunciations of it. The narrator's final comment reflects that view: "I was never so disgusted with anything in my life" (MS 40).

In "Private Property," O'Connor satirizes those who abandon their revolutionary idealism, placing personal economic interests above loyalty to "the secret revolutionary army" (DR 74). A squabble between two members of the secret organization over a clock leads to a police seizure of the brigade's weapons dump and the eventual dissolution of the organization. Joe Ward asks Tom Harrison, his brother-in-law and Brigade Adjutant, for a much-needed loan. When Harrison refuses, Ward steals a clock that he gave Harrison for a wedding present. Harrison reports Ward to the Free State police, who search Ward's house and retrieve the clock. Three weeks later the police raid the dump and seize all of the brigade's weapons.

The narrator, an idealistic youth of seventeen and Brigade Quartermaster, has tried to keep the peace in the organization for the sake of the revolution, but in the end he realizes that "there was no chance at all for idealism" (DR 88). He has learned that Harrison, in order to get the police to retrieve the clock, revealed to them the location of the Brigade weapons dump. Disgusted by the lack of idealism and loyalty in his fellow rebels, the narrator gives up his revolutionary activities and enrolls, ironically, in the School of Commerce—apparently to become a materialist himself.

This story also has an autobiographical element, specifically in the narrator's relationship to his father, who takes, as O'Connor's father had, a dim view of revolutionaries. The relationship provides a comic, self-mocking aspect to the story. The narrator and his father argue over the boy's night-time activities, resulting in this comic sentence: "He tried to keep me in check by making me be home at ten, but I felt that as a revolutionist as well as a wage-earner, I had to stick out for half past" (DR 74–75). O'Connor says that his father, upon going to bed at ten every night, would bolt the door so that O'Connor would have to knock when he came home, thus creating a ruckus that "stung . . . [his] pride as a soldier of Ireland" (OC 203). After the narrator learns the truth about the police raid, he "wonder[s] if there mightn't be something in Father's views" (DR 88), probably O'Connor's own insight after his experiences in the revolution. "Private Property" appears to be the last story O'Connor composed about the revolution. If so, then its final sentence has as much meaning for its author as it does for its narrator: "I was beginning to see that there was no future in revolutions" (DR 90).

Following O'Connor's lead, short-story writers in the next generation found much to satirize in the Troubles. Helen Lucy Burke's "Battles Long Ago" begins as a predictable and amusing satire on former rebels who live in the revolutionary past and drink away the present, but midway into the narrative it takes an unexpected, sharply-edged turn. Three former, now middle-aged revolutionaries, Tom, Cahal, and Paddy, return to Tom's house after an evening of drinking in town. Tom and Cahal, who are quite inebriated, exhibit all of the traits of the stereotypical drunken Irishman: Tom is bellicose toward two Englishmen on the bus home; both Tom and Cahal stumble and vomit on the walk from the bus stop to the house; and Cahal falls into a drunken stupor on the floor of Tom's home. Along the way to Tom's home, they sentimentally reminisce about their revolutionary days, singing the Ballad of Cloonbawn, in which both Tom and Paddy are mentioned for their supposedly heroic exploits during the War of Independence. But Tom is also, at times, lachrymose and bitter about the way he has been treated since the revolution: "In a low voice he sobbed that he should be coming home in a black Government Mercedes instead of a sixpenny busride" (SM 50).

When they arrive at the house, Tom's wife is cold but polite, offering the men cream crackers and smoked salmon prepared for her daughter and her daughter's fiancé who are expected shortly.

At this point, the light comic tone of the satire turns dark. As Tom watches men on the television talk blandly about the problems of world population and agricultural solutions, he begins to talk back to them, apparently in his drunken haze seeing them as interrogators accusing him of some revolutionary betrayal. Meanwhile, Paddy, who has managed to remain sober, slowly realizes from Tom's responses that what has long been rumored is, in fact, true. During the War of Independence Tom killed the Maguire brothers because they discovered that he had betrayed the rebels while he was being tortured by the Black and Tans. Paddy also remembers that Tom's betrayal of fellow revolutionaries had a family dimension: Tom's wife came from the Maguire family, and the two executed rebels were her cousins. Furthermore, the reader realizes that, judging from his wife's mouthing of Tom's drunken responses to the television, the responses must constitute a regular ritual. Tom's anguish is apparently her satisfaction for what he has done.

The story ends with another kind of ironic betrayal. As Cathal and Paddy leave, the daughter and her fiancé arrive. The young man, whom Tom and his wife have not previously met, is "tall, very blonde, healthy looking in a brutal sort of way, and unmistakably English" (SM 55). What has begun as a light but predictable satire of the boisterous, bellicose drunken Irish rebel has turned into a dark satire on betrayal in Irish life. Still, the reader cannot help but think that Burke approves of the daughter's engagement to the Englishman, perhaps as a symbol of how finally to end revolution and betrayal.

Most satire, as illustrated in the examples above, employs irony to reveal the reality under the appearance of things: the romantic revolutionary is really a coward, the idealist a materialist, the hero an informer, and so on. As satire moves from light to bitter, it also moves toward invective, that is, sheer vituperation with little or no irony.[20] Tom MacIntyre's

20. Frye, *Anatomy*, 223.

"An Aspect of the Rising" is a wonderful satiric mix of comic incident and invective, with the latter directed at one of the great leaders of the revolution. The story is set in 1966, the fiftieth anniversary of the Easter Rising. It is narrated by a Dubliner who relates his experience of picking up a flashy prostitute who calls herself Philomena. The two drive off to The Park beyond Kingsbridge to find a dark, quiet spot to have sex. But as the narrator moves next to Philomena, who is reclining against a tree, he finds her cold and unapproachable. When he asks what's wrong, she launches into a puzzling diatribe: "You crawthumpin' get of a Spaniard that never was seen . . . with your long features and your long memory and your two and twenty-two strings to your bow, what crooked eggs without yolks are you hatching between Rosaries tonight?" (TS 145).

At first baffled by this outpouring, the narrator suddenly realizes with "a skelp of joy" (TS 145) that the prostitute is looking out at a building, Arus an Uachtarian, the residence of the President of the Republic of Ireland, Éamon de Valera, and that her invective is directed against de Valera, presumably because he has not fulfilled the ideals of the revolution. The narrator's bafflement turns to admiration:

> Philomena roasted The Long Fellow. Practice graced her, rancours unnameable and a fury of the bones powered her—she left nothing out, there was nothing she didn't fit in: The Treaty, The Civil War, The Oath, The Hangings of the 'forties, Emigration, Inflation, Taxation, the Language, the lot. An eighth of a mile away, brooding or at his prayers, His Excellency heard not a word but, chosen by the gods, I heard, the ground heard and the wind and the sky's cupped ear. We listened to that alto scurrility leap the air, listened in ecstasy and heard. . . . (TS 145–46)

Philomena, the prostitute with the ironic name (Latin for "beloved") and perhaps an ironic version of Cathleen ni Houlihan, spews out all of de Valera's political sins in invective reminiscent of the ancient Gaelic poets satirizing the kings of Ireland. Like theirs, her invective seems intended to have a physical effect on the leader. Mercier explains that the Gaelic satirist was thought to have magical powers: *áer*, the Irish word used for lampoon or personal attack that eventually came to mean satire, "must originally have signified 'spell' or 'enchantment'. . . . an *áer* was believed to have power to cause facial blemishes, or even death, in its victim."[21] Most likely, however, Philomena's message will be ineffectual. Rather than looking for ways to effect the ideals of the revolution, the Irish people and government are fixated on the past: "in the city below, and all over Ireland, medals were being dusted, ribbons spruced, orations polished and artillery oiled for The Fiftieth Anniversary of The Insurrection" (TS 146).

V

Other targets of comic and satiric writers include the myths, symbols, and pieties that sustain the ideologies of both factions in the Troubles. Myths and the like are especially important in long-term rebellions in that they sustain insurgents even when all rational outlook for success is bleak. As noted in chapter 1, the central republican myth is that of blood sacrifice, evoked and enacted by Pearse and the heroes of 1916, according to which the Irish republic would be born of the self-immolation of its martyr-heroes. Loyalists have also exercised symbolism and myth-making in the service of their cause, first in their opposition to home rule and, since partition, in their opposition to unification of north and south. Richard Kearney observes that, while republicans have promoted the myth of blood sacrifice, loyalists have emphasized the symbols and myths of triumph. Although "the Unionist/Loyalist community has had its share of suffering," he points out, "it does not identify with this suffering as a fundamental symbol of its own specific tradition or ideology. Suffering for them is not transformed into sacrifice and martyrdom." Rather, "Loyalists tend more to identify with the triumphalist emblems of their historical victories: King Billy and Carson. The Apprentice Boys parade and Orange Day marches celebrate political and military success, not failure." Loyalist ideology is best expressed, Kearney says, in the catch phrase "Ulster will fight and Ulster will be right," which "is in stark contrast to the sacrificial ideology of Republicanism. . . ."[22]

21. Mercier, *Comic Tradition*, 106.

22. Richard Kearney, *Transitions: Narratives in Modern Irish Culture* (Manchester, England: Manchester University Press, 1988), 235.

Perhaps more than any other aspect of their ideologies, myths have sustained the determination of republicans and loyalists to continue the conflict. The compelling, irrational, and seemingly irrepressible power of myth makes any kind of rational challenge to it futile. Consequently, for those who reject these myths and believe that an end to the Troubles requires their deflation, finding a way to do so is not easy. The most promising challenge comes from the equally irrational and irrepressible forces of humor. Ridicule, comic desecration, mockery, and farce stand the best, perhaps the only possible, chance of dealing a blow to the great power of myth. O'Casey's *The Plough and the Stars* and Behan's *The Hostage*, for example, both demonstrate how the myth of blood sacrifice loses much of its allure when held up to the mockery and desecration of the comic dramatist. In the short story, Flann O'Brien and John Morrow attack the great allure of Troubles myths. O'Brien treats the myth of blood sacrifice with farce, and Morrow mocks the loyalist propensity to create mythic heroes where they do not exist. Both writers effectively deflate the myths of the Troubles, if only for the moment.

O'Brien's "The Martyr's Crown" is without a doubt the funniest of the comic stories of the Troubles: a farcical tale of a rebel ambush, a safe house, and sex. It is also a pub joke whose punch line turns on the sacred Irish myth of dying heroically for Ireland—but in this case the hero is born for Ireland. O'Brien frames the central story of the Troubles by having it related in a pub, years later, by Mr. Toole to his friend Mr. O'Hickey.

Mr. Toole's story is prompted by an unpleasant encounter the two shabby, middle-aged men have just had in the streets of Dublin. When walking with friends, Mr. Toole, we are told, has the habit of greeting well dressed, important-looking strangers in order to give the impression to his friends that, though poor now, he was once "a person of quality" (S&P 83). Startled, most of the strangers return his greeting, which always prompts Mr. Toole's companions to ask the identity of the important person. But this day Mr. Toole has predicted to Mr. O'Hickey that an elegant young man approaching them will "cut [him] dead" (S&P 84). Sure enough, when Mr. Toole salutes the young man with

"*How are we at all, Sean a chara?*" (S&P 84; italics in text), the young man refuses to acknowledge him in even the slightest way. The snub prompts Mr. O'Hickey to ask who he is. Coyly, Mr. Toole answers only that he knew well the young man's mother. Led to a pub and bribed by a drink to explain further, Mr. Toole tells Mr. O'Hickey about an adventure he claims to have had as a young man during the War of Independence. Mr. O'Hickey, however, knows "that Mr. Toole had never rendered military service to his country" (S&P 84).

Mr. Toole's story involves a Mrs. Clougherty, a Catholic widow and a captain in Cumann na mBan, the women's auxiliary to the Irish Volunteers. According to Mr. Toole, Mrs. Clougherty hid six rebels, Toole included, in her boarding house shortly after they had ambushed British soldiers in downtown Dublin. When a British officer, leading troops conducting a house-to-house search for the rebels, knocked on her door, Mrs. Clougherty ("a marvelous figure of a woman" [S&P 86]), invited the young officer in and, after some whispering, escorted him to a bedroom. Shortly thereafter the two emerged from the bedroom, the officer left the house, the troops drove off, and the rebels went safely to bed. The humor of the incident is enhanced by Mr. Toole's comment that the devout Mrs. Clougherty led the rebels in prayer before retiring for the night.

Mr. O'Hickey, as well as the reader, wants to know, of course, what Mr. Toole's story has to do with the haughty young man, which leads Mr. Toole (and O'Brien) to the punch line: "Do you not see it, man? . . . For seven hundred year, thousands—no, I'll make it millions—of Irish men and women have died for Ireland. . . . But that young man was *born* for Ireland. There was never anybody else like him. Why wouldn't he be proud?" (S&P 88; italics in text).

Ben Forkner has written that "The Martyr's Crown" demonstrates O'Brien's "brilliant powers of Irish farce at full strength."[23] Indeed, although the story lacks some of the more popular aspects of farce, such as

23. Ben Forkner, Introduction to *Modern Irish Short Stories*, ed. Ben Forkner (New York: Penguin, 1980), 39.

slapstick, horseplay, bawdy language, and broad ribaldry, it is built on that staple of farce, the bedroom scene, which O'Brien cleverly places off-stage. More to the point, the story resembles farce in that its mockery has a sacred object, namely, the republican myth of sacrifice. Krause says that, contrary to popular opinion, farce does not evoke laughter simply for its own sake; rather, its laughter is "efficacious . . . when it mocks and deflates whatever is excessively sacred in society. . . ."[24] Unlike typical farce, however, O'Brien's story is subtle in its mockery of the sacred. It does not blatantly attack the myth of sacrifice as, say, O'Casey and Behan do in their plays. Rather, it surprises the reader with the idea that an Irishman being born for Ireland is an immensely preferable alternative to Irishmen dying for Ireland—or, more to the point, sex is better than death.

Moreover, O'Brien gains additional force in his deflation of the myth of sacrifice by framing the farcical story of Mrs. Clougherty and the rebels. By having Mr. Toole tell it years later in a pub, the story becomes a pub joke, one that can be told over and over again, a recurrent mockery of the myth of sacrifice. Jokes, Freud says, "represent a rebellion against authority, a liberation from its pressure. . . . [T]hey make possible the satisfaction of an instinct (whether lustful or hostile) in the face of an obstacle that stands in its way."[25] "The Martyr's Crown," as farcical tale and pub joke, releases in the Irish reader the instinct for liberation from a repressive nationalist myth.

Morrow also directs his comic talents against the formidable power of myth, though his method is more direct and more sardonic than O'Brien's. While his pieces evoke laughter, it is a scathing laughter born of cynicism. Writing about the Northern Troubles, Morrow directs his mockery at both factions, nationalist and loyalist. In "Northern Myths" Morrow ridicules the tendency of loyalists to create hero-myths in defiance of reality. The story (actually more sketch than story) offers two ex-

24. Krause, *Profane Book*, 136.

25. Sigmund Freud, *Jokes and Their Relation to the Unconscious* (1905; reprint New York: Norton, 1963), 110, quoted in Krause, *Profane Book*, 19.

amples of such myth-making. In the first several paragraphs, Morrow's narrator compares the "truth of the matter" regarding Joe McConkey with the legend that blossomed after his death, and then in the remaining several pages he presents the mythic case of Tommy "Duncher" McAnuff.

Joe McConkey, Morrow's narrator tells us, was a "twenty-two year old unemployed caulker, under the influence of fifteen bottles of stout, God and Ulster," the last phrase deftly summing up so much of the inspiration for killing in Northern Ireland. When McConkey fired his gun at a patrol of British soldiers in the streets of Belfast, he was himself shot and killed by a wounded soldier, "a second generation coffee-coloured Welshman from Cardiff." If it seems odd that a Protestant, even a drunken one, would assault British soldiers ostensibly in Northern Ireland to protect Protestant rights, Morrow's narrator offers the following observation: "Judging by his last shouted remarks, Joe had been under the impression that the Pope was among the wounded" (NM 1).

In the myth that springs up after his death, Joe is transformed into "[f]ifteen-year-old Sergeant Joseph McConkey, 91st Company, Church Lads brigade" (presumably a unit of one of the Ulster militias). According to the myth, Joe was on his way home "with half-a-dozen baps for his Mammy—she's a widda woman, half crippled," when British soldiers stopped him. As he walked away, one (the Welshman, who now becomes a "Fenian bastard") shot him in the back. So McConkey becomes "an example of what happens to the unsuccessful thug: canonisation in the folk-memory as an innocent victim of the Khaki Hun" (NM 1–2). Had a ballad been written about Joe, the narrator says, there's no doubt that the patrol of British soldiers who killed Joe would have become a company of the IRA.

The case of "Duncher" McAnuff is as ridiculous as than that of McConkey. "Duncher," now serving out a "three year sentence in Crumlin Road Gaol" for an attack on the British army, is celebrated by Protestants for his exploits: "The Prod ghettoes abound with personal anecdotes illustrating the ruthlessness and cunning of 'Duncher', the Capo di Mafia, the right-wing Ché of the backstreets" (NM 2).

The truth of the matter is simply that Tommy McAnuff, "small, grey and more than half-deaf" (NM 2) was caught in the wrong place at the wrong time. An inveterate crowd-watcher, Tommy was observing a Belfast mob clashing with troops when a sniper came up behind him and steadied his rifle on Tommy's shoulder as he fired at the troops. When he finished, the sniper threw down the gun and ran off, leaving Tommy to be caught by the troops "standing beside [the gun], eyes tightly shut, pipe sagging between clenched teeth, his right cheek black with powder marks" (NM 4). As he was being arrested by a British corporal, Tommy reacted in the "heroic" way that earned him his nickname ("Duncher" is Belfast slang for a soft cap): "Lifting off his cap by the peak he gave the Corporal a back-handed swipe across his Pexiglass [sic] riot visor . . . 'Lave aff, y'ganch ye!' roared 'Duncher' McAnuff" (NM 4).

Although Morrow's ridicule in "Northern Myths" is largely concentrated on loyalist "heroes," he seems intent on exposing all hypocritical aspects of the Troubles. The following passage, representative of his acclaimed comic style, scathingly describes the various components of the Belfast mob that Tommy McAnuff watches clashing with British troops:

> The mob kept coming on until almost abreast of Tommy's vantage point, a stones-throw from the troop lines. As was the custom they had limbered up by smashing street lights on the way down. The main body of youthful marksmen, a berserk coalition of hirsute Pop idolators and dungareed skin-heads, centred around a colour-party of ancient winos in the middle of the road. Flanking them came a motley crush of Mums and sweethearts, religious maniacs, Aldermen, fly-men and prospective looters, all chanting gable-end lyrics of a hair-raising obscenity as the stones began to thunder on the riot shields of the troops. (NM 3)

The mordant humor in "Northern Myths" comes quite simply from Morrow's ability to point out the truth of the matter with directness, to deflate what has been inflated: sainted Joe McConkey is really a thug; "Duncher" McAnuff is nothing but a passive by-stander; Belfast protestors are berserk vandals, winos, religious maniacs, looters and the like. In its satirical intent, the story is somewhat hopeful: if the truth can be revealed, it seems to say, the sustaining myths of the Troubles may be abandoned and a resolution to the conflict may follow. "Northern

Myths" is probably the only comic story of the Northern Troubles that does have a touch of hope. The only other humor that appears in stories about the north is black humor, a humor that offers no hope.

VI

The Troubles in Northern Ireland, for a number of reasons, strike most people as far more ghastly and nightmarish than the Troubles of 1916–1923. The near-constant element of terrorism, the great many civilian casualties, and the conflict's exceptionally long duration (over a quarter century) all contribute to this nightmarish impression. For these reasons and because there has been no opportunity to view these horrible events from a clarifying distance, the most appropriate comic response seems to be black humor.

A primary element of black humor is the macabre, the portrayal of that which is grim and ghastly—in other words, horrible pain and death. The presentation of the macabre in the context of a joke or comic incident results in a laughter which, Mercier says, "is tinged with terror."[26] Mrs. Gogan's vision of the Irish rebels in O'Casey's *The Plough and the Stars* (quoted in the epigraph of this chapter) is an apt example of macabre humor applied to the Troubles: "I seem to be lookin' at each of yous hangin' at th' end of a rope, your eyes bulgin' an' your legs twistin' an' jerkin', gaspin' an' gaspin' for breath while yous are thryin' to die for Ireland!"

Unlike traditional comedy or satire, black humor refuses to hold out, or even hint at, a hopeful view of life. Instead, it "express[es] a sense of hopelessness in a wry, sardonic way that is grimly humorous."[27] Waters says that the macabre humor of the Irish is "directly linked to their acute consciousness of death," and she refers to Max Schultz (author of *Black Humor Fiction of the Sixties*, 1973) who believed that "in black humor there is no individual release or social reconciliation as there is in traditional comedy. . . ." Rather, black humor "reflect[s] not only anxiety but

26. Mercier, *Comic Tradition*, 47.

27. *The Bedford Glossary of Critical and Literary Terms*, ed. Ross Murfin and Supryia M. Ray (Boston: Bedford, 1997), s.v. "black humor."

ambivalence, a halfhearted willingness to submit to the inevitable. . . ."[28] Thus, black humor would seem to be the most appropriate—perhaps the only—humorous response to the grim and ghastly violence of the Northern Troubles.

Though it appears briefly in other stories, the only thorough-going example of black humor in a story of the Troubles is Morrow's "Place: Belfast / Time: 1984 / Scene: The only pub." As the allusion to George Orwell's *1984* in the title suggests, the story has a futuristic, dystopian theme (Morrow wrote the story in the 1970s): a united Ireland has come about—but it is not the ideal Ireland that nationalists envisioned. The story is a sustained monologue spoken by a nationalist to a companion in a pub, presumably, as the title notes, "The only pub" remaining in Belfast, suggesting that a united Ireland has brought some severe, unexpected restrictions with it. The Orwellian atmosphere is reinforced by the speaker's reminders to his companion that he had better keep his complaints about the political situation to himself because "you niver know who's listenin' . . ." (NM 92).

As the speaker tells it, the new nation has been achieved largely through the efforts of one man, who appears to be as sinister as Orwell's Big Brother. In a characteristic touch of humor, Morrow's speaker repeatedly refers to this Big Brother as "the wee man." The man has a club foot, wears black shirts and employs "Adverse Propaganda" tactics, which the speaker describes with great relish. He tells his companion that the wee man was able to unite Ireland by employing a cynical, chess-like tactic called "The Bishop's Game." The game consists of ten moves, beginning with the bombing of a Protestant pub, which is certain to provoke "Move two: angry Prods blow up a Taig pub the next Saturday night." Catholics then complain to the local Bishop about lack of protection. The Bishop appeals to the media, resulting in the British Parliament sending the army into the ghetto to protect Catholics. The Catholics then complain of harassment at army checkpoints, which prompts the Bishop to complain again to the media. The instigators of

28. Waters, *Comic Irishman*, 176–78.

the Bishop's Game then "shoot a sodger at a road check—or two . . . ," and the shooting results in howls in Westminster to get the troops out: "The Army withdraws from the ghetto an' Bob's yer Uncle! You've blown up a Prod pub, shot a sodger, made the Army look like a load of Boy Scouts, an' somehow it's all somebody else's fault! So you can start again at Move One . . ." (NM 93–94).

Described as such, the Bishop's Game would seem to be the epitome of cynicism: the escalation of violence in Northern Ireland is revealed to be brought about not simply by angry, spontaneous retaliation at each stage but by cynical premeditation and manipulation of the entire "game." Morrow increases the cynicism—and the black humor—when his speaker reveals how the wee man was cleverly able to manipulate the Bishop's Game to bring about a united Ireland.

A Catholic nationalist, in attempting to start the sequence again, bombs "the wrong [i.e., Catholic] school bus" by mistake. But it doesn't matter to the terrorist, "seein' they [the Catholic children] were goin' to a state school an' weren't confirmed anyway" (NM 94). Nor does it matter to the Protestant militants: they find it opportune to view the attack as if the victims were some of their own. But instead of bombing a Catholic pub in retaliation, they decide that "they're gonta put the lid on the wee man himself" (NM 94). When they arrive at his house, however, he isn't there. So instead they shoot his wife, a dog-breeder with a hair-lip, leaving "her spoutin' like a collander on the mat" (NM 95).

The speaker, the wee man, and another nationalist return just in time to kill one of the terrorists, but they are in a quandary about how to make the attack seem worse than it really is in order to keep the Bishop's Game going. The wee man knows that no one will really care that his wife has been killed. He certainly doesn't, remarking only that the killers "didn't half fix her lip." He had been "hopin' the Prods [would] do somethin' drastic in revenge for the school bus, like blowin' up a load of nuns . . ." (NM 95), something that would raise the ire of the Catholic population. The speaker then makes a proposal (worthy of Swift) to shoot the wee man's children, but the wee man has a better idea: shoot his wife's dogs. So the speaker does, and sure enough, when it gets into the papers that Protestant terrorists have killed dogs, there is outrage in London, which is full of dog lovers attending a week-long dog show:

> A hunnerd thousand dog-lovers from all over England . . . marches on Downing Street under the Tri-colour; Merlyn Rees [British politician who promoted direct rule in Northern Ireland] pelted with hot turds; the Government ready to topple; black-edged newspapers; Leyland shop stewards declare a four week mourning strike; special Capital Punishment Bill forced through Parliament in time to hang the two Prods who were supposed to have done it; and—the jackpot—a declaration of intent to withdraw in 1984! (NM 96)

The ploy works: Ireland is "A Nation Onct Again" (NM 96).

Morrow's story is a fitting comic response to the Northern Troubles. Its humorous blend of the macabre with bitter satire of those who would turn Ireland into a dystopian world evokes laughter but not liberation, insight but no sense of hope. If, as comic theorists say, frustrated emotions seek liberation in laughter, but the immediacy and intensity of the source of the frustrations, i.e., the violence and terrorism of Northern Ireland, preclude lighter comedy and satire and their implication of hope, then black humor seems the only comic mode by which to view the Northern Troubles and thereby release those frustrations.

Yet even black humor rarely appears in stories of the Troubles. In addition to Morrow, Eugene McCabe uses it sparingly in "Cancer," a story treated in the next chapter. And after the 1970s, it too disappears from the Troubles stories.[29] In tracing the uses of the comic in Irish writing, Waters makes an interesting observation about the absence of the comic in recent literature of Northern Ireland. After pointing out what is obvious to most observers—that "[t]here have been too many victims, too many brutal injuries [and, it might be added, too many deaths] on both sides" for Northern Irish writers to take a comic view of life—Waters points out that in one story of terrorism the comic has been perverted

29. Black humor does appear, however, in recent novels about the Northern Troubles. Laura Pelaschiar analyzes the uses of black humor in Colin Bateman's novels in *Writing the North: The Contemporary Novel in Northern Ireland* (Trieste: Edizioni Parnaso, 1998), 22–30.

and reemerges as the tragic grotesque. She suggests that in "Proxopera," a story by Benedict Kiely (taken up in chapter 5 of this study), "the clown has put on the faceless mask of a modern gunman. . . . A laughing boy has become a madman. The Black pig has reemerged as a prophecy of terror and destruction. A humorous song about a drunken adventure becomes a grotesque counterpoint to real acts of violence."[30] If Waters' perception of comic elements lying buried beneath the guise of terrorism is accurate, then it would seem that the on-going grim and ghastly nature of the Troubles has ultimately resulted in the suppression of the comic impulse, that even the laugh "tinged with terror" is no longer possible.

30. Waters, *Comic Irishman*, 179–80.

4

Border and Sectarian Tensions

Realism and Irony

Do you know the word endogamein? *It means to marry within the tribe. And the word* exogamein *means to marry outside the tribe. And you don't cross those borders casually—both sides get very angry.*

—Jimmy Jack, *Translations* by Brian Friel

I

In the period between the end of the Civil War in 1923 and the outbreak of sectarian violence in Northern Ireland in the late 1960s, Irish writers crafted somber stories about Ireland's Troubles, in addition to the humorous and satiric ones. A few of these stories look back to the revolutionary events of 1916–1923; most depict more contemporary events related to the issue of partition and the simmering tensions in sectarian relations. A study of these stories provides insight into the hostilities and tensions that flowed out of the partitioning of Ireland and the ensuing Civil War and that remained in Ireland for decades, often just below the surface, finally erupting in a renewal of sustained violence in the late 1960s. Thus, these stories serve as an important link between the romantic and naturalistic stories of the early Troubles and the stories of violence and terror that were to follow. The stories fall into two broad categories, those that treat IRA activities and those that examine sectarian relationships. Most are written in a realistic style, though the IRA stories also often include elements of the romantic and naturalistic stories, and the sectarian stories have a strong component of irony.

During these decades the IRA was driven underground, having been declared illegal in 1936 by the Irish Free State. It was also greatly reduced in strength, its membership decimated by prison terms, resignations, defections, and the deaths of members. Consequently, much of its activity was directed to restoring and training its membership and restocking its weapons, the latter task often accomplished through raids on police and army barracks and magazine forts. In order to maintain its reputation as a revolutionary organization with nationalist aims, the IRA also conducted attacks on selected targets, such as the custom huts along the border between north and south. Much of this activity was sporadic, but there were two periods of intense, concentrated aggression, a bombing campaign in England in 1939 and a border campaign against the north waged from 1956 to 1962.

In January 1939, the IRA issued an ultimatum to the British to get out of Ireland entirely and, to back up its demands, conducted a bombing campaign in English cities, including Manchester, Birmingham, and London. IRA members planted bombs in letter boxes, telephone booths, public lavatories, and railway cloakrooms, conducting over 127 attacks in England in the first half of 1939. The intent of the IRA in these attacks was not to kill people but to disrupt British life by destroying property. Nevertheless, British citizens were at times killed, including five people in an explosion in Coventry in August 1939. In response to the campaign, the Irish government enacted new laws that effectively crippled the IRA. Authorities in Ireland and England conducted widespread sweeps: IRA members were tracked down, arrested, and interned; some were convicted, and a few executed. The most intensive sweep came after a daring and briefly successful IRA raid in December 1939 on the Magazine Fort in Phoenix Park, Dublin, during which over one million rounds of ammunition were stolen by the IRA but then quickly recovered by authorities. Despite a few successes, the bombing campaign was ill-planned, largely ineffectual, and effectively over by early 1940. Tim Pat Coogan says that "[t]he arrests and internments following the [Magazine Fort] raid sapped the strength of the organisation," and the resulting turmoil within the IRA, including the Stephen

Hayes' affair, related later in this chapter, "finished it off as a serious force of subversion for the duration of the second world war."[1]

The 1940s were a low point for the organization. According to J. Bowyer Bell, "[m]ost of the active IRA men spent the war years in British prisons, in detention camps and prison ships in Northern Ireland and in de Valera's 'Republican' Ireland."[2] When they were eventually released from prison after the war, many were tired of the struggle and left the IRA, so once again the organization was forced to rebuild its membership.[3] In the early 1950s, in order to restock its arms and ammunition, the IRA began another series of raids on police and army barracks in Ireland and England. It also received financial support from America. The money, often funneled through the Irish-American revolutionary organization Clann na Gael, was used to purchase weapons in Paris, Manchester, and elsewhere that were then smuggled into Ireland.[4] The IRA was thus able to begin a second concentrated period of aggression in 1956. "Operation Harvest," a campaign against the Northern Ireland government, was intended to force an end to partition and bring about reunification. The plan called for attacks on "BBC transmitters, bridges, oil refineries, radar stations, RUC barracks, and the destruction of the North's transport and communications system," though in the end very few of these objectives were achieved.[5] The governments of both the north and the south dealt harshly with the militants, tracking down and interning suspects. Furthermore, the campaign, condemned by the Catholic hierarchy, was not supported by northern Catholics. As a result, Operation Harvest was a political failure as well as a military one.[6] In 1962 the IRA called an end to it.

1. Timothy Patrick Coogan, *Ireland Since the Rising* (New York: Frederick A. Praeger, 1966), 273.

2. J. Bowyer Bell, "Case Study IV: The Irish Republican Army," in *Contemporary Terror: Studies in Sub-State Violence*, ed. David Carlton and Carlo Schaerf (New York: St. Martin's, 1981), 218.

3. J. Bowyer Bell, *The Secret Army: The IRA 1916–1970* (New York: John Day, 1971), 239, 242.

4. Coogan, *Ireland,* 278.

5. Ibid., 281.

6. Alvin Jackson, *Ireland 1798–1998: Politics and War* (Malden, Mass.: Blackwell, 199), 358.

II

Several stories about the IRA written in this period treat the themes of rebuilding membership and weapons stores, raiding police and army barracks, and re-establishing the IRA as a serious revolutionary force. Mary Lavin's "The Patriot Son," Michael McLaverty's "Pigeons," Mary Beckett's "The Master and the Bombs," and Sean O'Faolain's "No Country for Old Men" all portray some such IRA activity. Lavin's story, for example, treats the twin themes of recruiting new members and attacking a police barracks. Lavin sets her story, not in the 1940s or 1950s as the publication date of 1956 might suggest, but in the early part of the twentieth century, probably before the Easter Rising. Her references to the growing influence of the Gaelic League, established in 1893, and to the presence of the RIC, disbanded in 1922, confirm that the story takes place sometime between those dates. Furthermore, the absence of any reference to any current rebellion suggests that it is set before the 1916–1923 Troubles. Despite this early twentieth-century setting, much about the story evokes the climate contemporary with its publication. The story is set in a period of relative peace, much like that of the 1940s and 1950s. The protagonist's mother, for example, expresses hope that there will be no return to the "Fenian bitterness" (PS 8) of the past. Also as in the 1940s and 1950s, rebels are secretly drilling in the hills and preparing for revolution. The main action of the story, a raid on a police barracks, was also a common occurrence in mid-century Ireland. Hence, when the story was published in 1956, it must have evoked for readers the contemporary situation in Ireland.

The story focuses on the involvement of the young protagonist, Matty Conerty, in a failed attack on the police barracks across the street from his mother's village store. His friend, Sean Mongon, and Sean's fellow rebels intend to use parafin oil from the Conerty store to set fire to the barracks. When Matty reveals to Sean that he knows what the rebels are up to, Sean asks for Matty's trust and silence so as not to jeopardize the attack. Despite his mother's expressed allegiance to the RIC—the police provide business and security for her—Matty is drawn to Sean and the rebel cause. When he realizes, during the attack, that Sean is in danger of being captured or shot, Matty tries to create a diversion so that his friend can escape. He dons a trench coat and scrambles over sheds to attract the attention of the police. His efforts fail, however; Sean is shot, and possibly killed, and Matty is cut by the edge of an iron roof. In the moment when he feels the searing pain from the cut and thinks he has been shot, he also feels elated by his involvement in the rebel cause. Despite its elements of romantic nationalism—the rebel raid, the attempted escape, the protagonist's feeling of revolutionary idealism—the story leaves unstated whether or not Matty will become a full-fledged rebel. In fact, the reader might just as well assume that the reality of Sean's fate will steer Matty in a less idealistic direction.

Sean O'Faolain's "No Country for Old Men," which takes its title from Yeats's great poem "Sailing to Byzantium," is arguably the best of these stories about IRA activity in the years between the early and later Troubles. O'Faolain reprises the narrative conventions of romantic nationalism from his early career, but he uses them to explore new, more realistic themes. The story, which takes place some time during the border campaign of 1956–1962, consists of an IRA raid on a police barracks over the border in Northern Ireland. In the course of the raid, a policeman and an IRA youth are killed, and the two main characters attempt to get the youth's body back across the border to bury it before the RUC can identify it. Their escape becomes harrowing when, pursued by the police, the two men are unable to navigate the confusing border roads in the dark. Finally, they resort to seeking help from a cottager, who willingly guides them on foot through the woods and across the border into the south. The raid, the daring escape at night, the sympathetic cottager, the rural setting, and the rising dawn as the story ends—all recall the old story of romantic nationalism.

But O'Faolain is only partially interested in reviving the revolutionary feelings of romantic and idealistic fervor. The two men who drag the dead youth across the border, Joe Cassidy and Freddy Wilson, are not current members of the IRA, nor were they involved in the actual raid. Decades earlier both participated in the Easter Rising and War of Independence, but they are now successful, middle-aged business men (Joe, 63, owns a corset business, and Freddy, 57, is his accountant). It is Joe's son, Frank, who took part in the raid, and Joe has followed him into the north because Frank took one of his corset vans, not because Joe wants to be involved in the raid. Furthermore, it is revealed in the course of the story that Freddy has accompanied Joe in the van because he intends to abscond through Northern Ireland to France with bearer bonds worth four thousand pounds stolen from the corset company. As a final blow to romanticism, the adventure ends, not in the fashion of the romantic stories, but more realistically: after disposing of the youth, Joe and Freddy inadvertently walk back across the border and are arrested.

O'Faolain further complicates matters by revealing a long, suppressed conflict between Joe and Freddy, stemming from the Civil War, which accounts for Freddy's decision to steal the bonds from Joe. As they make their escape south, carrying the dead youth on their backs, the two men engage in a heated argument about the past. After the Treaty of 1921, Joe had joined the Free State side in the Civil War, while Freddy had fled to Manchester, England, where for years he managed a trick-and-joke shop owned by a widow. Freddy says that, had he stayed in Ireland during the Civil War, he would have joined the rebels and, consequently, Joe probably would "have plugged [him] for it" (CSO 695). Joe, whose life Freddy once saved during a dangerous moment in the War of Independence, adamantly denies that he would have killed Freddy, or that he killed, as Freddy claims, one of Freddy's rebel friends. The moment is intense because both men have guns. Joe has the dead youth's Webley, and Freddy has Joe's old gun, which he has kept all these years and now points at Joe. The tension is defused when Freddy becomes weary of pressing the matter and says that he will just have to take Joe's word about their friendship.

O'Faolain frames the story of the raid and escape with reports of the consequences. He begins the story with a newspaper item that reports the trial of the two men. The two have been convicted and sentenced to light terms—Joe to a year; Freddy to six months—for their peripheral roles in the incident. Both have been convicted of illegal entry into

Northern Ireland and (erroneously) of belonging to the IRA, an illegal organization. Joe has also been convicted of illegal possession of a weapon (Freddy threw his gun away). The story ends with a paragraph relating that Freddy is out of prison and back at work at Joe's corset business. He visits Joe every week in the Belfast prison and brings with him a manuscript of a biography of Joe that he is writing. As Joe listens intently to "the latest couple of pages, the prison walls fade, and Death flowers exquisitely again" (CSO 699). The former rebels are content to experience revolution through writing rather than through actual experience.

O'Faolain's central theme is the one evoked by his title: Ireland—or, more precisely, revolutionary Ireland—is "no country for old men." The dead youth that Joe and Freddy carry across the border to bury is symbolic of their revolutionary youth, dead but in need of final burial. Both men, however, have conflicting feelings about relinquishing their rebel idealism, partly because of unresolved issues created by the divisive Civil War and partly because of the unsatisfying, albeit financially successful, lives they have lived since the Troubles. Joe's corset business and Freddy's work in the trick-and-joke shop stand in obvious ironic contrast to the ideals of their revolutionary youth. In a moment of realization that it is best to leave the revolutionary past behind, Freddy says to Joe, "Come on! It'll soon be a new day. Leave us bury him [the youth]. Leave us bury everything we ever believed in and be shut of them forever" (CSO 696). But just a short time later when they find themselves "safely in the South," he shouts at Joe: "Leave us go up North for God's sake and let off a couple of rounds at somebody. . . . It's our last chance to do something decent before we die" (CSO 697). Despite these conflicting sentiments, both men know it is too late: "'It's a pipe dream,' Joe sigh[s], and [feels] his hip tenderly. 'Our dancing days are done'" (CSO 698). They have recognized in the end that the actual world of revolution is "no country for old men." Like "The Patriot," O'Faolain's romantic story that best expressed disillusionment with the betrayed ideals of the revolution, "No Country for Old Men" expresses a similar disillusionment, one that has been complicated by the deep divisions wrought by the

Civil War and the materialistic gains of the relatively peaceful era that followed.

Another type of IRA story that appears in the period between the Civil War and the Northern Troubles is the execution story, in which an IRA member, accused of being an informer, is executed by other members. Several times in this period, particularly during the 1939 bombing campaign, the IRA was thwarted in carrying out its activities by sweeps conducted by Irish and English authorities, resulting in the arrest and internment of its members and the loss of weapons. Coogan, in *The IRA*, says that a belief arose among IRA members that these misfortunes were caused by treachery and deceit within the organization. That belief led to reprisals in which informers were severely punished.[7] As one example, Coogan mentions the case of Michael Devereaux, an IRA battalion officer, who was court-martialed *in absentia* and then executed for allegedly revealing the location of arms dumps and informing on members of the organization.[8]

Most of these cases of betrayal, court-martial, and execution must have occurred without much public awareness, but one incident, in which betrayal was suspected though never proven and execution was ordered, gained a great deal of publicity. It occurred in 1941 and involved Stephen Hayes, the IRA Chief of Staff. Under Hayes' leadership, the IRA suffered a series of drastic setbacks: attacks failed, members were killed or arrested and imprisoned, and weapon dumps were uncovered by authorities. Consequently, Hayes was suspected and accused by IRA leaders in the Northern Command of providing Irish authorities with information about IRA members and activities. He was detained and interrogated, and, according to his version of events (contradicted by his captors), tortured and forced to write out a confession of his disclosures, for which he was to be executed. In order to gain time to attempt an escape, Hayes wrote out an excessively long confession, "admitting" to treachery as far back as 1935, which included providing

7. Tim Pat Coogan, *The IRA*, rev.ed. (New York: Palgrave, 2002), 149.
8. Ibid., 156–57.

information to authorities about the bombing campaign of 1939. Hayes finally signed the confession, but his captors were still not satisfied with his disclosures. The delay gave him the opportunity he needed; he escaped and turned himself in to the Irish police. His captors then published his confession, despite it being filled with contradictions and improbabilities. The Hayes affair had the effect of demoralizing other IRA members and of creating further dissension within the movement. For years after, IRA men were bitterly divided over the question of Hayes' guilt.[9]

The stories of IRA executions are told in a spare realistic style, but they also resemble the earlier naturalistic stories, both in their theme of betrayal and in their stark description of brutality. Moreover, they evoke some of the poignancy of O'Connor's tragic story, "Guests of the Nation," in their portrayal of a narrator who, to at least some extent, is morally sensitive to the execution. In Brendan Behan's "The Execution," the narrator relates how he and several other IRA men are charged with executing a man named Ellis, who, under pressure from the police, has betrayed the organization by revealing the location of an arms dump. Keeping their purpose hidden from Ellis, the executioners drive him out into the country and, at one point, stop for a drink in a pub in order to allay his suspicions. Once they arrive at the lonely, wooded spot where he is to be executed, Ellis realizes what is happening, begins to cry, and then kneels to pray. The others kneel with him, but the narrator can't pray, thus revealing that his part in the cold-blooded killing has unsettled his moral values: "I tried to pray for his soul. I couldn't. It seemed awful to think of souls just then" (P&S 9). Nevertheless, he and the others shoot Ellis and then bury him.

To convey the ruthless world of the IRA, Behan employs the spare, stark style shared by naturalism and realism. His lean description and minimal dialogue imitates Hemingway's particular style of realism,[10]

9. For detailed accounts of the Hayes affair, see Bell, *Secret Army*, chapter X, and Coogan, *The IRA*, 150–59.

10. Colbert Kearney, *The Writings of Brendan Behan* (New York: St. Martin's, 1977), 28.

while his account of the shooting and burial recalls the naturalistic style of earlier Troubles stories. Behan does not give a date or time period for the action of his story, but it most likely takes place in the late 1930s or early 1940s when he claims to have been involved in the IRA.[11]

Patrick Boyle's "The Lake" is another example of the execution story. Jim, the narrator, and Mac take their prisoner, a fellow IRA member, out in the country to shoot him and dump him in a mountain lake. The prisoner has been court-martialed and found guilty of betraying the organization, but his long and faithful service dating as far back as the Easter Rising makes Jim worry that he might be innocent. In the end Jim shoots the prisoner but then throws up, a physical revulsion symptomatic of his moral revulsion.

Boyle very likely had the Hayes affair in mind when he wrote the story. He gives to Jim and Mac the opposing arguments that divided IRA members over the prosecution of Hayes. For Mac, unquestioning of IRA authority, the court-martial verdict is enough proof of the prisoner's guilt, while for Jim the man's years of loyalty and service, including prison terms for IRA activities, cast strong doubt on his conviction. The amoral Mac argues that attempts by authorities "to smash the Movement with every kind of blackguardism" (AN 249) demand equally harsh counter-measures, including the execution of suspected informers. The morally sensitive Jim, beset with guilt over his role in the execution, wants to—but cannot—tell Mac that such retaliation "is merely evil vindicated by evil. And that it will go on and on until nothing is left but a hard core of bitter hatred" (AN 249). More so than Behan's story, "The Lake" takes a realistic look at the organizational problems that plagued the IRA at mid-century and, more importantly, the moral issues raised by these problems.

11. When he was arrested in 1939 for making bombs in a Liverpool boarding house, Behan may have been acting on his own, not on IRA orders. For a brief account of Behan's involvement in IRA affairs, see Raymond J. Porter, *Brendan Behan* (New York: Columbia University Press, 1973), 5–6.

III

Although the stories of IRA activity are valuable for the insight they provide into the state of that organization during the middle decades of the twentieth century, the most interesting stories written during and/or about this period are those that explore the effects of sectarianism, with its implicit threat of violence, on the citizens of Ireland in both the north and the south. These stories, written in the modern realistic style characteristic of the best mid-century Irish fiction, present poignant insights into the tribal qualities of sectarianism, particularly the ways in which it drives rifts within communal, social, familial, and marital relationships.

The sectarian divide between Catholics and Protestants in Ireland has its roots in the latter half of the sixteenth century when England began to "plant" Protestant settlers in Munster, Ulster, and the Dublin area in order to solidify its colonization of the island. However, sectarianism did not become a sustained, seemingly intractable problem until the latter half of the twentieth century. Until then, with few exceptions, the nationalist/unionist divide was not so cleanly demarcated in terms of religious affiliation. The Williamite war, fought in Ireland in the late seventeenth century between James II, the deposed Catholic King of England, and the Protestant William of Orange, who was crowned William III of England in 1689, did widen the sectarian divide, as did the anti-Catholic Penal Laws that followed the war and the rise of the Protestant "Ascendancy" in the eighteenth century. Even then, however, the division between Catholics and Protestants was not absolute. David E. Long points out, for instance, that "a degree of affinity developed between Ulster Presbyterians and Catholics in the eighteenth century" because Anglicans, who controlled the Irish parliament established by William III, treated the Scottish Presbyterians, who made up a good portion of Ulster Protestants, almost as poorly as they did the Catholics.[12]

12. David E. Long, *The Anatomy of Terrorism* (New York: The Free Press, 1990), 44.

Furthermore, the nationalist leaders who arose in the late eighteenth century—Wolfe Tone, Lord Edward Fitzgerald, and Robert Emmet—were, in fact, Protestant. Tone, "the founding father of Irish Republicanism," called for the abolition of sectarian division as a means of achieving Irish independence: "To unite the whole people of Ireland, to abolish the memory of all past dissensions, and to substitute the common name of Irishmen in place of the denomination of Protestant, Catholic, and Dissenter—these were my means."[13] His appeal was effective. The United Irishmen, who fomented the rebellion of 1798, were comprised of both Catholics and Protestants. So were the members of the Young Ireland movement who instigated the rising of 1848. In the latter part of the nineteenth century, Parnell, the pre-eminent Irish politician, and the great nationalist writers, Yeats, Lady Gregory, Hyde, and Synge, were also from the Protestant tradition, thus helping to discount the sectarian factor in the nationalist movement of their day.

Sectarianism, however, began to gain strength in the north at the beginning of the twentieth century. This development came as a result of the movement, supported in England, toward home rule, which would have established a separate Irish parliament. Ulster Protestants, particularly members of the Orange Order, a Protestant society formed in 1795 to commemorate William of Orange, were adamant in their opposition to home rule because they feared that, given the Catholic majority in the south, it would result in Catholic control of an Irish government. Protestants organized such violent groups as the UVF to oppose home rule. World War I delayed the movement, but the start of the War of Independence in 1919 once again raised the possibility of home rule, perhaps even complete independence, and revived the specter of sectarianism.

The partition of Ireland into the Free State and Northern Ireland, proposed in the Government of Ireland Act of 1920 and enacted by the Anglo-Irish Treaty of 1921, further exacerbated sectarian relations. Partition effectively gave governmental control to majority Catholics in the

13. Quoted in Bell, "Case Study IV," 215.

Free State and to majority Protestants in Northern Ireland. The Protestant majority who took power in Northern Ireland were determined to maintain it by excluding Catholics from government as much as possible, relegating them to second-class citizenship, and discriminating against them in jobs and housing. Protestants were all too keenly aware that the Catholic minority of the north were supported by a large Catholic population in the south, many of whom desired reunification. That fact nourished in the Protestants a state of mind that emphasized the divide between Catholics and Protestants. As Paul Wilkinson notes, "The truth is that Ulster Protestants have the mentality of a beleaguered minority. They have never shaken off the fear that someday the overwhelming Catholic Republic of Ireland will try to absorb or annex them."[14]

There are valid reasons for this fear: the Free State Constitution of 1937 laid claim to the north, and the IRA periodically demonstrated violent opposition to partition by attacking targets along the border and in the north, attacks which intensified during the border campaign of 1956–1962. The sectarian aspect of the nationalist/unionist divide was also heightened by the fact that the 1937 Constitution was Catholic in character, and, furthermore, a particularly conservative brand of Catholicism, proscribing, for example, divorce, contraception and abortion. This fact has given Protestants "an abiding fear of religious intolerance under [C]atholicism."[15] They see the prospect of unification with the south as a threat to their religious and social freedoms, as well as to their political independence.

For their part, Protestants have aggravated sectarian relations over the years by observing, with annual marches and triumphal displays, the historical events of the late seventeenth century that pitted the two reli-

14. Paul Wilkinson, "The Orange and the Green: Extremism in Northern Ireland," in *Terrorism, Legitimacy, and Power: The Consequences of Political Violence*, ed. Martha Crenshaw (Middletown, Conn.: Wesleyan University Press, 1983), 111.

15. Yonah Alexander and Alan O'Day, "Introduction: Dimensions of Irish Terrorism," in *The Irish Terrorism Experience*, ed. Yonah Alexander and Alan O'Day (Brookfield, Vt.: Dartmouth Publishing Co., 1991), 3.

gious groups against each other, particularly the successful Protestant defense against the Siege of Derry and the Williamite victories at the Boyne and Aughrim. Sponsored by the Orange Order and featuring bands playing Lambeg drums and flutes, these marches continue today, their routes often taking them through or near Catholic areas, thus heightening sectarian tensions.

In the late 1960s the tensions, which had simmered for nearly a half century, boiled over, though at first over the issue of civil rights in Northern Ireland rather than over unification of north and south. Adopting the strategies of the civil rights movement of the United States, Northern Catholics belonging to NICRA took to the streets of Belfast and Derry with marches and demonstrations and demanded an end to discrimination in jobs and housing. There were early attempts by Northern Catholics to keep the civil rights movement nonsectarian by inviting disenfranchised Protestants to take part, and the UDA apparently made overtures to Catholics to "work out a new Northern Ireland which [would] be suitable and admirable for [Catholics and Protestants] both."[16] Soon, however, the movement was characterized by violent sectarian strife. Militant Protestants attacked Catholic marchers in January 1969 while the mostly Protestant RUC stood by and watched. That event set off riots in Derry and Belfast, and soon Catholic and Protestant neighborhoods in both cities were turned into virtual fortresses, "no-go" areas where the other sect dared not enter. British troops, at first welcomed by Catholics in 1969 as protection against Protestant aggression, began searching Catholic homes for arms in 1970 and interning Catholics as suspected IRA members, actions that further exacerbated sectarianism.[17] Thus began the longest period of sustained sectarian conflict in Ireland's history.[18] Sectarian tensions gave way to

16. Quoted in Adrian Guelke, "Loyalist and Republican Perceptions of the Northern Ireland Conflict: The UDA and the Provisional IRA," in *Political Violence and Terror: Motifs and Motivations*, ed. Peter H. Merkl (Berkeley and Los Angeles: University of California Press, 1986), 102.

17. Guelke, "Perceptions," 98–99.

18. Alexander and O'Day, "Dimensions," 1.

sectarian violence, which soon spread through Northern Ireland and extended into the Republic of Ireland and England as well.

IV

Although sporadic acts of sectarian violence occurred during the middle decades of the twentieth century and are represented in some stories of this period, the focus in the stories is not so much on the violence as it is on other pervasive and debilitating effects of sectarianism, especially the divisions created between friends, neighbors, family members, even lovers and married couples. These stories are especially poignant in the way that they represent the insidious effects of sectarianism in the everyday lives of ordinary people, most of whom are not actively committed to sectarian division.

Benedict Kiely's "Bluebell Meadow" depicts the ways in which the demands of sectarian loyalties can thwart personal relationships in a community, especially, as in this case, young love. The story is set in a small, unnamed town in Northern Ireland in the years just before World War II. A young man named Lofty, a Presbyterian, is attracted to a Catholic schoolgirl, who often sits reading by the waters where he fishes. The story opens in the home of the girl's aunt and uncle, with whom she lives, where a police sergeant questions her about six bullets that were found in her possession. Kiely then moves back in time to recount the young couple's courtship and the trouble that arises because of it.

Kiely enhances the charm of the relationship by portraying Lofty as easy-going, handsome, and popular and the girl, who is never named, as intelligent and witty but somewhat reclusive, perhaps because she is handicapped (she wears a leg brace). He also describes the place where the courting takes place in idyllic terms. It is an island park, created by the confluence of a river, a mountain stream, and a millrace. The park is called Bluebell Meadow after the flowers that grow nearby. Children play in the sand and water, and upstream "[t]he river comes out of deep water, lined and overhung by tall beeches, and round a right-angled bend to burst over a waterfall and a salmon leap" (SI 275). Although they have been attracted to each other for a while, the two young people meet for the first time when Lofty, wearing waders and carrying a fishing rod and a bag full of fish, offers the girl a trout. Thus the youthful love affair begins.

Then one day, as she is sitting on the park bench, the girl is approached by the local butcher, Samuel McClintock, a man she thinks of as "black" because he is "a member of the black preceptory . . . , a special branch of the Orange Order" (SI 284). He is, in fact, "the Worshipful Master of the [Orange] Lodge" (SI 287), and he has come to tell her to break off the relationship with Lofty. McClintock tells the girl that Lofty is a member of the B Specials branch of the Ulster Special Constabulary and that his standing in the Orange Order is in jeopardy because of his relationship with a Catholic. He could be expelled if the relationship continues. The girl responds to McClintock in a feisty manner, refusing to take his talk about the B Specials seriously. She also has a hard time imagining how "lazy, freckled, lovable Lofty" (SI 290) could be a member of a group that "went about at night with guns and in black uniforms, holding up Catholic neighbours and asking them their names and addresses—which they knew very well to begin with" (SI 287).

But the relationship has already been doomed by the six bullets found by the police. At the end of the story, Kiely returns to the opening scene in the aunt and uncle's home. The girl refuses to say where she got the bullets (an innocent gift from Lofty), so the sergeant asks her to come to the barracks to make a statement. When they arrive, Lofty is there being questioned by the police and McClintock, who have figured out that Lofty gave the girl the bullets. They have also led Lofty to believe that the girl has betrayed him, thus sealing the fate of their relationship.

Much of the poignancy of Kiely's love story derives from the hard fact that sectarian loyalties, created by the highest levels of religion and politics, can come between the most innocent of lovers. Before McClintock confronts her, the girl cannot imagine that sectarian differences could ever come between her and Lofty. Early in their relationship, *Romeo and Juliet*—an appropriate literary analogue for the lovers' situation—springs to her mind, but her reflection is that, unlike her, "Juliet

. . . didn't have to wear a school uniform [and] [i]f she had . . . Romeo wouldn't have looked at her." She then quickly dismisses any idea "that they are star-crossed lovers or Lofty any Romeo" (SI 280). The implication is that such an idea would be melodramatic, but, as the reader can see, the analogy is apt. On her way home after her encounter with McClintock, the idea that their relationship might be affected by higher authority gains more force, though she still wants to believe that it is absurd. As she passes the Orange hall with its large medallion of William of Orange on his white horse crossing the Boyne, she thinks that it is "crazy . . . that a man on a white horse, riding across a river two hundred years ago could now ride between herself and Lofty. Or for that matter . . . [could] another man on a chair or something being carried shoulder-high in the city of Rome" (SI 290). She cannot fathom what kings and popes and the sectarian allegiances they inspire have to do with common lovers.

The girl also finds it hard to accept the reality of sectarian interference in her own life because others she knows seem to escape it. Not everyone in the town is as zealously sectarian as McClintock. Lofty's mother, for instance, is a free-spirited woman, who vacations with Catholics in the resort town of Bundoran on the Donegal Coast. Kiely writes: "As a rule Protestants didn't go west to Bundoran but north to Portrush. The sea was sectarian" (SI 278). As she travels with a train full of Catholics to Bundoran, Lofty's mother tells jokes about Catholics, confession, and sex, which make all of the Catholic passengers roar with laughter. Even McClintock's daughter, Gladys, "a fine good-natured brunette with a swinging stride, a bosom like a Viking prow, and a dozen boy friends of all creeds and classes," had "[n]othing sectarian about [her]" (SI 289–90).

Kiely enriches the realistic style of "Bluebell Meadow" with symbolic analogies that reveal, sometimes subtly, sometimes in obvious ways, the themes and motifs of his story. The theme of tribal loyalty is foreshadowed early on by a brief incident involving tinkers, the wild, gypsy-like people who wander Ireland in caravans, and the local sergeant who questions the girl about the bullets. Five tinkers, stumbling drunk out of a pub, begin fighting with one another, but when the sergeant tries to break up the fight, the tinkers, "united by foreign invasion," give him "an unmerciful pounding" (SI 277). The incident is a small reminder that tribal loyalties are strong and that members will violently fend off outsiders in order to keep the tribe intact.

Kiely also uses an analogy for the intrusion of ugly sectarianism into the love affair. As McClintock and the girl are talking on the park bench, a wind carries the stench of the local shambles located just beyond the river: "She smelled blood and dirt and heard screams and knew, with a comical feeling of kindness, that she had been wrongly blaming him for bringing with him the stench of the shambles." She is thinking literally—McClintock is a butcher and very well might have the odor of meat on him—and he speaks literally when he also catches the odor and says, without irony, "It's a sin, shame and scandal to have a piggery beside a beauty spot" (SI 288). But the passage has a rich figurative overtone: he has brought the stench of sectarianism into the beauty of a love affair.

The island park that gives rise to the love affair also has rich overtones. At first it seems idyllic, removed, even protected, from the realities of life, but that is not really the case. Kiely signals such in the exchange between the lovers when Lofty offers the girl the trout. She asks him who she should tell her aunt and uncle gave her the trout, and Lofty responds: "Tell them nothing. Tell them you whistled and a trout jumped out at you. Tell them a black man came out of the river and gave you a trout." His remark evokes a mythical world where everything is possible, but the real world stares the lovers in the face: "The trout, bloody mouth gaping, looked sadly up at the two of them" (SI 276).

Although the main action of "Bluebell Meadow" takes place in the 1930s, at the end of the story the reader realizes that it has been told from the perspective of the 1970s. Thus, the main action serves as a foreshadowing of the sectarian violence that was to come in that decade. All of the story, except for the last four paragraphs, is seemingly told in the third-person point of view, leading the reader to believe that the narrator is an impersonal voice. But in those final paragraphs the narrator reveals himself, in fact, to be a first-person observer of the action. He tells us that after a while the girl went to London for work. She and Lofty met a couple of times when she came home from London on holiday, but nothing ever came of it. Then the World War came, she met and married an American, and the couple moved to Detroit. Now, as the narrator (it is, perhaps, Lofty himself) recounts that long-ago shattered romance, the Troubles—"bombings and murders"—have begun: "soldiers go about in bands, guns at the ready, in trucks and armoured cars. There are burned-out buildings in the main streets—although the great barracks is unscathed—and barricades and checkpoints at the ends of the town" (SI 293). Strabane, Newry, and Derry, the narrator tells us, are worse. Tragically, sectarian violence is everywhere in Northern Ireland, but the sectarian-thwarted love of Lofty and the girl—a love that might have bloomed into a marriage of Protestant and Catholic—somehow seems even more tragic.

The state of sectarian tensions in Northern Ireland in the years leading up to the outbreak of violence in the late 1960s is the subject of John Montague's "The Cry." Originally published in *Kilkenny Magazine* in 1961, the story portrays the reluctance of the people of Northern Ireland to admit to, or deal with, the growing problems of sectarianism, including discrimination in civil rights matters, and it presciently foreshadows the sectarian violence that came to the North just a few years later.

The story relates the experience of Peter Douglas during a visit to his hometown of Moorhill, a small, mostly-Catholic town in Northern Ireland. Despite its English-sounding name, Peter's family is Catholic and nationalist. His father is "violently anti-English" (DC 60) and has "centuries of republicanism stirring in his blood" (DC 59). When he was younger, Peter himself considered joining the local unit of the IRA, but instead he went to England for work and is now a reporter for *The Tocsin,* a newspaper in London. His experience there has all but eliminated his sectarian prejudices and made him acutely aware of Irish provincialism. He speaks to his father of the decency of the English people, "the great freedom of living in London," and the absence there of sectarian views: "Nobody on *The Tocsin,* for instance would dream of asking if you were Catholic or Protestant . . ." (DC 59). Irish Catholic religious practices, such as the family saying the rosary together, now seem odd and embarrassing to him: "English Catholics did not believe in loading themselves down with inessentials" (DC 61).

On the first night of his visit home, Peter hears a row outside his bedroom window and, looking out, witnesses an incident in which B Specials beat up a young man and arrest him. They apparently suspect that he is a member of the IRA, at that time engaged in the border campaign. The young man is crying out for help, but no one comes to his rescue. The only protest comes from the local schoolteacher, who is warned by the police that he will "get a touch too" if he doesn't "[k]eep [his] bloody nose out of it . . ." (DC 64). When Peter's father complains the next morning about the incident and challenges his son to "do [something] about it" (DC 66), Peter declares that he will write an article of "[m]oral protest" (DC 67) about it for his newspaper, exposing the brutal treatment of Catholics by the Protestant police. However, Peter is thwarted in his less-than-aggressive efforts to gather information for the article, first at the police barracks where the County Inspector assures him that the young man is fine and that the incident was merely a matter of disturbance of the peace (the Inspector never mentions the IRA), and then at the country cottage of the victim where neither the parents nor the young man will make a complaint. They are afraid of bringing more trouble to themselves. The victim is silent, but his mother explains: "we'd as lief the matter was forgotten. It would be better for all of us, like" (DC 83). Peter's mother is also concerned. "That thing you're writing will create bad blood," she tells him. "I've seen too much fighting between neighbours in this town already" (DC 71). The story ends as "the village idiot," with the prophetic name of Joe Doom, holds up a placard outside Peter's bedroom: "NOSY PARKER GO HOME" (DC 86). The obvious and ironic implication is that Peter's naïve belief that sectarianism could be eliminated has made him no longer at home in Northern Ireland.

Montague suggests that the treatment of the young man is not an isolated incident but part of a pattern of growing sectarian hostilities that, if not confronted, will develop into an intractable problem. In his parents' copy of *The Ulster Nationalist*, Peter reads an "editorial [that] spoke with dignified bitterness of the continued discrimination against Catholics in the North of Ireland in jobs and housing" (DC 62) and an article that reports a minor but nasty dispute in a court case between a Protestant and his Catholic neighbor, a woman who reportedly threw a bucketful of water on the man after he spoke harshly to her. The magistrate's comment on the case might serve as the story's theme: "the RM said it was a difficult case to disentangle but he felt both parties were to blame" (DC 62).

The story also comments on the ineffectuality of moral protest and argument as means of dealing with sectarian hatred.[19] Peter initially expresses faith in the power of journalism to address the problem. He tells his father, "I can do more than you or a whole regiment of the IRA. I can write an article in *The Tocsin* which will expose the whole thing. Good, decent—yes, English—people will read it and be ashamed of what is being done in their name. Questions will be asked, maybe in Parliament, if not this time, then the next. . . . [T]he ruling classes in Ulster will come to their senses" (DC 67). But Peter's belief that his newspaper could sound an effective alarm bell to the problem is naïve, and his efforts are futile. The refusal of police and victim to speak candidly and Peter's lack of aggression as an investigative reporter prevent him from gathering facts to write about the incident. Although his early draft of the article forcefully points out that the arming of the Ulster police and the hiring of 12,000 B Specials have turned Northern Ireland into a police state, his later draft expresses a resignation that comes with accepting the status quo and raises only the weakest of alarms: "*There is a way of dealing with such incidents of course. . . . The charge is dropped or minimised, the too zealous police or soldiers reprimanded, any public fuss avoided. Perhaps as the authorities claim, it is the best way in the end. But one is left wondering in how many small Ulster towns such things are happening, at this moment, in your name!*" (DC 84; italics in text).

19. John Wilson Foster, *Forces and Themes in Ulster Fiction* (Totowa, N.J.: Rowan and Littlefield, 1974), 286.

The title of Montague's story refers specifically to the unanswered cry of the young man as he is being beaten by the B Specials, but more generally it refers to the futile cry, as illustrated in the last sentence of Peter's draft, of those citizens of Northern Ireland who sincerely desire an end to sectarian hatred. As John Wilson Foster suggests, the story makes clear that there will be no lasting solutions, particularly ones based on argument and moral protest, to the cry for help in Northern Ireland "until the tribal realities of Ulster life are broken down."[20]

V

Sectarian hostility in the decades before the renewal of the Troubles was not limited to Northern Ireland. The south, where the Catholic population has held a commanding majority, also experienced its share of tension and hostility, though not to the degree or intensity of the north. With the outbreak of violence in Northern Ireland in the late 1960s, and then in England and the south in the early 1970s, sectarian tensions increased dramatically, and provided the subject matter for the stories of Terence de Vere White and William Trevor.

White's "Someone's Coming" is set in the Republic of Ireland, just after violence has broken out in the north. Like "The Cry," it focuses not on the violence itself but on the suspicions and dissension sectarianism created among Irish people. White blends an air of mystery with touches of irony and humor to develop a serious theme about the deep rifts caused by sectarian tensions on both social and personal levels.

The Irish narrator, Hugh Perry, and his English wife, Joan, live near an isolated cove on the Kerry coast with a beautiful view of Dingle Bay, Mount Brandon, and the Blasket Islands. The location satisfies Hugh's need for uninterrupted seclusion to do his unspecified but sedentary work and his wife's desire for a life of guarded isolation. They are on friendly but reserved terms with their nearest neighbors, Matt and Siobhan O'Sullivan. As the story opens Joan announces, "'Someone's coming' . . . in a voice of dread" (FG 229). The unexpected visitor turns out

20. Ibid., 287.

to be Hugh's long-lost brother, John, now seventy-two and living in America. John was "the family rebel" who, having been named by his father after "the youngest of the Royal Family at the time, the one who died of haemophilia," later changed his name to Sean (FG 231). He was packed off to Canada after a violent altercation with a co-worker in a brewery and was not heard from thereafter by his family. John tells Hugh that he has been in Killarney looking for business opportunities and that a man he met by chance in Killarney told him that Hugh lived nearby. Hence, he has decided to renew families ties. During his week-long visit, however, John spends more time out on a boat fishing and taking photographs with Hugh's neighbor, Matt O'Sullivan, who is—John says—the brother of the man he supposedly met in Killarney. John's visit and his activities with Matt make Joan suspicious.

Joan is suspicious by nature. Hugh says, "When I'm not at work I welcome visitors, but my good wife, except for a small group—which includes none of my relations—suspects the motives of the world in general, and is delighted when she can demonstrate the soundness of her prejudice by pointing at gates left open and litter lying about" (FG 229). The latter comment is a reference to Joan's propensity for making deductions based on circumstantial evidence. Her suspicious nature has been exacerbated by the fact that she is an Englishwoman living in Ireland, convinced that "people here don't like her" (FG 233), and by frequent news of the Troubles in the north and in England. A radio report of explosions, dead horses, and dead Guardsmen in London Parks, for example, greatly disturbs her. Near the end of John's visit, she tells Hugh that she suspects John has been gathering photographic information about their concealed cove. Though she does not state it outright, she implies that John is an IRA sympathizer, perhaps even an operative, gathering information to be used to smuggle arms into the country.

Hugh thinks Joan is imagining things. He refers to her "mania" and "crazy suspicions," dismisses her charges, and tells her "to keep [her] mouth shut about this" (FG 234). Whether or not she does report her suspicions to anyone remains a mystery, but after John leaves, the Garda Sergeant arrives to ask Hugh questions about his brother, including

John's address. The reader is left wondering whether Joan has reported her suspicions to the police, or whether the police have their own suspicions of John. In an amusing irony, Hugh, who has dismissed his wife's deductions based on circumstantial evidence as "crazy," deduces—probably correctly—from circumstantial evidence that Joan has been to see the Sergeant. Earlier in the day of the Sergeant's arrival Joan has served lettuce for lunch, a rare treat in their area but grown by the Sergeant in his garden and shared with neighbors. Also, Hugh notes that during his visit the Sergeant makes no mention of Joan and she does not appear to greet him, but later "she [comes] back looking as if she ha[s] laid an egg" (FG 237). All of this is strong circumstantial evidence that Joan has spoken to the Sergeant about John, but it also lends validity to the process of making deductions from circumstantial evidence, which is exactly what Joan has done.

The question of whether or not John is involved in clandestine IRA activities remains a mystery, even at the end of the story. After he departs, he is not heard from again. There is some circumstantial evidence to support Joan's contention, including John's sudden and unexpected arrival, the inordinate amount of time he spends with Matt O'Sullivan photographing the coast, and his past rebellious nature and interest in Irish identity, such as changing his name to Sean. (Interestingly, John never mentions, and Hugh does not ask, whether or not he still calls himself Sean.) Furthermore, arms smuggling was still being supported by pro-Irish Americans in the 1970s, the time in which the story is set. But White characterizes John in such a way as to make any claims that he is involved in rebel activities seem almost comical. He is "dressed in a lemon and grey checked suit" and wears a "Texan hat" that makes him look "like a mushroom" (FG 230). Furthermore, his advanced age of seventy-two and a recent prostrate operation hardly make him the typical rebel.

If the story fails to resolve the mystery of John's involvement in the Troubles, it does emphasize the social and personal effects of the Troubles. John's visit has produced dissension both in the community and in Hugh and Joan's marriage. Joan's likely revelation to the Sergeant is sure to place the O'Sullivans under suspicion, and it has produced a permanent frost in Joan and Hugh's relationship. They have, Hugh says in the last paragraph, "adopted a new manner of elaborate politeness towards each other" (FG 237), itself a polite way of saying that all intimacy has gone out of their relationship.

William Trevor also explores the theme of sectarian tension in several short stories, including "The Distant Past" and "Another Christmas." The first of these takes place in the south, while the second is set in England, the effect of which is to emphasize the geographical extent of the problem. "The Distant Past" explores the renewal of sectarian tensions in a small southern town after decades of peace and amity between Catholics and Protestants. The story illustrates how the animosity of the distant past never really disappears but rather remains just below the surface of seemingly amiable social relationships, ready to surface again given the right provocation. The story is set in the late 1960s, just as the Troubles in the north are breaking out, news of which has a profound effect on the people of the town.

Trevor relates the story through the point of view of a brother and sister, now in their mid-sixties, the Protestant Middletons of Carraveagh. Once a grand Anglo-Irish estate "built in the reign of George II" (CST 349), Carraveagh has gradually fallen into decay. Rumors circulate that the Middletons' father had mortgaged the estate "in order to keep a Catholic Dublin woman in brandy and jewels" (CST 349), and thereby brought about its ruin. In addition to the decaying estate, their father, who had once met Queen Victoria, also bequeathed them a strong Anglo-Irish heritage, which they have preserved over the years. They regularly attend St. Patrick's Protestant Church; stand when they hear "God Save the King" on the BBC; keep in their hall the family crest, a portrait of their father in his Irish Guard uniform, and the Cross of St. George; and prop a small Union Jack on the rear window of their English Ford Anglia in honor of the coronation of Queen Elizabeth II. To the townspeople, including the new Anglo-Irish minister, Reverend Bradshaw, the Middletons' displays are anachronistic and amusing.

In the fifty years of relative peace since the end of the Troubles, the

Middletons have grown friendly with their Catholic neighbors, including Mrs. Gerrity, owner of both a grocery store, where they bring eggs to be sold, and a bar, where they have drinks with her. They also patronize the shop of Fat Cranly, the butcher who once, during the War of Independence, stood armed with two other men in the hall of Carraveagh, waiting to ambush British soldiers while the Middletons, then children, waited locked in an upstairs room with their mother. The soldiers, however, did not appear and so nothing came of it. Now the Middletons joke about the incident with the butcher, as they share drinks with him in Healy's hotel.

The post-World War II years have brought prosperity to the town, primarily from tourism, which, in turn, has brought a multicultural flavor. The grocer stocks foreign wines and cheeses; the hotel, renamed the New Ormonde, serves Japanese crackers and martinis; and English and American accents float through the town. Such changes give the impression that sectarian differences have been eroded and that peace and good will between Catholics and Protestants have been realized. The perceived improvement in sectarian relations, however, is attributed by the townspeople, not to their financial good fortune, but to "living in a Christian country" (CST 352). Meanwhile, as the Catholic middle class prospers, the Middletons' Anglo-Irish estate of Carraveagh continues to decline.

Then comes news of the bombings of post offices in Belfast. The townspeople, Catholics and Protestants alike, disavow the violence: "We don't want that old stuff all over again" (CST 353), Fat Cranley remarks. They refer to the Troubles as "bad business" (CST 353), a phrase that is literally truer than they realize. As the violence increases, spreading from Belfast and Derry to Fermanagh and Armagh, and British soldiers are sent into Northern Ireland to quell disturbances, tourists stop coming to the town, which is located just sixty miles from the border. The townspeople become angry and the distant past surfaces: "As anger rose in the town at the loss of fortune so there rose also the kind of talk there had been in the distant past. There was talk of atrocities and counter-atrocities, and of guns and gelignite and the rights of people. There was bitterness suddenly in Mrs Gerrity's bar because of the lack of trade . . ." (CST 354; Trevor does not use the period after Mrs or Mr in his stories).

Catholics begin to treat the Middletons coldly. People are silent in their presence, Canon Carter snubs them, and Mrs. Duggan doesn't respond when they address her in the hotel. The Middletons grow melancholy and depressed as the sectarian divide widens and they become more and more isolated from the townspeople. They remove from their hall the anachronistic Anglo-Irish symbols that have sustained them over the years of decline: the family crest, the Cross of St. George, the portrait of their father, the Union Jack. They mourn the loss of "the *modus vivendi* that had existed for so long between them and the people of the town" and that "had given them a life, and a kind of dignity" (CST 355). The story ends poignantly with the Middletons thinking that their present state is "worse than being murdered in their beds" (CST 356). The last image, in both its symbolic evocation of the past and its foreshadowing of the future, poignantly captures the pain brought on by sectarian divisions.

Trevor also explores the effects of sectarian hostilities in "Another Christmas," particularly the rifts created in social and marital relationships. The story is set in Fulham, England, in the rental home of an Irish couple a few days before Christmas in the mid-1970s. Shortly after their marriage in 1953, Norah and Dermot emigrated from Waterford to England for work and have lived there for more than twenty years, raising their children and enjoying a relatively comfortable and peaceful existence. Up until the time just prior to the opening of the story, they had a special relationship with their landlord, Mr. Joyce, an elderly Englishman. For years, he came for tea and watched the Friday evening television news with them, and each Christmas he dined with them and brought presents for their children.

Then the relationship changed. When reports of IRA bombings in Birmingham, Guildford, the Tower of London, and elsewhere appeared on the television, Mr. Joyce began to make terse, scornful comments about Irish terrorists. Out of respect for their friendship, neither Norah nor Dermot said anything. But after hearing Mr. Joyce comment on the madness of the terrorists following still another television report of violence, Dermot responded. He said that people "mustn't of course forget what the Catholics in the North had suffered. The bombs were a crime but it didn't do to forget that the crime would not be there if generations of Catholics in the North had not been treated as animals" (CST 519). Obviously offended, Mr. Joyce remained silent at the moment but then stopped coming on Friday evenings. Norah now fears that he will not come for Christmas, a visit she greatly treasures. She is convinced that, if Dermot would just apologize, Mr. Joyce would once again come for Christmas, but Dermot refuses. He believes that what he said is the truth and that people have to hear it.

The story ends, not only with it highly unlikely that Mr. Joyce will visit them on Christmas, but also with a deep rift opening up in Dermot and Norah's marriage. Their landlord's friendship is very important to Norah—he may be their only real friend in England—but the truth, at least as he sees it, is more important to Dermot. When Norah tells Dermot that "[y]ou couldn't say [what Dermot has said] . . . because when you did it sounded like an excuse for murder," Dermot counters: "You have to state the truth, Norah. It's there to be told" (CST 520). Dermot's attitude angers Norah, but she lacks "the courage to urge her anger to explode in their living-room" (CST 520). She realizes, however, that "[f]or the first time since he had asked her to marry him in the Tara Ballroom she did not love him." She sees her husband as "a man with an Irish accent in whom the worst had been brought out by the troubles that had come, who was guilty of a cruelty no one would have believed him capable of" (CST 521).

The split in their marriage over sectarian tension is all the more regrettable because Norah and Dermot had been living in a kind of peaceful sectarian co-existence. Mr. Joyce, the Englishman with the Irish name, had treated them more as friends than tenants. And while Dermot and Norah still keep scenes of Waterford on their walls and refer to Boxing day as St. Stephen's Day "in the Irish manner" (CST 515), their children have been assimilated into English culture, speaking "with

London accents" (CST 518). Their two oldest, Patrick and Brendan, work for English firms, and Patrick has married an English girl. Now, the incident with Mr. Joyce has moved Dermot back toward his Irish identity and Norah further away from hers. Norah has "begun to feel embarrassed because of her Waterford accent." When she fantasizes that "she should be out on the streets, shouting in her Waterford accent, violently stating that the bombers were more despicable with every breath they drew" (CST 520), Norah is apparently searching for a way to disown publicly her Irish identity.

Trevor's overriding point is that sectarian violence, by inflaming tensions among people not directly affected, causes as much social and personal tragedy as it does death and destruction. The point is reflected in Norah's final thought: "the bombers would be pleased if they could note the victory they'd scored in a living-room in Fulham. And on Christmas Day, when a family sat down to a conventional meal, the victory would be greater" (CST 521).

VI

Like Trevor's "Another Christmas," the final two stories to be discussed, Mary Beckett's "A Belfast Woman" and Eugene McCabe's "Cancer," take place in the 1970s, well after sectarian tension gave way to sectarian violence. But, like "Another Christmas," these stories focus, not so much on the devastation of the violence, which will be discussed in the next chapter, as on the insidious social and personal effects of sectarian hatred.

Perhaps no story of the Troubles illustrates so well the burden of living in a sectarian-divided society for one's entire life as does Beckett's "A Belfast Woman." The Catholic narrator, Mrs. Harrison, recounts her life in the violent-prone neighborhoods of sectarian Belfast. When she was a child in 1921, her family was burned out of its home and forced to move into her grandmother's house. In 1935, she and her mother (her father and grandmother were dead by then) received a letter warning them that they would be burned out again if they didn't move, so they picked up their belongings and moved again. Now in the mid-1970s, as the story opens, she receives a note, written with a red felt pen on a sheet ripped out of an exercise book: "Get out or we'll burn you out" (BW 111). Despite her fear, she decides to stay, thinking that, since she has Protestant neighbors on both sides, it is unlikely that she will be burned out. But her unidentified tormentors foil her. They trash her house, ripping out plumbing to cause water damage, destroying her furniture, and depositing filth throughout. Her son, Liam, and his friends repair the damage, and then something strange happens: her Protestant neighbors, having themselves received threatening letters, begin to move out, and Catholics move in. The story ends with the narrator still in her home.

Beckett's portrayal of sectarian relations in "A Belfast Woman" is, like the portrayals in other stories in this chapter, mixed with complexities and small ironies. Divisions are not always clear-cut, nor are they necessarily adhered to or preferred by every member of the sect. Sometimes Catholics and Protestants do get on well together, and even intermarry. The narrator's deceased husband, for instance, came from a mixed marriage. After his Catholic mother died when he was a boy, his Protestant father raised him a Catholic, fulfilling a promise to the mother. Mrs. Harrison sees that sectarian identity does not dictate whether or not one is good or even pleasant. She calls her Protestant neighbors "good decent people . . . ready to help at any time" (BW 113), and, ironically, prefers them to her new Catholic neighbors who "open [her] door and walk in at any hour of the day" (BW 127). She also prefers Protestant ideas regarding childbearing. After her daughter, Eileen, was born she thought, "*If I was a Protestant now we'd have just the two and no more and I'd be able to look after them and do well for them*" (BW 114; italics in text). As a Catholic, expected to produce a large family, she was reduced to marital subterfuge: "So I didn't act fair with William at all" (BW 114). Her own mother's attitude also illustrates the contradictions inherent in sectarianism: "She had a horror of my Protestant neighbors even though she liked well enough the ones she met" (BW 118).

Another strength of "A Belfast Woman" is Beckett's use of understatement. Although Mrs. Harrison recounts some moments of hysteria brought about by the Troubles, such as when her son's wife, Gemma, screams at the sight of the threatening note, or when Liam shouts at the soldiers who have failed to protect his mother's home, the characteristic tone of the story is one of quiet understatement, signaling that Mrs. Harrison and other people of Belfast are quietly determined to survive the Troubles. An example is her remark about her state of mind the day she receives the threatening letter: "I remember thinking while I was dressing myself that it would be nice if the Troubles were over so that a body could just enjoy the feel of a good day" (BW 111).

Beckett also uses two understated analogies for the persistence with which some people have struggled against the Troubles. Mrs. Harrison recounts the first time she met her husband's father, "a good man" though "cross-looking" (BW 115). He was pulling weeds out of his garden, and the first thing he said when he saw the couple was, "Sitfast and scutch! Sitfast and scutch! They're the plague of my life. No matter how much I weed there's more in the morning" (BW 115). She then told him about her grandfather's obsession with an elderberry tree that blocked the sunlight from his small cottage home. He cut it down, but it grew new shoots. He then tried to dig the stump out, but he was never able to get it out entirely. Her father-in-law's fight with weeds and her grandfather's with the stump subtly symbolize the refusal of people to succumb to the Troubles.

The story also ends with understatement, though with a hopeful one. A man comes to sell Mrs. Harrison venetian blinds to cover her windows. She declines, saying she prefers to see the sunsets, and points out "the sunset behind Divis—bits of red and yellow in the sky and a sort of mist all down the mountain that made it nearly see-through" (BW 128). The salesman tells her that Belfast sunsets are the most beautiful in the world because the sun is filtered through the pollution and dust of the city. "'And it seems to me,' he said, 'it seems to me that if the dirt and dust and smoke and pollution of Belfast just with the help of the sun can make a sky like that, then there's hope for all of us'" (BW 128). And Mrs. Harrison agrees: "I started to laugh, for it's true. There is hope for all of us. Well, anyway, if you don't die you live through it, day in, day out" (BW 128).

Beckett's story also conveys the theme of survival through another analogy. Mrs. Harrison had been told, after the birth of her second child, that her hard, swollen stomach was probably cancerous and that she might die if she did not have an operation. She had refused, fearing that the operation itself might be fatal. Much later she was told by another doctor that the condition was probably not cancerous. Beckett's point seems to be that it is possible to survive under the worst possible threats if one has the determination to do so.

Eugene McCabe's "Cancer" also uses the analogy of that disease, but in an ominous way. The story is a distressing depiction of the way in which the sectarian-bred Troubles have infected every aspect of the lives of ordinary citizens in Northern Ireland—their work, home life, relationships with friends, family and neighbors, even their sense of humor and their sense of physical health. The title refers to both the literal cancer of one of the characters and the metaphorical disease of the Troubles.

The central narrative of the story, told through flashback and framed by the present action, relates a car trip taken by James Boyle and Dinny McMahon a week prior to the opening and closing scenes of the story. The two men drive through the northern county of Fermanagh to the town of Enniskillen to see Dinny's brother, Joady, who lies in the hospital with terminal cancer. The journey from the McMahon home in Gawley's Bridge to the hospital is fraught with tension, heightened by a recent bombing near Trillick, which lies between Enniskillen and Omagh. Presumably the work of the Provos, the explosion has killed two BBC officials and three workers riding in a Land-Rover to a television transmitter station. Boyle and Dinny, both Catholics, are harassed along the way to Enniskillen, first by a British helicopter that, at one point, swoops down and blocks their path in order to record their license plate number, and, further on, at a British Army check point where their car is searched and they are extensively questioned. Combative by nature, Dinny doesn't take the harassment passively. He shouts obscenities at the helicopter and drops a pointed remark about the Trillick bombing while being questioned by the soldiers at the checkpoint.

The tension is not just with the British occupation troops. When they decide to stop for a drink in Linaskea, Boyle and Dinny discover too late that the pub they have chosen is a hangout for members of the UDR (Ulster Defence Regiment, successor organization to the B Specials that were disbanded in 1970). Again, Dinny refuses to be passive, ordering "Irish" whiskey so that the Protestant patrons are certain to know his affiliation. That, in turn, provokes an anti-Catholic tirade from one of the patrons. But Dinny has the last word: "I'd as lief drink with pigs" (HE 60), he says, pouring his whiskey into the bar sink and walking out. We also get an insight into Catholic-Protestant relationships when Dinny recounts for Boyle how a co-worker, a Protestant whom Dinny considered a friend, said to him in all seriousness one day as they were having a drink after work, "Fact is, Dinny, the time I like you best, I could cut your throat"—this despite the two of them having talked "not one word of politics or religion" (HE 56).

In addition to capturing the tension created by sectarian divisions, McCabe also displays in "Cancer" flashes of black humor, resembling that in Morrow's story "Place: Belfast / Time: 1984 / Scene: The only pub," discussed in the last chapter. A printed notice in the pub where Boyle and Dinny stop for a drink lists various bounties offered by the local development association for the extermination of vermin, from a shilling for each magpie to a pound for a fox. Underneath the list a patron has scribbled: "For every Fenian Fucker: one old penny" (HE 59). In the hospital, Boyle jokingly tells Joady that a nurse has told him that Joady has received a blood transfusion from a Protestant: "Black blood, she told me you got Paisley's blood" (HE 65)—an allusion, of course, to the Reverend Ian Paisley, perhaps the "blackest" of all Protestant extremists. As discussed in the previous chapter, such humor serves as temporary comic relief from the sectarian tensions while at the same time revealing a deep resignation to the Troubles.

The analogy implicit in the story's title signals its central theme: the Troubles are a cancer in the body politic of Northern Ireland and are no less devastating than the literal cancer that ravages Joady. McCabe points up his analogy several times in the story. During their drive to the hospital, for example, Dinny says to Boyle that a doctor once told him that cancer "could be in the blood fifty years, and then all of a shot it boils up and you're a gonner" (HE 58). The period of fifty years is roughly the period between the Treaty of 1921 and the renewal of Troubles in Northern Ireland, a stretch of time in which the sectarian symptoms went unattended, so that now the cancer has finally surfaced. Later at the hospital, as Dinny and Joady discuss the state of his cancer, Boyle reads a newspaper account of recent incidents related to the Troubles, which again underlines the analogy.

Joady's case turns out to be hopeless and he is sent home, supposedly to live out his few remaining days in relative ease and comfort with the companionship of his only brother. Instead, the two brothers are at odds with each other, still yet another effect of living under the strain of sectarian strife. They are unable to talk about their feelings and are probably beyond any kind of reconciliation. Dinny stays out late at night to avoid facing his dying brother. Joady resents this behavior and, in the story's final paragraph, expresses his feelings in words that apply as well to the sectarian strife in Northern Ireland: "What would you call it, when your own brother goes contrary, and the ground hungry for you . . . eh! Rotten, that's what I'd call it, rotten" (HE 67). It is a bitter, despairing comment on the state of Northern Ireland.

McCabe's story serves as a link between the stories that focus primarily on sectarian tensions and divisions and the stories of terrorism that followed. More than the other stories of sectarian tension discussed in this chapter, "Cancer" brings to the forefront the violence of the Troubles. The blown-up body parts of the men killed at Trillick have been brought to the morgue attached to the hospital in Enniskillen, and Joady relates to Dinny and Boyle what he has heard from the nurses: "Army doctors tryin' to put the bits together, so's their people can recognise them, and box them proper" (HE 62). His gruesome description leads to a bizarre discussion about using bloodhounds to find other missing body parts so that they won't be left "to rot in a bog" (HE 63). But the passage is brief, and McCabe returns to his primary focus on the more subtle consequences of sectarianism. In the stories treated in the following chapter, violence and its terrible consequences become the primary focus.

5

Sectarian Violence

The Story of Terrorism

The thought of violence a relief,
The act of violence a grief;
Our bitterness and love
Hand in glove.
—Seamus Deane, "Derry"

I

In the 1970s and 1980s a new type of Troubles story appeared: the story of sectarian violence and terrorism. In these stories Irish writers represent the brutal phenomenon, then frequently occurring in Northern Ireland and occasionally in the Irish Republic, of violence perpetrated by Catholic and Protestant militants. Using a style of stark realism that depicts fictional characters in situations that resemble real-life incidents, these authors probe the many facets of sectarian violence and terrorism: the roots and causes, the traumatic social and psychological impact on innocent victims, the moral choices forced upon people, and the extraordinary acts of moral courage and cowardice resulting from these choices.

Terrorism, sectarian and otherwise, was of course not new to Ireland. It dates back centuries, though often carried out as much for agrarian change by such secret societies as the Protestant "Peep o' Day Boys" and the Catholic "Defenders," as for—or against—the overthrow of government. It played a significant role in the Troubles of 1916–1923, notably in Michael Collins' strategy to defeat the British during the War of Independence. However, with the exception of William Carleton's "Wildgoose Lodge" (1833) which depicts the terrorism used by secret societies in the nineteenth century, terrorism did not become a major theme in the Irish short story until the 1970s.

Violence, on the other hand, has been a feature of Troubles stories from the beginning. However, in depicting the violence of the 1916–1923 Troubles, O'Connor and the other short-story writers portray it neither as terrorism, nor as sectarian in nature. In the romantic stories, violence is muted or presented in an acceptable manner: the romantic revolutionaries are "freedom fighters" who use violence as a legitimate means of overthrowing an oppressive colonial power. In the naturalistic stories, violence is depicted as the deplorable but inevitable consequence of a misguided idealism. In both cases, the violence portrayed is restricted largely to combatants in the normal course of military operations. In the few stories in which the victims are civilians, the violence is portrayed more as a by-product of the fighting (as, for example, the destruction of the tavern in O'Flaherty's "The Mountain Tavern") than as an act of terrorism.

In the 1970s and 1980s Irish writers made sectarian violence and terrorism the primary focus of their stories. In doing so, they portrayed violence in a context larger than the ideological one that viewed terrorism as the means necessary for militant nationalists to pursue a united Ireland, or for militant loyalists[1] to prevent Northern Ireland's absorption into the Republic of Ireland. These stories rise above ideology to examine the violence and terror from a human perspective. Hence, the focus is not on the political issues—partition, unification, civil rights, and the like—that have spurred violence and terrorism, but on the attendant human issues: the dehumanizing aspects of sectarian violence; the disruption and loss of lives caused by the violence; and the profound physical, social, and psychological effects inflicted on its victims. Some of these stories hint at human, rather than political, solutions to this seemingly intractable problem, but their real value lies in their larger, human per-

1. I use the terms "unionist" and "loyalist" interchangeably, as many scholars do. For a distinction between the two, see Michael MacDonald, "Blurring the Difference: The Politics of Identity in Northern Ireland," in *The Irish Terrorism Experience*, ed. Yonah Alexander and Alan O'Day (Brookfield, Vt.: Dartmouth Publishing Co., 1991), 86–87.

spective that enables them to raise moral questions about terrorism, its causes and its aims, and ultimately to question the claims of sectarian and cultural identity that triggered the violence and terrorism in the first place.

Terrorism became commonplace in Northern Ireland and spread sporadically to the south shortly after the civil rights marches and demonstrations began in Derry and Belfast in the late 1960s. The anger of Northern Catholic demonstrators demanding political and economic equality was met by the violent responses of Protestants unwilling to give up their long-held power. Catholics, in turn, rioted in their Belfast and Derry neighborhoods. Soon, the spontaneous violence of citizens, Catholic and Protestant, gave way to planned, organized violence—namely terrorism—of the militant extremist groups of both sides. Moreover, the terrorism was often motivated more by the interests of nationalists and unionists than by those of civil rights marchers. The goal of nationalist terrorism was the end to partition, the unification of north and south, while the goal of loyalist terrorism was the solidification of the northern state.

Sectarian terrorism was carried out on both sides by organized, trained groups. The Provisional IRA, which had split from the "Official" IRA in 1970 over philosophical differences and policy differences, became the primary terrorist organization on the nationalist side. The UVF, with roots back to 1912, and the UFF, the violent subgroup of the ostensibly legal UDA, took the lead in terrorist activities for the unionists. During the quarter century of sustained terrorism in Northern Ireland, from the late 1960s through the mid-1990s, militant groups proliferated into a bewildering array of organizations: the INLA, the Contingency IRA, and the Real IRA, on the nationalist side; and Ulster Resistance, the Red Hand Commando, the LVF, Tara, and others on the unionist side—all contributing in one way or another to terrorist activities.

Violence, of course, is endemic to any revolutionary enterprise, but not all of it can be labeled terrorism. It is helpful, therefore, to distinguish terrorist violence from other types of violence that occur during armed conflicts. Definitions of terrorism abound, yet scholars of the subject agree that no single definition that strives for any kind of precision is likely to embrace all forms of terrorism. There are, nevertheless, certain characteristics that most scholars identify as essential to terrorism, and that have been present in Irish terrorism.[2] First, terrorism involves acts of violence or force—mayhem, arson, murder, assassinations, bombings, kidnappings, hijackings—designed to achieve political goals, such as the overthrow of a ruling power or, conversely, the prevention of a revolutionary group from ascending to power. Secondly, many terrorist acts are committed against innocent people rather than against combatants. By committing such acts, terrorists acknowledge that it may not be possible to defeat or destroy the enemy militarily; instead, their purpose is to intimidate the opposition into making political concessions through the ever-constant threat to the property and lives of innocent people. Still another prominent trait is what Robert Tabor calls "political theatre"[3]: terrorist acts designed to gain widespread publicity and, thereby, convey the trauma of terrorism not only to those victims immediately and severely affected, but also to all others in the terrorist arena who see or hear the news of the terrorist act. One final important characteristic of terrorism is that it is organized: it is carried out in planned, controlled, and systematic ways by organizations, rather than spontaneously executed by unaffiliated individuals.

Irish terrorism on both sides of the sectarian divide reflects all of these characteristics. Although groups on each side have other motives, such as the civil rights issues mentioned above or control of the drug trade and other flourishing criminal enterprises,[4] their major goals are

2. For definitions and characteristics of terrorism see *Terrorism Experience*, ed. Alexander and O'Day; David E. Long, *The Anatomy of Terrorism* (New York: The Free Press, 1990); and *Terrorism, Legitimacy, and Power: The Consequences of Political Violence*, ed. Martha Crenshaw (Middletown, Conn.: Wesleyan University Press, 1983).

3. Robert Tabor, *The War of the Flea: A Study of Guerrilla Warfare, Theory and Practice* (London: Granada Paladin, 1970), 31, quoted in Richard Davis, "Northern Ireland Political Papers and the Troubles, 1966–90," in *Terrorism Experience*, ed. Alexander and O'Day, 29.

4. See Adrian Guelke, "Loyalist and Republican Perceptions of the Northern

political and their methods are the standard terrorist ones: mayhem, murder, assassination, and bombings intended to destroy property and cause pain, suffering, and death. The only standard terrorist method underutilized in the Irish experience is hijacking. Irish terrorism is also typical of terrorism generally in that it is "essentially propagandistic," that is, "waged with the media in mind."[5]

Another characteristic that makes Irish terrorism typical is that many of the estimated thirty-six hundred victims of the Troubles have been civilians. Although some of these victims may have been targeted because they were actively supportive of one side or the other, others were chosen simply for their sectarian affiliation. Adrian Guelke provides a chart showing that, of the 2204 deaths recorded in the years 1969 through 1982, 1565 (71%) of them were civilian.[6] (The chart, however, does not distinguish truly innocent civilians from those actively involved in sectarian affairs.) Guelke also quotes a UDA leader as saying that the UDA followed the IRA method of killing civilians for their sectarian affiliation: "In 1972 almost 500 people were killed and we have little doubt now that most of these people died, whether they were Protestant or Catholic, because they were of the wrong religion in the wrong place at the wrong time."[7]

Finally, Irish terrorism is organized terrorism. Both Catholic nationalists and Protestant loyalists have long had organized militant groups that have periodically resorted to terrorism. The IRA goes back at least to the 1916 Easter Rising, when the rebels became known as the Irish Republican Army, though many historians argue that its roots go back

---

Ireland Conflict: The UDA and the Provisional IRA," in *Political Violence and Terror: Motifs and Motivations*, ed. Peter H. Merkel (Berkeley and Los Angeles: University of California Press, 1986), 100; Paul Wilkinson, "The Orange and the Green: Extremism in Northern Ireland," in *Terrorism, Legitimacy, and Power*, ed. Crenshaw, 120; and Long, *Anatomy*, 46–47.

5. Yonah Alexander and Alan O'Day, "Introduction: Dimensions of Irish Terrorism," in *Terrorism Experience*, ed. Alexander and O'Day, 2.

6. Guelke, "Perceptions," 103.

7. John McMichael interview in *Marxism Today*, December 1981, quoted in Guelke, "Perceptions," 106–7.

to the Fenians of the nineteenth century, perhaps even farther back. Most other contemporary nationalist terrorist groups, such as the Provos and the Real IRA, are off-shoots of the original IRA, though they are often in conflict with the parent organization over both philosophy and methods. Similarly, most loyalist groups trace their lineage back to the Orange Order, formed in the late eighteenth century and named after William of Orange. The UVF, originally formed in 1912 to resist home rule, resurfaced in the 1970s. Long says that it was organized out of various street gangs, as were the UDA, Red Hand Commandos, and the UFF.[8]

The five stories analyzed in this chapter represent, in terms of depiction of subject matter, treatment of theme, and literary quality, the best of the stories of sectarian violence and terrorism. Together they also present a balanced perspective of the Northern Troubles in terms of both sectarian representation and geography. Three are told from the perspective of the Catholic community and two from the Protestant perspective. Two take place in Belfast, two in smaller towns in Northern Ireland, and one in Dublin. These stories also illustrate the various types of terrorism common in Ireland in the last three decades of the twentieth century. There is a bombing in downtown Dublin and a proxy bombing planned in a small town in the Northern county of Tyrone; a British Army officer is murdered in Belfast and his wife is raped by terrorists; two members of a local Protestant militia are targeted and gunned down by IRA terrorists and, in retaliation, another member of the militia butchers two innocent Catholic farmers; and an innocent Catholic Belfast fruiterer is randomly chosen for execution in retaliation for the recent killing of a Protestant. Most impressively, the five stories poignantly examine the human issues related to terrorism. Each one treats in depth one or more of those issues noted above: the root causes of sectarian hatred and violence; the devastating physical, social and psychological effects on innocent people; and the moral decisions and actions that acts of sectarian violence and terrorism force upon civilians.

8. Long, *Anatomy*, 46–47.

II

The central event of Val Mulkerns' "Four Green Fields" is a terrorist attack in downtown Dublin, a car bomb that kills twenty people and injures dozens more. Among the victims is a family of four on its way to feed the ducks in Stephen's Green: a young husband and wife and their two children, one "[a] flaxen-haired toddler" (AQ 23) holding her father's hand and the other in a pram being pushed by the mother. Just prior to the sudden blast, Emily, one of the central characters, has noticed the family as she shops in Talbot Street. After the explosion, which has stunned but not seriously injured Emily, she sees the father being carried off on a stretcher clutching what she takes to be his child's hand. The children have been "blown into fragments" (AQ 26).

The explosion inflicts devastating physical havoc at its point of impact, but like many terrorist acts it is also "political theatre," designed to be felt beyond its immediate victims. Mulkerns' focus, in fact, is the response of Irish people to the blast, as news of it is brought to a dinner party being held that night by Siobhán O'Sullivan and her husband. The O'Sullivans' guests include Emily, who arrives straight from town "white-faced, bloodstained, [and] filthy" (AQ 26); Emily's husband, Denis; and an American couple in Dublin to research the topic of revolution in Anglo-Irish literature. Denis brings along Mary Kate, an American girl studying Irish literature, who has been living with Denis and Emily.

The center of attention, however, is another guest, Feardorcha O'Briain, a hard-drinking and often drunk raconteur, "a senior counsel who [takes] mostly Provo briefs" (AQ 24). O'Briain displays his Republican sympathies with his Gaelic name and his Gaelic endearments ("Siobhán, a chroí" [AQ 24], he addresses the hostess) and by regaling the American couple with stories of the 1916 Easter Rising and the IRA Coventry bombing of 1940. He frequently interrupts his own stories to sing snatches of rebel ballads, such as the one whose title Mulkerns borrows for the title of her story. He is treated politely by the other guests, even when, in his boisterous and drunken fashion, he defends IRA terrorism as necessary to bring about "an end to the effects of seven hundred years of foreign domination" and "the ultimate aim of a United Irish Socialist Republic" (AQ 27). The strongest verbal response to O'Briain's insensitivity is Emily's pointed question, "Is bombing babies in prams north and south a permissible means to this end?"—to which he blithely answers: "Regrettable but inevitable, my treasure" (AQ 27).

One of Mulkerns' themes is that tolerance, or at best mild rejection, rather than moral outrage, is the typical Irish response to such violent ideology. While O'Briain goes on about the need for a "total reshaping of [Irish] society" (AQ 28) through a bloody civil war that will rage in the south as well as in Belfast, the hosts and other guests respond—as dinner hosts and guests are wont to do—in polite, tolerant ways. The American couple and Emily quietly leave the table, while Denis, sympathetic to the man if not to his views, offers to drive O'Briain home. "Nobody would be sorrier or quicker to phone with his apologies in the morning than the same parlatic madman" (AQ 29), Denis remarks to the others.

Meanwhile, in another room Emily switches on the television to hear of more Irish terrorist violence, general all over Ireland, and spreading to London and Paris as well: "two Catholics had been shot dead in a village pub in Armagh and four Protestants seriously injured when masked raiders sprayed a Sandy Row lounge with machine-gun fire. A member of the Westminster opposition had been slightly injured in a car bomb explosion outside his Mayfair flat, and news had just come through of the death in mysterious circumstances of an Irish student in Paris" (AQ 29). The point of the story is quite clear: Irish terrorism is thriving, in no small part due to an Irish public that feels helpless and is unable to challenge even the most ineffectual proponents like the drunken O'Briain. Mulkerns' story damns the dinner guests nearly as much as the terrorists.

The story also points to one of the fundamental—and vexing—paradoxes of politically motivated violence, captured in the oft-quoted aphorism, "one man's terrorist is another man's freedom fighter."[9] To those, such as O'Briain, who believe that their political goals will come

9. Regarding this aphorism, see Alexander and O'Day, "Dimensions," 2.

about only through violent means, the perpetrators of the violence are political guerrillas or freedom fighters, while to those who abhor and condemn violent means, whether or not they believe in the political goals, the perpetrators are terrorists. Although it is clear that the dinner guests do not accept O'Briain's view that the Irish terrorists are freedom fighters engaged in "guerilla warfare" (AQ 28), apparently many in Ireland do agree with that view, judging from O'Briain's popularity. His popularity is reflected in Emily's comment about him that ends the story: "'When I was ten,' she said shivering, 'I had that man's picture pinned up on my wall at home. With Pearse and Dev and Yeats and Bold Robert Emmet'" (AQ 29).

In a skillful literary strategy, Mulkerns uses a subsidiary plot thread to reinforce her theme that subtle acquiescence can lead to disaster. "Four Green Fields" begins with Denis and Mary Kate returning home from a trip to Shannon airport where Mary Kate had hoped to reunite with her father. She aborted that plan, however, when she saw that he was drunk. When they go upstairs they find a dead pigeon lying on one of the beds. Puzzled by its presence, Mary Kate suggests that it was done in by a hawk, but Denis rejects that explanation, preferring instead to believe that the pigeon flew through the open window and crashed into the mantelpiece, leaving only the pigeon to blame for its death.

The complications that this narrative thread creates are only subtly suggested: a couple of times Mary Kate wonders aloud how Emily will respond to her return, and as he stoops to pick up the family cat, she kisses Denis on the back of the neck, a gesture that he ignores while calling her "child." The implication is that Mary Kate has brought sexual conflict into Denis and Emily's home and that, perhaps, Emily has asked her to leave. But, later at the dinner party when Emily discovers that Mary Kate has returned, her response is just what Denis has predicted: she says that Mary Kate can continue to stay in their absent daughter's bedroom. In this personal matter, as in that of the larger political one, Emily and Denis are too tolerant to confront the issue head-on; they thereby acquiesce in the potential destruction of their marriage. Furthermore, Denis' refusal to admit the possibility that the hawk, or more probably the cat, is responsible for the ominous death of the pigeon symbolizes the Irish public's refusal to probe the real causes of the great terrorist violence in their land.

III

Benedict Kiely's "Proxopera" (Latin for proxy operation) has the length and depth of a novella but the intensity of a short story. Kiely's plot revolves around a terrorist operation in which three members of the IRA intend to explode a bomb in a small town in Northern Ireland by having it delivered in a car driven by an innocent man. The Binchey family—a widower, his son and daughter-in-law, and his two grandchildren—arrive home on Saturday after a holiday in Donegal to discover three IRA terrorists have taken possession of their home and made their housekeeper a prisoner. The terrorists tell the elder Mr. Binchey, a retired Latin teacher, that he is to drive his car with the bomb—"One hundred pounds of ammonium nitrate mixed with fuel oil and about three pounds of gelignite" (SI 362)—into town on Sunday morning and leave it either between the post office and town hall or, if security makes that impossible, near the home of Judge Flynn. The terrorists' intent is to destroy much of the town while the townspeople are at Church services, an act of reprisal for the killing by Protestant militants of a Catholic who owned a pub frequented by IRA members.

To force the elder Binchey to comply with their demands, the terrorists threaten to harm his family and the housekeeper if he does not carry out the operation. Thus Kiely sets up the moral dilemma of his protagonist: either carry out the terrorists' orders and thereby destroy much of the town and perhaps injure, even kill, innocent people, or allow his own family to be harmed by the terrorists. Binchey's dilemma is further complicated by the fact that he is Catholic (though neither an IRA sympathizer nor an overt nationalist), and the town, though set in the heart of a "well-planted Presbyterian countryside" (SI 336), seems at the moment relatively free of sectarian tension and strife. Furthermore, Judge Flynn has a reputation for peace and justice and would be an innocent victim. Hence, carrying out the proxy terrorism would likely re-ignite sectarian conflict in this town where Catholics and Protestants currently co-exist in relative peace.

Reluctantly, Binchey agrees to the terrorists' demands and on Sunday morning, fully resigned to carry out the proxy bombing, he begins his trip into town. As he drives toward town, he is stopped at an intersection by a young policeman he knows who tells him that several fires have been started in the area, perhaps, the policeman says, as diversions for a possible terrorist attack. After driving on for a short while, Binchey thinks more deeply about the potentially devastating effects of the bombing and decides not to carry it out. He turns his car around and drives away from the town. At a military checkpoint, he tells two British soldiers about the bomb and then drives off toward a bog. As the car approaches the bog, he gets out and the bomb goes off, knocking him unconscious. Two weeks later, in the hospital, he learns that the terrorists set fire to his home and shot his son in a kneecap, but his family is otherwise safe. He also learns that two of the terrorists died when a bomb in their car accidentally exploded, and the third was found shot to death, probably by the leader for insubordination.

Kiely filters the story through the mind of his protagonist, the elder Binchey, which enables us to see how he comes to his difficult moral decision to abort the proxy operation. Because Binchey has had a long life, is a well-educated man, and has been reared in the town, his mind is rich with memories, local images, and historical and cultural allusions. He recalls memories of growing up in the town, of his courtship and marriage, and of his wife's death of cancer. He conjures up images of his wife's gravesite; of the white house that he admired as a boy, eventually purchased, and now lives in; and of the nearby lake, which has played a prominent role in his life as well as in the current incident. He also evokes allusions to historical events of sectarian strife, such as the Siege of Derry; to myth and song; and to Irish poetry, such as Yeats's "September 1913" with its allusions to the Irish heroes Tone, Emmet, and Fitzgerald, who, Binchey thinks, would "not have died by proxy" (SI 367).

These free-floating and seemingly random bits of memory, feeling, and knowledge coalesce in Binchey's mind and lead ultimately to his decision not to carry out the bombing. "Now I see," he repeats to himself three times as he realizes what the town, its history, and his life there all mean: "I see there my town and all its people, Orange and Green, and the post office with all its clerks and postmen and red mail vans, and the town hall and its glass dome and everybody in it—from that fine man, my friend, town clerk, or mayor, for forty-odd years, down to the decent tobacco-chewing man who swabs out the public jakes in the basement, my people, my people." How could he, he wonders, "ever submit to what the madmen are now trying to force on [him], and go on for the rest of his life remembering that to save his own family he had planted death in his own town which is also his family?" (SI 379).

Of all the images that run through Binchey's mind, the lake is imbued with the greatest significance. It was once a "paradise," where as a youth Binchey would go to get away from the occasional sectarian hatred that would threaten to flare up in town. From the lake he would view the great white house that he admired and eventually bought: "long and white, an air of aristocratic age about it" with "a small brook" cutting through the lawn and "tumbling down to join the lake" (SI 339). But now the lake has become eerie, a reminder of death. The body of the Catholic pub owner killed by the Protestant militants was dumped in the lake, where it became badly decomposed, broke loose from the weight that held it down, floated up, and was discovered by a fisherman. This event, Binchey thinks, has caused the lake to become "dark and still" (SI 336), so that the "lake would never be the same again" (SI 335), a phrase Binchey repeats to himself several times.

Binchey's mind also plays with the name of the lake, Lough Muck, Gaelic for "lake of the pig." In a beautifully rendered stream-of-consciousness passage, Binchey remembers verses of a comic song about two drunks who, having fallen harmlessly into a small lake, think they are in the ocean: "*And that was the start of our ill-fated cruise on the treacherous waves of Loughmuck.*" But the once-comic chorus of the song ("*oh the sights that we saw as we waited for death*" [SI 361–62; italics in text]) now has tragic reverberations with the recent killing of the Catholic pub owner. Lough Muck has changed forever: "Laughter and innocence were gone. The shadow of the monstrous mythological pig brooded over a landscape that could never free itself from vengeance and old wrongs" (SI 362). Binchey's ultimate choice to abort the proxy operation is in one sense, then, his determination to do his small part to reverse this history of "vengeance and old wrongs," to help drive away that "shadow of the monstrous mythological pig." His allusion here is to the legendary Irish belief in an apocalyptic battle that will take place in the valley of the Black Pig in Ulster and will pit the forces of Ireland against its enemies.[10]

"Proxopera" portrays two conflicting aspects of terrorism: the terrorists' need for anonymity and the victims' need to establish a human connection with their attackers and maintain a sense of self-esteem. Anonymity is essential for terrorists, not only because it deters their later identification, arrest, and imprisonment, but also because it precludes the establishing of a personal bond between them and their victims and maintains "the barrier of dehumanization."[11] Conversely, if victims can break down this barrier by dissolving the anonymity and establish a personal bond with their captors, they can help to ensure their own survival. As Long points out, "when a personal bond is established between a terrorist captor and a hijack or kidnap victim, it becomes increasingly difficult for the terrorist to continue to mistreat him or her." He adds that the self-esteem of the victim, which can grow out of the personal bond, is particularly important "for psychological and physical survival."[12]

Kiely's fictional terrorists are at first anonymous to their victims. They disguise themselves by wearing caps and masks, including one in a gasmask. But the elder Binchey refuses to accept their anonymity. At

10. See W. B. Yeats's note to his poem "The Valley of the Black Pig," in *W. B. Yeats: The Poems*, rev. ed., ed. Richard J. Finneran, vol. 1 of *The Collected Works of W. B. Yeats*, ed. Richard J. Finneran and George Mills Harper (New York: Macmillan, 1989), 593–94; and Steven Putzel, "The Black Pig: Yeats's Early Apocalyptic Beast," *Éire-Ireland* 17 (fall 1982): 86–102.

11. Long, *Anatomy*, 134.

12. Ibid., 134–35.

first, he bestows identity on them through their appearance, referring to them in his own mind as Gasmask, Soldier's Cap, and Corkman, the first two for their apparel and the last for his Cork accent. Gradually, though, the real identities of Gasmask and Soldier's Cap come to him. He recognizes Gasmask by his poor feet as Bertie, the son of a man he knows and despises for his sectarian hatred, and Soldier's Cap by his eyes, which show through his mask, as Mad Eyes Minahan, another local militant nationalist. Although the real identity of Corkman, the leader and outsider, remains unknown, Binchey's determined and otherwise successful effort to identify the terrorists and thus destroy their anonymity helps to frustrate their terrorist intentions.

Binchey and his son also confront the terrorists in small, though brave, ways, which helps to bolster their self-esteem. They mock them as "Irish heroes" (SI 347) who "tar and feather a few girls" (SI 351) and kneecap innocent civilians. They call them a "gang," implying that they are nothing but thugs, thus contesting Soldier's Cap's claim that they are "freedom fighters" (SI 347). The younger Binchey, a boxer in his youth, suggests to Corkman that they "step outside" (SI 351). At another point he punches Soldier's Cap and knocks him through the backdoor into the yard, momentarily creating a crisis. The elder Binchey, alone at one point with Bertie, slips up and calls him by name. He then continues to call him by name once he senses that, for all his bravado, Bertie is a coward who does not want Corkman to know that Binchey has identified him, lest things get out of hand. Though each attempt at confrontation is ineffective, each is an expression of self-esteem and a statement to the terrorists that not everyone acquiesces to their ideology and methods.

The relatively successful resolution of the crisis brought on by the proxy operation perhaps belies the harsh reality of terrorism and offers at best a wistful view of how it might be confronted and even defeated through brave moral acts. Binchey and his family have escaped the crisis with a minimum of injury, the town has avoided a devastating explosion, and the terrorists have all been killed. Nevertheless, Kiely's examination of the moral issues inherent in the terrorist experience is profound.

IV

If Mulkerns and Kiely focus on moral responses to terrorism, David Park illustrates the social and psychological impact of random and unexpected terrorism in "Oranges from Spain." Park deftly recreates for the reader the shock such terrorism brings to its victims and bystanders by giving no warning of the violence to come and by describing it in full graphic detail in the last four paragraphs of his story. The first-person narrator, a young married man looking back to the summer of his sixteenth year, provides a bit of foreshadowing in the opening pages by alluding to his nightmares and vaguely attributing them to the death of his first employer, the Catholic fruiterer Gerry Breen. But he makes no mention of the Troubles or terrorism despite the story taking place in contemporary Belfast. So engrossing is the narrative of his personal relationship with Gerry Breen that we are completely swept up in it and are thus unprepared for the violence when it comes: the brutal sectarian execution of the fruiterer.

The narrator relates that, when he started working for Breen, he "didn't like the man much at first," and he didn't think that Breen "liked [him] much either" (OS 178). He thought the fruiterer "was one of the meanest men [he had] ever met" (OS 183); he was always correcting the way the boy did his chores. Breen also hassled suppliers if the fruit was damaged, and he flattered and joked with women customers to induce them to buy his produce, behavior the boy thought embarrassing and unpleasant. Gradually, however, fruiterer and employee grew to appreciate each other and began to develop a warm relationship. Eventually Gerry Breen revealed a personal side to the young narrator that had the effect of drawing the boy close to him. When Mrs. Breen, "all dressed up in a blue and white suit . . . on her way to some social function" (OS 186), appeared in the shop one day and treated her husband with disdain, the fruiterer told the boy, "Never get married, son—it's the end of your happiness," and then remarked, "My wife's ashamed of me" (OS 186).

The boy learned that Gerry Breen was a complex person. He was, for example, thrifty to the point of being stingy, saving every "bit of string or . . . piece of wood" (OS 183) and grousing when a local priest asked him for free fruit for some hospitalized parishioners ("The church'll be the ruin of me" [OS 184]). But he also had a generous streak in him. The narrator learned that for fifteen years he had regularly supplied free fruit to an elderly woman who had once done him a favor.

It was Gerry Breen's revelation of his dream, however, that did the most to establish a close relationship between the two. Embarrassed that he might seem foolish, the fruiterer nevertheless told the narrator, upon being asked, that his fondest dream was to visit the countries that supplied his produce: "Oranges from Spain, apples from New Zealand, cabbages from Holland, peaches from Italy, grapes from the Cape, bananas from Ecuador . . ." (OS 190). At the time of his revelation, the boy did not respond, but in retrospect he tells us that he regrets not having told Gerry Breen what he felt, that he "would have gone with him" (OS 190).

Breen is executed in his fruit shop, while holding a tray of oranges, by a Protestant extremist in a blue crash helmet who arrives suddenly and departs just as swiftly on a motorbike. The random execution, apparently in retaliation for the IRA execution of a Protestant, is described in all of its gruesome detail:

> Suddenly, the man pulled a gun out of his tunic. . . . The first shot hit Gerry Breen in the chest, spinning him round, and as he slumped to the floor the oranges scattered and rolled in all directions. He lay there, face down, and his body was still moving. Then, as I screamed an appeal for mercy, the man walked forward and, kneeling over the body, shot him in the back of the head. His body kicked and shuddered, and then was suddenly and unnaturally still. I screamed again in fear and anger and then, pointing the gun at me, the man walked slowly backwards to the door of the shop, ran to the waiting bike and was gone. Shaking uncontrollably and stomach heaving with vomit, I tried to turn Mr Breen over on to his back, but he was too heavy for me. Blood splashed his green coat, and flowed from the dark gaping wound, streaming across the floor, mixing with the oranges that were strewn all around us. Oranges from Spain. (OS 191; Park does not use a period after Mr)

This is a vivid, revolting portrait of brutal and senseless terrorism.

Gerry Breen is "another bystander, another nobody, sucked into the vortex by a random and malignant fate that marked him out . . . a casualty of convenience, a victim of retribution, propitiation of a different god. . . . Just one more sectarian murder—unclaimed, unsolved, soon unremembered but by a few" (OS 190). Park, however, goes beyond the dramatic impact of terrorism, its "political theatre," and uses the story to explore the range of effects brought on by an isolated act of sectarian violence. The random and brutal execution of Gerry Breen ends his life, of course, as well as his dream of visiting all of the countries that supply his produce. But the violence also has serious social effects in the community and psychological effects in the narrator, though these effects may at first appear insignificant compared to the fruiterer's death.

The narrator tells us that, after Gerry Breen's death, the widow sold the fruit shop to people who turned it into a fast-food restaurant: "You wouldn't recognise it now—it's all flashing neon, girls in identical uniforms and the type of food that has no taste" (OS 177). The symbolism implicit in the change from fresh fruit and vegetables to tasteless fast food and from the personable, quirky Gerry Breen to uniformed (and uniform), impersonal waitresses conveys the social loss the violence has wrought. More significantly, Breen is no longer mentioned by the narrator's parents in the boy's presence, obviously because they are afraid of recalling to their son's mind the horror of the fruiterer's execution. The social effect of such reticence is great. "It's almost as if he never existed" (OS 178), the narrator states. Terrorism has not only taken the physical life of a person; it has obliterated his memory in society.

The psychological impact of the violence, felt by the narrator, is more prominent than the social impact. Shortly after witnessing the execution, the boy began to have nightmares. Now a married man, he continues to have the nightmares, though less frequently, requiring his wife to cradle him "in her arms like a child" (OS 178). The nightmares might be explained by the sheer horror of witnessing the execution, an effect that might have come about even had the narrator witnessed the execution of a stranger, but the narrator's trauma is all the greater for the loss of his relationship with Gerry Breen.

V

No short story conveys the unspeakable horror of terrorism in Northern Ireland more powerfully than William Trevor's "Attracta." One of Trevor's purposes in writing this story is quite clearly to make the violence so brutal and so repugnant as to force the reader to reflect on the nature of terrorism and solutions to it. Trevor, however, is not interested in proposing political solutions to terrorism; in fact, he is rarely if ever political in his perspective, even when he writes about the Irish Troubles. His focus is always on the human aspects of suffering.[13] In this story, as Suzanne Paulson notes, Trevor's "interests transcend the political"; his primary focus, she remarks, is on the female protagonist's "imaginative response to life and her capacity to empathize, especially in response to suffering."[14]

The actual violence that the story treats—murder, decapitation, rape, and suicide—would be repellant enough even if reported just once, but Trevor wants the reader to imagine it in all of its astounding detail, and so he repeats the gruesome account several times. We first learn of the violence through the consciousness of the protagonist, Attracta, a sixty-one-year-old Protestant schoolteacher in a small town close to Cork. Shortly after the story begins, the narrator relates how Attracta is reviewing a recent newspaper account with which she has become obsessed. The account is about a young Englishwoman, Penelope Vade, who has committed suicide by swallowing a bottle of aspirins after having been raped repeatedly by seven men, her husband's murderers. The men, probably IRA terrorists, murdered and then decapitated her hus-

13. Trevor has stated, "The struggle in Ireland—and the sorrow—is a good backdrop for a fiction writer, but it is not for me any sort of inspiration. . . . What seems to nudge me is something that exists between two people, or three, and if their particular happiness or distress exists for some political reason, then the political reason comes into it—but the relationship between the people comes first." William Trevor, "The Art of Fiction CVIII," interview by Mira Stout, *Paris Review* 110 (1989): 118–51, quoted in Suzanne Morrow Paulson, *William Trevor: A Study of the Short Fiction* (New York: Twayne, 1993), xi.

14. Paulson, *Trevor*, 21.

band, a British army officer stationed with peace-keeping forces in Belfast. They then sent the severed head, "wrapped in cotton-wool to absorb the ooze of blood, secured within a plastic bag and packed in a biscuit-tin" to Penelope Vade in England. The horror of such an act seems unsurpassable, until we learn that "[s]he hadn't known that he was dead before his dead eyes stared into hers" (CST 676). Her courageous response to this horrific act is "to make the point that neither he nor she had been defeated": she joins the Women's Peace Movement in Belfast. But her husband's murderers learn of her gesture and retaliate by raping her, an act which provokes her suicide: "*From the marks of blood on carpets and rugs,* the [newspaper] item said, *it is deduced that Mrs Vade dragged herself across the floors of two rooms. She appears repeatedly to have fainted before she reached a bottle of aspirins in a kitchen cupboard*" (CST 676; italics in text).

The newspaper account triggers in Attracta memories of her own victimization decades earlier. When she was three years old, during the War of Independence, her parents were accidentally killed in a rebel ambush of Black and Tan soldiers. At the time she was not told of the killings or of those responsible; instead, relatives simply told her that her parents had inexplicably left town. But when she was eleven a vengeful Protestant neighbor, Mr. Purce, revealed to her the truth of the incident: her parents had been killed by two townspeople, Mr. Devereux, a Protestant who had sided with the rebels, and his Catholic companion and lover, Geraldine Carey. This knowledge, however, did not evoke in Attracta a hatred of her parents' killers, as Purce had hoped it would, because by this time the two rebels, out of remorse for their violent actions, had changed their violent ways and had drawn themselves close to Attracta. From the time of the accident, Devereux had doted on her, giving her birthday and Christmas presents and spending Saturday afternoons with her. The ironic effect was that when she "kiss[ed] him good-night . . . [s]he imagined it was what having a father was like" (CST 680). Geraldine Carey, by then Devereux's housekeeper, had also changed, living a quiet life and attending daily mass. With her coiled hair and dark clothes (she had worn men's clothing as a rebel), she looked like a nun to Attracta. But when Attracta asked her why she did not become a nun, "Geraldine Carey replied that she'd never heard God calling her. 'Only the good are called,' she said" (CST 679). Now, in present time, Attracta looks back on her life and considers that, despite her tragedy, "she had not suffered. People had been good to her" (CST 676).

Inspired by this recollection of her own tragedy and its ultimate effects on her, Attracta realizes that she has not taught her students—sixteen Protestant children—anything really important about life, namely, about evil, human suffering, guilt, and the possibility of reconciliation. The portraits on the walls of her schoolroom, of "England's kings and queens" *and* Irish heroes of the past, "Niall of the Nine Hostages, Lord Edward FitzGerald, Wolfe Tone and Grattan" (CST 675), now seem a pathetic attempt to instruct the children about the enormous suffering that has resulted from the long history of Ireland's relationship to England and the legacy of the Troubles. In an effort to teach her students something significant, she decides to inform them about Penelope Vade's tragedy.

She begins by reading the newspaper report to the class and then going back over it: "Again she read them the news item, reading it slowly because she wanted it to become as rooted in their minds as it was in hers. She lingered over the number of bullets that had been fired into the body of Penelope Vade's husband, and over the removal of his head" (CST 686). Then to insure that they are grasping the full import of this shocking story, she asks the children to visualize the incident: "Can you see that girl? Can you imagine men putting a human head in a tin box and sending it through the post? Can you imagine her receiving it? The severed head of the man she loved?" (CST 686).

The children, however, are unmoved by the account, apparently because they have grown accustomed to reports of violence and cannot truly imagine it. "Sure, isn't there stuff like that in the papers the whole time" (CST 687), one child remarks. The children's inability to be moved by Penelope Vade's story leads Attracta to tell them about her own experience, again trying to make them visualize the tragedy, something she herself was unable to do at age eleven when Purce told her about it. She asks them to "imagine . . . [her] mother and father shot dead on the Cork road, and Mr Devereux and Geraldine Carey as two monstrous people, and arms being blown off soldiers, and vengeance breeding vengeance" (CST 687). She also wonders aloud whether Devereux's men who committed acts of atrocity felt the same things that those who murdered and decapitated Penelope Vade's husband felt. Then she speaks of her imaginative identification with Penelope Vade, made possible by her own tragedy:

> My story is one with hers. . . . Horror stories, with different endings only. I think of her now and I can see quite clearly the flat she lived in in Belfast. I can see the details, correctly or not I've no idea. Wallpaper with a pattern of brownish-purple flowers on it, gaunt furniture casting shadows, a tea-caddy on the hired television set. I drag my body across the floors of two rooms, over a carpet that smells of dust and cigarette ash, over rugs and cool linoleum. I reach up in the kitchen, a hand on the edge of the sink: one by one I eat the aspirins until the bottle's empty. (CST 688)

Attracta's intent in merging the two tragic stories, hers and Penelope Vade's, is to "tell [the children] . . . never to despair" (CST 688). She believes that her story illustrates the lesson that redemption is possible, that killers can become remorseful and, through remorse, better people. She wonders about the terrorists who have wreaked their violence on Penelope Vade: "Will those same men who exacted that vengeance on [Penelope Vade] one day keep bees and budgerigars? Will they serve in shops, and be kind to the blind and the deaf? Will they garden in the evenings and be good fathers? It is not impossible" (CST 688). But her musings only leave the children bewildered. Later she realizes that "[t]he gleam of hope she'd offered had been too slight to be of use, irrelevant in the horror they took for granted, as part of life" (CST 689). The only tangible effect of her lesson is that parents and school officials are upset and she is asked to resign from her teaching position.

Critics have praised "Attracta" as a story of reconciliation and hope. Dolores MacKenna, calling it "arguably Trevor's most complex exploration of the nature of reconciliation," says that the story "manifests how the human capacity for forgiveness makes it possible for people to have hope no matter how adverse the circumstances,"[15] and Paulson says that Attracta's message is that "we must develop the capacity to mourn for strangers and that no human being is truly a stranger to human suffering of any kind."[16] Indeed, Attracta's insight is the romantic (i.e., hopeful) notion about the relationship of imagination, empathy, and reconciliation—that the act of imagining the suffering or guilt of others enables us to empathize with them and to mourn them or forgive them.

But Attracta's message, strong and hopeful as it is, is counterbalanced by an equally bleak one. The harsh facts and implications of the story stare the reader in the face: the husband of Penelope Vade was murdered and decapitated; she was raped and driven to suicide; Attracta's students have not responded to their teacher's message; and for her act of "moral courage"[17] Attracta is forced into retirement. Furthermore, Attracta's conviction regarding the power of the imagination to bring reconciliation is based on her own experience that resulted from the Black and Tan war. Whether a factor of the distance of history or the conventions of representation in literature, the violence of that war, even the specific representation of the death of Attracta's parents, pales in comparison to the gruesome contemporary violence enacted upon Penelope Vade and her husband. It is extremely difficult for the reader, let alone people victimized by terrorism in Northern Ireland, to view Attracta's solution of forgiveness and reconciliation as viable.

VI

Eugene McCabe explores the roots of sectarian hatred that feed terrorism in Northern Ireland in his long, poignant story "Heritage." He finds those roots in family, religion, and the land, as well as in the instinct for survival that humans have inherited from animals.

Eric O'Neill, McCabe's young protagonist, lives with his parents in

15. Dolores MacKenna, *William Trevor: The Writer and His Work* (Chester Springs, Penn.: Dufour Editions, 1999), 111.

16. Paulson, *Trevor*, 22.

17. Gregory A. Schirmer, *William Trevor: A Study of His Fiction* (New York: Routledge, 1990), 141.

the northern county of Fermanagh on a fifty-acre farm very near the border. At the urging of both his mother and her brother, his Uncle George Hawthorne, he became a member of the Ulster Defence Regiment (UDR), a branch of the British army that functions as a local militia. His mother urged him to join as much for economic as sectarian reasons; the money he earns helps the family. His uncle urged him purely for sectarian reasons: George is a rabid unionist who marches in the Orange parades as a drummer and has portraits in his kitchen of the Queen; Edward Carson, the prominent Ulster Unionist during the partitioning of Ireland; and the militant loyalist minister, Ian Paisley. George speaks disparagingly of Catholics: "a rotten race. . . . Good for nothin' but malice and murder; the like of Hitler would put them through a burnhouse and spread them on their sour bogs and he'd be right, it's all they're fit for" (HE 72).

Not all members of Eric's family are fervently sectarian. Eric's brother, Sam, married a Catholic woman and then left the area to avoid conflict, and his father, John Willie, is tolerant of, even friendly with, neighboring Catholics and willing to take odd jobs from them, such as fixing gutters and patching slates. In contrast, George has lost the business of Catholics in his forge because of the rude way he has treated them.

This split in family attitudes toward Catholics has created a rift between John Willie and his wife, Sarah. Much of the bad feeling between the two resulted from the fact, known by Sarah, that John Willie fathered a son, the idiot boy Willie Reilly, through a liaison with Maggie Reilly, a poor Catholic woman who works on the farm (George calls her a "proper Papist hedge whore" [HE 72]). Rather than feel guilty, however, John Willie feels aggrieved. He tells Eric, who suffers the burden of his parents' dissension, that since the birth of the two boys he has not seen his wife's naked body, which he attributes to Sarah's cold Protestant views: "[She] hates bodies, her own and mine . . . even food, hates that. . . . She could live on black bread, water, the bible and hating Catholics; that's enough to keep her happy, makes me sick" (HE 82). The marital estrangement was made worse by Sarah's refusal to attend Sam's wedding to Maisie because it was held in a Catholic Church. And Sarah and John Willie quarrel frequently over Eric's membership in the

UDR. She thinks that it is right for Eric to be involved; he thinks that Eric is foolish for joining because, in his view, the leaders are greedy men who get others to do the killing and be killed.

Shortly after the story opens on a Sunday morning, Eric finds a death threat tied to a milk can, which causes him to question the wisdom of his membership in the paramilitary organization. He knows that the threat is a very real one: twenty-five UDR members have been killed by militant nationalists since he joined the organization. But when his father, having learned of the death threat, urges Eric to leave the area as his brother has, Eric dismisses the idea. Later that morning at church his girlfriend, Rachel Robinson, tells Eric that IRA terrorists stopped her the previous night, threatened her with rape, and warned her that her brother Joe might be their target. This news further frightens Eric, but he is reluctant to leave the fields of Fermanagh that he loves so much.

That afternoon Eric and Rachel join a hunting party, led by Colonel Armstrong, pursuing otters with dogs along a river. As the group begins to close in on an otter, Dinny McMahon, a Catholic, appears with a shotgun, threatens them, and orders them off his land. Armstrong, a rich Protestant land owner, argues that he has "hunting and shooting rights for this townland" (HE 113), but when McMahon points the gun at the Colonel the group decides to leave. One of Armstrong's party interprets McMahon's warning to the Colonel not to call the police as a terrorist threat: McMahon, he says, has them all "afeered to tell police, for fear we'd be blown up or burnt out . . ." (HE 117).

That night, when George and Eric are driving their assigned UDR patrol, they see smoke and flames over the town of Lisnaskea. British soldiers tell them that terrorists have shot and killed Joe Robinson and fatally wounded his father in the head. Eric and George drive to the Robinson home where Rachel sits passively by the covered body of her brother. George lifts the cover to reveal "Joe's face, a mass of congested blood, unrecognisable" (HE 129). George is enraged. He bullies a Catholic neighbor who has come to express his sympathy into leaving the Robinson home, and he attempts, unsuccessfully, to intimidate the District Inspector, who happens to be a Catholic.

On the drive home, George tells Eric to stop outside the farm of Martin Cassidy, a Catholic active in politics and the civil rights movement but "respected by both sides" (HE 74). George walks from the road to the farm and, out of Eric's view, kills Cassidy and his helper, the idiot boy Willie Reilly, with a farm implement. Suspicious, Eric follows George and discovers Willie's body and then sees George "driving a graip into what looked like a dung heap; again and again and again, and again" (HE 134). Eric is sickened by George's bloodlust. But later in his kitchen, George exalts in it; he tells Eric that "our side'll be glad some men had guts to act; blood for blood, this is a celebration son" (HE 135).

The next morning Eric gets up early and, apparently believing that there is no way out of the vicious cycle of sectarian hatred and bloodshed but also realizing that "there was nothing left to fear" (HE 146), drives his truck through an Army roadblock, deliberately provoking British soldiers to shoot and kill him.

McCabe's title, "Heritage," is as rich in its associations as is the title of his story "Cancer," discussed in the previous chapter. The most common meaning of the word *heritage* is some tangible property, such as a house or piece of land, or some intangible characteristics, such as family traditions, rights, personality traits, even responsibilities and burdens, handed down from one's ancestors. The word is related to *heredity* (*heritage* comes from the Latin *hereditare*, to inherit) and, thus, carries the meaning of birthright. In a broader sense, it means what humans generally pass down to each other through the ages, and even more broadly what humans have inherited from animals, our ultimate ancestors.

McCabe draws all of these meanings into his narrative in order to probe the roots of sectarian hatred, violence, and terrorism. The heritage of land plays a particularly prominent role in the story, and it almost always has a sectarian connotation. There are frequent descriptions of the Fermanagh countryside and the nearby border, as seen through Eric's consciousness, some lush and beautiful, others harsh and barren. From his farm Eric can see "Shannock and Carn Rock, a dim, hidden country, crooked scrub ditches of whin and thorns stunted in sour putty land; bare, spade-ribbed fields, rusted tin roofed cabins, housing a stony faced people [i.e., Catholics] living from rangy cattle and Welfare handouts" (HE 72). In another direction, he observes "the orchard and beech copse planted by his grandfather in 1921 to block off the view of the Fenian South" (HE 72–73). During the otter hunt, the Catholic Dinny McMahon defends his meager three acres of riverside property against the intrusions of Colonel Armstrong, whose Ascendancy estate of Inver Hall dominates the local area. Later that night, as he and Eric drive by Cassidy's farm, George wonders aloud how a Catholic got enough money to buy "Protestant land." When Eric suggests that he has earned the money through hard work, George counters that it is "[m]urder money" received for informing on his Protestant neighbors (HE 126). Later, when George senses that he has lost Eric's allegiance by killing Cassidy and Willie Reilly, he tries to regain it by telling Eric that he intends to leave him all of his land that the Hawthorne family has owned for eight generations. Despite his great love for the land, Eric rejects the offer. The heritage of the land has become more a curse than a blessing for him. Although it represents much of what he loves, the land is also a source of hatred and killing.

The title also refers to the instinct to survive, which at times necessitates the killing of others, that humans have inherited from the animal kingdom. McCabe incorporates numerous images of animals, literal and figurative, into the story, all of them quite natural to the country setting of the story and almost all of them related to the basic instinct for survival and, therefore, to the sectarian conflict. The story opens with a pigeon crashing through a window in the dairy of Eric's family farm in a desperate but fatal attempt to escape a hawk who then swerves away "towards the border river" (HE 71), as if it were a terrorist from the Irish Republic striking into the north. Meanwhile, a family hound carries the pigeon away, a reminder that even domesticated animals have predatory instincts. Moments later Eric sees "the hawk perched in rigid silence" in a tree, and when he looks at it, the bird "stare[s] back sullen" (HE 72). This is a foreshadowing of Eric's notion, when he finds the death threat on the milk can, that the terrorists "could be watching ten fields away or further, in a hedge, up a tree" (HE 74). Other animal images include a "scald crow feeding on the carcass of a run-over dog" (HE 126) observed by Eric and George as they drive by Cassidy's farm on their UDR patrol, a gruesome foreshadowing of George's later killing of Cassidy.

McCabe also uses figurative images of animals to convey the theme that humans have inherited bestial instincts. When Eric goes to see Rachel after her brother and father have been shot, she is described as having "frightened animal eyes" (HE 130), and John Willie says that Joe and Tom Robinson were killed "like rats burned in a cage" (HE 142). The scriptural words read by the minister, Reverend Plumm, which Eric and others hear at church that morning, sum up well the theme of bestial heritage: "I said in my heart concerning the sons of men, that God would prove them, and show them to be like beasts. Therefore the death of man, and of beasts is one; and the conditions of them both is equal . . ." (HE 89).

The otter hunt raises the question of whether or not humans can disinherit the animal instinct for killing. Colonel Armstrong has gathered together dogs and a large group of people, including several Catholics and an American, to hunt otters along a tributary of the river Finn. Their reason for hunting and killing otters is that the animals eat trout, a reason that Protestants and Catholics alike do not seem to question since trout is a source of food, i.e., survival, for humans. But Rachel questions the killing ritual. When Eric describes the otters as "[b]ig water squirrels, brown fluffy fellows, whiskery, with bit tails," Rachel responds, "They sound nice" (HE 110). Eric agrees, though he also points out that "[t]hey'll fight if they have to, a whole pack, so they say" (HE 110), a hint of the instinct for self-defense in prey, also passed on to humans. Rachel's admiration for the animal leads her and Eric to allow an otter to escape the hunting party. When Eric spots the otter that the dogs have been chasing, he is about to shout to the others but instead motions to Rachel its location: "Her mouth opened in wonder and pity; she whispered: 'Don't Eric! don't! Let it live, let it live'" (HE 112). Her sympathy for the otter stands in stark contrast to the bloodlust expressed by George.

Finally and most prominently, the title of the story refers to the heritage of sectarian hatred and strife developed in Ireland over hundreds of years. Because the story is told from the perspective of Protestant characters, their sectarian heritage is emphasized. George's participation in Orange parades and his display of portraits of the Queen, Carson, and Paisley are the most obvious and innocuous expressions of his heritage, but McCabe offers subtle and ominous clues as well. When George attends church, as he does faithfully, and listens carefully to Reverend Plumm's scriptural readings, ambiguous in their application to the Troubles ("If thou shall see the oppression of the poor, and violent judgments, and justice prevented in the province, wonder not at this matter, for he that is high hath another higher, and there are others still higher than these"), he is described as being like "a daw listening for worms" (HE 89). This image of George as a bird "listening" for prey suggests both the bestial heritage of killing for survival and the way in which humans look for justification of even their basest instincts.

Sarah, also, has rigid sectarian beliefs that have destroyed her familial relationships. She admits to Eric that her views appear hypocritical. She goes to church and prays and is against hunting animals ("God's creatures") on Sunday, but she refuses to meet Sam's wife and, most appalling of all, says that she would "sooner [Sam] was dead" than father a Catholic child: "It's wrongful I know, and I've prayed God to help me but . . . the children of my first born . . . Papists." She has been taught that "we should beget as God intended [and] work hard and pray . . . that's what I was taught: I believe it, I abide by it" (HE 124).

The views of George and Sarah are contrasted, though not forcefully countered, by those of Rachel and Eric. Both wish to hold more tolerant views of Catholics, but circumstances make it difficult to do so. Rachel tells Eric that she "didn't want to hate [Catholics]," despite her parents' harsh views of them. But her work in the hospital delivery ward aroused a disgust in her for the many Catholic mothers: "I heard them talk, so coarse and stupid, holy magazines and rosaries and this fuzzy headed priest going about blessing their labours and their babies, and the horrid way they sucked up to him" (HE 118–19). Her experience the previous night, being threatened by Catholic terrorists with rape and warned that her brother might be killed, makes her admit to Eric an "ugly" thought she had a month previously when she was on duty in the infant ward: that if she started a fire, she could kill many Catholics.

Eric also is conflicted in his views. He sees the self-destructive quality of his mother's and George's extremist views, but he loves his mother and wishes to please her, and he genuinely likes George. He adheres closely to his mother's religious views, especially with regard to sexuality. When Rachel asks him why he has not "touched" her, he uses his mother's words: "It's wrongful" (HE 120). He also feels guilty when his mother finds out that he has joined the Sunday hunting party. He recognizes a hatred in himself for Catholics, especially the terrorists who have threatened him. He tells Rachel: "I've seen them [Catholics] look at me in streets, marts, I don't want to hate or kill any of them, but a body must do something when the thing's gone the way it has" (HE 119). He knows that the only real hope for a normal life is to leave the area, but his love of the land prevents him from doing so. In the end, Eric makes the only choice possible, given his heritage, and the choice that will thwart the passing on of his heritage to the next generation: he commits suicide.

The stories of sectarian violence and terrorism mark a significant development in the Irish stories of the Troubles. They are the first stories of the Troubles to depict in stark and graphic realism the horror that has occurred in the everyday lives of Irish people over the last three decades of the twentieth century. Yet they also examine with poignancy and compassion the many causes and effects, both traumatic and subtle, of violence and terrorism. In denying the reader a political or ideological stance, and instead providing a human perspective of the victims, these stories may be said to point the way, not only to civilian disavowal of violence and terrorism, but to the flight from the sectarian and cultural identity that has been at the source of the violence. In the stories that followed, there is a distinct, albeit incipient, theme of the disavowal of sectarian and cultural identity. Such a disavowal may bring to an ironic close both the Troubles and the stories in which they are represented.

6

Gender and Nationalism

Women and the Troubles

we are stepping into where we never
imagine words such as hate
and territory *and the like—unbanished still*
as they always would be—wait
and are waiting under
beautiful speech. To strike.
—Eavan Boland, "Writing in a Time of Violence"

I

Throughout Irish history, and especially since the late nineteenth century, women have played significant, albeit unsung, roles in the revolutionary struggle for Ireland's independence. And ever since the first stories of the Troubles in the early twentieth century, women have been depicted in revolutionary roles. In actual life, Irish women have served in various revolutionary capacities—though rarely as the equals of men. In the early stories of the Troubles, they are represented mostly as secondary characters who support the male rebels and rarely as central characters, heroic in their own right. Often too, as discussed in the first chapter, women characters in the early Troubles stories are made to symbolize Ireland, and are vaguely reminiscent of Cathleen ni Houlihan or the Aisling figure, a tendency that feminist critics decry.[1] In sto-

1. For example: "In Ireland, such clichéd literary representations of women [as Cathleen ni Houlihan and the Shan van Vocht] have been absorbed by political discourses, which then recast them as patriotic emblems: the process has limited possible identities for Irish women to those represented in an archaic national identity. Today's Irish women argue that their political and social effectiveness is constricted by the

ries of the latter part of the twentieth century, a time when women writers increasingly contributed to Troubles short fiction, female characters are frequently cast in the role of protagonist, though far more often as passive victim than as active heroine.

The actual roles that Irish women have played in the nationalist movement have been many and significant. In *Unmanageable Revolutionaries: Women and Irish Nationalism*, Margaret Ward traces the roles Irish women have played in the pursuit of national independence over the one hundred years from the land agitation of the 1880s to the Northern Troubles in the 1980s. Ward shows how women often exercised those roles through their own organizations and institutions. The Ladies' Land League, for example, was founded in 1881 to support the work of the male-dominated Land League, which had come into existence two years earlier to address Ireland's agrarian crisis through agitation. Although the Land League's principal goal was land reform, not independence, many of its members, such as the Fenian Michael Davitt, were avowed nationalists. So were some of the women, such as Anna Parnell, "the driving force behind the Ladies' Land League."[2] Sister of Charles Stewart Parnell, the leading advocate of home rule, Anna Parnell exceeded her brother's avowed goal by espousing complete independence for Ireland. In 1900, Irish women founded Inghinidhe na hÉireann (Daughters of Ireland), electing Maud Gonne as president. Jackson calls Inghinidhe na hÉireann a "radical nationalist organization designed by women for women" whose most important contribution was that it "provided a republican environment acceptable to women."[3] One of the goals of the organization was "the complete independence of Ireland."[4]

continuing tendency of Irish public discourse to clothe the idea of woman in the antiquated garb of a sentimental, patriarchal version of cultural history." Katherine Martin Gray, "The Attic LIPs: Feminist Pamphleteering for the New Ireland," in *Border Crossings: Irish Women Writers and National Identities*, ed. Kathryn Kirkpatrick (Tuscaloosa: The University of Alabama Press, 2000), 269–70.

2. Margaret Ward, *Unmanageable Revolutionaries: Women and Irish Nationalism* (London: Pluto Press, 1983), 4.

3. Alvin Jackson, *Ireland 1798–1998: Politics and War* (Malden, Mass.: Blackwell, 1999), 189.

4. Quoted in M. Ward, *Unmanageable Revolutionaries*, 51.

The ideas of Inghinidhe na hÉireann were promoted in *Bean na hÉireann* (Women of Ireland), Ireland's first women-operated newspaper. An editorial in that paper, which first appeared in November 1908 and ran until February 1911, "declared their battle cry to be 'Freedom for Our Nation and the complete removal of all disabilities to our sex.'"[5]

This mix of nationalist and feminist goals by women nationalists raised the question of priorities, an interesting question in examining the portrayal of women in the stories of the Troubles. Some women, such as Hanna Sheehy-Skeffington, co-founder of the Irishwoman's Franchise League, believed that the goal of female equality in Irish society should be placed above that of independence. But, although Inghinidhe na hÉireann was "fully aware of the realities of women's oppression and . . . dismissive of any idealisation of women's position in a traditionalist Irish culture," the organization held that national independence must be the primary goal; female equality, it believed, would be addressed once independence came.[6]

In 1915 Inghinidhe na hÉireann, dwindling in numbers, became a branch of the quickly growing Cumann na mBan, which soon became the most prominent women's organization in the Irish nationalist movement. Founded in April 1914 as the women's auxiliary of the Irish Volunteers, Cumann na mBan declared Irish liberty as one of its constitutional aims and, accordingly, went on to play a significant supporting role in the Easter Rising, the War of Independence, and the Civil War. Although a relatively small group at the time of the Easter Rising, it grew rapidly thereafter. According to Ward, local branches increased from 100 in 1917 to 600 in 1918 and to 800 by 1921. Total membership in Cumann na mBan is estimated to have grown to 3000 during the War of Independence.[7]

In the first couple years of its existence, Cumann na mBan devoted much of its energy to raising funds for the Volunteers, often through the staging of *tableaux vivants* and other forms of entertainment. Branches also trained women in first aid and related supportive skills.

5. M. Ward, *Unmanageable Revolutionaries*, 69.

6. Ibid., 71–72, 86–87.

7. Ibid., 94, 131, 153, and 157.

Training women in military skills, on the other hand, was not a top priority. Although the organization's 1914 constitution suggested rifle practice as an activity, very few branches included it in their training. When the Rising came in 1916, about sixty women of Cumann na mBan and another thirty from the Irish Citizen Army actively participated, though only a few women were involved in actual fighting. Of these, Ward mentions Margaret Skinnider, a member of both the Glascow branch of Cumann na mBan and the Irish Citizen Army. Employed as a sniper at Stephen's Green, Skinnider was seriously wounded by an enemy sniper. The most famous—and flamboyant—of the militant women was Countess Markievicz (Constance Gore-Booth), who was placed second-in-command of the Irish Citizen Army at Stephen's Green. She was reputed to be especially proficient in "tackl[ing] any sniper who was 'particularly objectionable'" and "in commandeering vehicles for use as barricades." She created a striking image: "Passers-by were confronted by the awesome figure of the 48-year-old countess in full military uniform, revolver in hand, with her best hat with plumed feathers perched jauntily on her head."[8]

Notwithstanding the Countess' prominence, most of the women of Cumann na mBan and the Irish Citizen Army were relegated to supporting roles in the Easter Rising: procuring food and ammunition, cooking, nursing the wounded, and carrying dispatches between outposts. They carried out these tasks extremely well. Ward says that communications between the GPO headquarters and the outposts were maintained largely through the work of women and that without their "invaluable work" as couriers "the Rising would have been an even more confused venture than it was."[9] Of all the male leaders, apparently only de Valera, in charge of the outpost at Boland's Mill, refused to allow women to join his command—because, in his words, they were "untrained for soldiering."[10]

8. Ibid., 102–4, 111–13.

9. Ibid., 108.

10. Dail Eireann, *Official Report*, vols. 67–68, 13 May 1937, 462, quoted in M. Ward, *Unmanageable Revolutionaries*, 110.

When the Easter rebels finally surrendered to the British, many women asked to be allowed to surrender with the men, a request not always granted by the leaders. At the GPO, for example, Pearse ordered the women to leave before the surrender took place. Of the seventy-seven women arrested and jailed, all but five were released within a short period of time. The most famous woman prisoner was Countess Markievicz. Tried, convicted, and sentenced to die for her role in the Easter Rising, she was spared the death penalty because she was a woman, her sentence being commuted to life in prison. She was sent to an English prison and subsequently released.[11]

Following the failed Easter Rising, the women of Cumann na mBan threw themselves into the work of furthering the nationalist cause. They raised funds, held meetings to demand the release of imprisoned rebels, worked to secure support for the cause from the international community, and generally were instrumental in creating nationalist propaganda throughout the country. When the War of Independence started in 1919, Cumann na mBan members, according to Ward, wished "to become the military equals of the Volunteers, rather than their handmaidens," an attitude that resulted in friction between the women and the men, many of whom opposed the idea. Although some funds were provided to arm women during the War of Independence, "the military activities of Cumann na mBan clearly remained supportive and therefore of necessity under the direction of the [male] Volunteers."[12] These supportive activities included hiding fugitives, sheltering and nursing the wounded, scouting, and providing intelligence and logistical support for the rebels' flying columns. According to Jackson, the women also "were crucial to the success of the *Irish Bulletin*,"[13] Erskine Childers' highly influential republican propagandist newspaper. Tom Barry, the famous flying-column leader, gave tribute in his memoir, *Guerilla Days in Ireland*, to the women of Cumann na mBan in West Cork for their "indispensable" work of "nursing the wounded and sick, carrying dispatches, scout-

11. M. Ward, *Unmanageable Revolutionaries*, 114–17.
12. Ibid., 120, 131–32.
13. Jackson, *Ireland 1798–1998*, 251.

ing, acting as Intelligence agents, arranging billets, raising funds, knitting, washing, cooking for the active service men and burying our dead."[14]

In 1919, Cumann na mBan was proscribed by the British, along with the IRA and Sinn Féin. Nevertheless, it continued to operate. By 1921, the organization was realigned more closely with the IRA; branches of Cumann na mBan were attached to most IRA units. However, new branches of Cumann na mBan were founded only when IRA units lacked such branches. This practice ensured that "Cumann na mBan's main function was to service the needs of the local Volunteers."[15]

Most of the organization's membership took an anti-Treaty stance during the negotiations to end the War of Independence. At its conference on 5 February 1922, Cumann na mBan became "the first nationalist organisation to reject the treaty" and thereby positioned itself to support the republicans in the coming Civil War. Women in favor of the treaty formed their own, non-militant organization, Cumann na Saoirse (Society of Freedom).[16]

During the Civil War, Ward says, "[t]he work of the women became even more vital for the small roving guerrilla bands struggling against the remorseless advance of the Free State." Their work was "important and dangerous," particularly since the women, rather than the men (who were often well known to the Free State soldiers), had to do the work that required appearing in public.[17] Nevertheless, their work continued to be largely supportive of the men. They sheltered fugitives and the wounded, acted as secretaries and couriers, and engaged in other such supportive activities. Their work as "handmaidens" did not, however, create an unmitigated impression of passivity. Some men thought of the women as hard and ruthless as male rebels. P. S. O'Hegarty, a Free State polemicist, remarked that "[t]he women were the implacable and

14. Tom Barry, *Guerilla Days in Ireland: A Firsthand Account of the Black and Tan War (1919–1921)* (New York: Devin-Adair, 1956), 278.

15. M. Ward, *Unmanageable Revolutionaries*, 147, 158.

16. Ibid., 171, 173.

17. Ibid., 187, 190.

irrational upholders of death and destruction. . . ."[18] In *Vive Moi!* O'Faolain says that republican women "were power-hungry, temperamental but with few warm emotions, ruthless, abstract in discussion, and full of a terrifying sentimentality" (VM 214–15). Ward took the title of her book from de Valera's comment that "[w]omen are at once the boldest and most unmanageable revolutionaries."[19]

For their roles in the War of Independence and Civil War, some women were imprisoned, often without trial because it was difficult for authorities to gather convincing evidence of their revolutionary activities. Ward says that about fifty women were imprisoned during the War of Independence, admittedly a relatively small number in contrast to the 4000 jailed men. After the Civil War, women constituted 400 of the 12,000 prisoners. These included such well-known nationalists as Maud Gonne, Grace Plunkett, Nora Connolly, and Mary MacSwiney.[20]

II

The authors of the romantic and naturalistic stories treating the 1916–1923 Troubles often portray female characters in one or more of the actual roles assigned to the women of Cumann na mBan, though they rarely mention the organization by name. In a couple of his stories Corkery does explicitly mention the women of Cumann na mBan and characterizes their work as supportive and daring. For instance, his narrator in "An Unfinished Symphony," a Volunteer on the run, remarks, "I had no doubt at all I would find a very efficient Cumann na mBan in the place [to which he is fleeing], ready for all emergencies; I would find them learning Irish, learning First Aid, learning how to cook on an open fire . . ." (HB 154). Similarly, Corkery's female narrator in "Seumas," a member of the women's organization, says, "As ladies of the Cumann na mBan our part was to be cool, business-like and brave" (HB 99).

Whether or not their authors meant to represent them as members of

18. P. S. O'Hegarty, *The Victory of Sinn Fein* (Dublin: Talbot Press, 1924), 104–5, quoted in M. Ward, *Unmanageable Revolutionaries*, 177.

19. Quoted in M. Ward, *Unmanageable Revolutionaries*, viii.

20. M. Ward, *Unmanageable Revolutionaries*, 145, 190, 192.

Cumann na mBan, the women in many of the romantic stories perform the work of that organization. It is women, for instance, who usually offer shelter to rebels on the run, as in O'Connor's "September Dawn" and "Nightpiece with Figures," O'Faolain's "Fugue," and Corkery's "The Price." Nan Twohig, the heroine of "The Price," also acts as a nurse by administering to the wounded Volunteer she shelters. In Corkery's "Seumas," women of Cumann na mBan attend a First Aid lecture and provide food for imprisoned Volunteers. Helen Joyce, in O'Connor's "Soirée Chez une Belle Jeune Fille," serves as a courier, delivering a dispatch from Cork to republican soldiers in the nearby hills. Two women play typical Cumann na mBan roles in O'Faolain's "The Bombshop." Old Mother Dale has turned over her house to Volunteers, allowing it to become a bombshop, and Norah, a younger woman, serves as courier and housekeeper for the three Volunteers who make the bombs. When two of the male bomb-makers run off, Norah helps the third make the bombs, a role occasionally played by the Cumann na mBan women.

Most of these female characters are secondary as well as stereotyped, and sometimes they are as much symbolic as representative of real women. Only in a couple of these early stories are the women characters given lead roles, and even then their stature is undercut. O'Connor treats Helen Joyce, the protagonist of "Soirée Chez une Belle Jeune Fille," with amusing irony, and Corkery makes Nan Twohig, the heroine of "The Price," a rather cloying saintly figure.

Set during the Civil War, "Soirée Chez une Belle Jeune Fille" recounts Helen Joyce's initial experience as a courier for republicans operating in the mountains near Cork. While sitting in a college lecture hall, bored by her professor, Helen receives a mysterious note instructing her to call at The Western Milk and Butter Emporium and to bring her bicycle. She goes to the designated place, where a little man gives her a manila envelope and instructions for delivering it. Helen hides the envelope under her clothing and bicycles out into the country through rain and mud to deliver it to republicans staying in a safe house. She does all of this with great enthusiasm; her idealism is described by the narrator as she bicycles out of town: "At last she was doing the work she had always longed to do, not her own work but Ireland's. The old stuffy, proprietary world she had been reared in was somewhere far away behind her; before her was a world of youth and comradeship and adventure" (GN 182).

Although Helen's task appears to be an exciting and heroic one, not unlike those of his male romantic rebels, O'Connor treats it with irony and humor. He portrays Helen as a naïve participant in the Troubles, who, at almost every turn, is disabused of her romantic notions about revolution. The man at the Emporium who gives her the dispatch, a dwarfish cripple with a woman's voice, jars against her idealized image of a rebel: "Somehow she had not imagined revolutionaries of his sort" (GN 180). The nonchalant response of Michael Redmond, the republican to whom she gives the dispatch, brings her "perilously close to tears . . . [because] it appeared as if the dispatch she had carried was of no importance to anyone" (GN 185). And most "incredulous" to her, May Crowley, the young woman whose family owns the safe house to which Helen has traveled, opens it to republicans and Free State soldiers alike. She tells the astonished Helen that on one occasion both Tom Keogh, a rebel, and Vincent Kelly, a Free State soldier, were in her house at the same time. When Helen asks May why she doesn't "bang the door in [the Free State soldiers'] faces" (GN 189), May responds that she has known Vincent since they both were children, and she is certain that Vincent and Tom, once "thick as thieves," will "be as thick again—unless they shoot one another in the meantime." May's concluding rhetorical question—"And you think I'm going to quarrel with one about the other?" (GN 189)—neatly distinguishes her pragmatic view of the Civil War participants from Helen's overly idealistic perspective.

The story's amusing, if rather gruesome, climax is a further source of disillusionment for Helen. Dr. Considine, a Free State medical officer, arrives at the house and asks if one of the rebels will ride to Cork with him. He has a corpse in his car, a youth who was wounded that morning in a skirmish and has died on the way to a hospital. Considine is not ashamed to admit that he doesn't like driving alone with the corpse and wants company. However, despite his assurances that he will not allow the rebels to be apprehended by Free State authorities, neither Redmond nor Jordan is willing to ride in the car with a corpse, the implication being that both are as squeamish as the doctor is. Finally, Jordan agrees to go—motivated not by any altruistic sense but by the overwhelming desire (mocked by May) to see his wife and family. Meanwhile Helen, having seen the true colors of the Irish revolutionaries, bicycles back to town on her own.

If O'Connor's amusingly ironic portrayals of the women—Helen as a naïve romantic and May as an opportunist, willing to entertain men of both sides—seem patriarchal in tone, they are balanced by his portrayals of the men, both the rebels and the Free State doctor, as hollow romantics. Jordan is "suave" and "fiery" with "dark, smoldering eyes," and Redmond is "urbane" and "complacent," "a Don Juan of sorts" (GN 186). They revel in relating to Helen their experience that day of being hunted and attacked by Free State soldiers, and then of making a bold escape. But their dashing appearances and romanticized exploits are ironically undercut by their cowardly reaction to the dead man in the doctor's car. In many ways, the men come off less favorably than do the women.

While O'Connor deliberately undercuts his heroine, Corkery unintentionally does so in "The Price," a story that takes place during the War of Independence when the British auxiliaries and Black and Tans terrorized the Irish community by sacking and burning towns.[21] His depiction of Nan Twohig is ultimately far too idealized to be the least bit convincing. Portrayed as having fused her republican ideals and religious piety, Nan is widely admired by the Volunteers for boldly praying aloud in church for the soul of Roger Casement, executed for his role in the Easter rebellion, and for secretly nursing a wounded Volunteer in her home. While these actions realistically represent those of a republican woman in Nan's position, Corkery stretches probability in the climactic scene in

21. The American Commission on Conditions in Ireland reported that British forces sacked and burned, at least partially, 98 towns in 1920. "Memorandum on British Atrocities in Ireland 1916–20," Interim Report (Washington, D.C.: n.p., n.d.). Cited by M. Ward, *Unmanageable Revolutionaries*, 143.

which Nan saves her small town from destruction by frightening off anonymous terrorists. The terrorists, probably auxiliaries or Black and Tans, have come in the middle of the night to burn the town down because of its republican sympathies. Nan deters them by appearing next to a stone cross on the hill above the town, illuminated by the light given off by burning petrol. Apparently her saintly appearance is enough to stop the terrorists from carrying out their destructive intentions.

These portraits of women nationalists in the first wave of Troubles stories are fair enough representations in the sense that they depict women engaged in roles—sheltering rebels, nursing the wounded, acting as couriers, even assisting in the production of bombs—that actual women of Cumann na mBan engaged in. They are also accurate in the impression they give that women, for the most part, played subsidiary roles that, though essential to the nationalist cause, were not considered as "heroic" or sacrificial as the roles that men played. What they do not portray, however, is that some women, particularly those of Cumann na mBan, actually were the fighting equals of men. In fact, none of the women characters in the early stories even *expresses* a desire to become involved in the actual warfare, let alone actually participates. There are, in fact, no portraits in these stories of women as heroic fighters, modeled for instance after Countess Markievicz or Margaret Skinnider, the sniper in the Easter Rebellion.

This less-than-full picture of women revolutionaries can, of course, be attributed to the fact that the first stories were written exclusively by men. In all likelihood, these male writers viewed the role of women in the struggle for independence as did the majority of Irish men who led or constituted the nationalist forces, namely, as supportive of male fighters. Furthermore, the absence of a full picture of women revolutionaries can be attributed to the fact that the nationalist myth of blood sacrifice, requiring that one be willing to die for Ireland, was considered by Irish nationalists, men and women alike, as an exclusively male preserve. As Ward notes, this elevation of the role of male rebels to "the cult of martyrology" had the effect of "obscur[ing] the continual yet less dramatic sacrifices made by women working for the same cause" and "perpetuated an artificial distinction between man the leader and woman the auxiliary, not least in the consciousness of women themselves."[22] It is fair to say that the early stories of the Troubles perpetuate that distinction.

III

Since the middle of the twentieth century, and especially in the last quarter of it, more and more Irish women writers have published stories about the Troubles, thereby broadening the range of fictional representation of women in these stories. In addition to Burke, Lavin, Beckett, and Mulkerns, whose stories have been discussed, their numbers include Anne Devlin, Fiona Barr, Brenda Murphy, Maura Treacy, Jennifer Johnston, and Anne-Marie Reilly, among others. Focusing primarily on the Troubles in Northern Ireland, women writers have explored sectarian tensions and hostilities with great insight and have treated terrorism as graphically as have male writers. In some stories, such as Burke's "Battles Long Ago," Johnston's "Trio," and Beckett's "The Master and the Bombs," women writers have explored the roles of men in the Troubles. But most stories by women focus on women, their roles in the conflict and the impact of the Troubles on them. The remainder of this chapter discusses the various ways in which women have been involved in the Northern Troubles and how women writers have represented them in short stories.

The issue of how women's roles in the Northern Troubles are represented is complicated by several factors, including a lack of substantial evidence about the actual, real-life roles that women have played. In *Shattering Silence: Women, Nationalism, and Political Subjectivity in Northern Ireland*, Begoña Aretxaga writes that the literature of social science, which one might expect to provide a full and inclusive account of women's involvement in the Northern Troubles, largely "portray[s] women as victims of a violent conflict over which they have little control."[23] In fact, as Aretxaga and other scholars have begun to show re-

22. M. Ward, *Unmanageable Revolutionaries*, 193–94.

23. Begoña Aretxaga, *Shattering Silence: Women, Nationalism, and Political Subjectivity in Northern Ireland* (Princeton: Princeton University Press, 1997), 9.

cently, Irish women have played a variety of active political and militant roles in the Northern Troubles. In Aretxaga's words, they have

> walked the streets of their neighborhoods at night to prevent their menfolk from military detention, organized marches to protest arbitrary arrests, [taken] arms against the state, defied the penal system by smearing their prison cells with feces and menstrual blood, clad themselves in blankets and traveled the world to break the silence on state violence, [and] argued to assert a distinctive feminist voice within male-dominated organizations.[24]

The reality of their lives, Aretxaga says, "challenge[s] the assumption that women are the passive bystanders of a war between male factions."[25]

Evidence of women's involvement in the Northern Troubles is especially scant with regard to the issue of women acting as paramilitaries on either side of the sectarian divide. Valerie Morgan and Grace Fraser note that "it is extremely difficult to get quantitative information about the actual number of either women or men who have been active in paramilitary groups. From what evidence is available [e.g., prison records] it seems that only a very small number of women have been active members of either the Provisional IRA or the Protestant paramilitary groups."[26]

Suzann Buckley and Pamela Lonergan do find some evidence of the steady, if low-level, involvement of women in paramilitary and terrorist activities in Northern Ireland since the early 1970s. "The new year for female terrorists was rung in on January 1, 1973," they state, citing seven incidents in February and March alone of that year and another six from June through October, in which women were either involved, or suspected of being involved, in terrorist-related acts.[27] Ward says that, un-

24. Ibid., 10.

25. Ibid.

26. Valerie Morgan and Grace Fraser, "Women and the Northern Ireland Conflict: Experiences and Responses," in *Facets of the Conflict in Northern Ireland*, ed. Seamus Dunn (New York: St. Martin's, 1995), 87.

27. Suzann Buckley and Pamela Lonergan, "Women and the Troubles, 1969–1980," in *Terrorism in Ireland*, ed. Yonah Alexander and Alan O'Day (New York: St. Martin's, 1984), 80–81.

like their predecessors, young women coming into Cumann na mBan in the early years of the Northern Troubles were trained for combat. Their acceptance as fighting equals of the men was, she says, "the result of a combination of female insistence and male recognition of the necessity of having some militarily trained women."[28] Martin Dillon describes the "honeytraps" used by women of the IRA, a tactic of sexually enticing British soldiers in pubs and inviting them to their apartments so that IRA gunmen might kill them.[29] One such incident in 1971 involved the killing of three Scottish soldiers, members of the Royal Highland Fusiliers. They were invited to a party by two women they had met in a pub and then were fatally shot on the way by IRA operatives in collusion with the women.[30] The most publicized female Irish terrorist was Mairead Farrell, who spent ten years in prison for her part in the IRA bombing of a hotel in Northern Ireland and then was assassinated in 1988, along with two male companions, in Gibraltar by an elite British anti-terrorist team.[31]

The activities of loyalist women in the Northern Troubles are even less documented than those of republican women, resulting in a "far more obscure" picture of their involvement.[32] There is apparently no prominent Protestant women's organization comparable to Cumann na mBan, though reports are conflicting as to whether or not loyalist women have been admitted as members of Protestant paramilitary groups. Ward and Marie-Thérèse McGivern state that "the Loyalist paramilitary organizations—the UDA and UVF—do not include wom-

28. M. Ward, *Unmanageable Revolutionaries*, 258.

29. Martin Dillon, *The Dirty War: Covert Strategies and Tactics Used in Political Conflicts* (New York: Routledge, 1999), chapter 9.

30. Ibid., 214–15.

31. J. Bowyer Bell, *The Irish Troubles: A Generation of Violence, 1967–1992* (New York: St. Martin's, 1993), 753–54.

32. Margaret Ward and Marie-Thérèse McGivern, "Images of Women in Northern Ireland," in *The Crane Bag Book of Irish Studies*, ed. Mark Patrick Hederman and Richard Kearney (Dublin: Blackwater, 1982), 584; Morgan and Fraser, "Women and the Northern Ireland Conflict," 87; and Patrick Grant, *Literature, Rhetoric and Violence in Northern Ireland, 1968–98: Hardened to Death* (New York: Palgrave, 2001), 104.

en amongst their ranks."[33] On the other hand, Grant cites Rosemary Sales' claim that the UDA did, in fact, have a women's branch, disbanded in 1974 because of a brutal murder by its members. Grant also quotes from an anonymously written UDA report claiming that loyalist women have played an active role in the UDA, transporting weapons, supplying 'safe' houses, and performing other paramilitary duties for the loyalists. Grant says that the group, Women's Action, apparently still functions, though at a reduced level.[34]

In addition to being victims, political activists, and paramilitaries, women of Northern Ireland have also played the risky role of peacemaker during the Troubles. Women have founded and directed large, nonsectarian peace organizations, including Women Together, established by Monica Patterson, an English Catholic, in 1970; Women for Peace, founded in 1972 by Margaret Dougherty of Derry; and the Peace People Movement, begun in 1976 by Mairead Corrigan, Betty Williams, and Ciaran McKeown. (Corrigan and Williams shared the Nobel Prize for Peace in 1977 for their work.) In addition to the efforts of these peace organizations, the sectarian Loyalist Women's Association turned its focus to peace in 1972, collecting 90,000 signatures under a petition for an end to the violence.[35] According to Buckley and Lonergan, women, particularly mothers of hunger strikers, also played a significant role in bringing to an end the hunger strikes of IRA prisoners in the early 1980s, although "the IRA perceived the women's intervention merely as female acquiescence to [Catholic] religious authority,"[36] rather than as evidence of the women's ability to bring a peaceful resolution to the Troubles.

Despite the prominent role of women in pursuing peace in Northern

33. M. Ward and McGivern, "Images of Women," 584.

34. Grant, *Literature, Rhetoric and Violence*, 104. Grant cites Rosemary Sales, *Women Divided: Gender, Religion and Politics in Northern Ireland* (London: Routledge, 1997), 71, and an anonymously written work, *A Brief History of the UDA/UFF in Contemporary Conflict* (Belfast: Prisoners Aid and Post Conflict Resettlement Group, 1999), 52.

35. Buckley and Lonergan, "Women and the Troubles," 78–79, 82.

36. Ibid., 85.

Ireland, however, scholars point out that there is very little empirical evidence to support the popular stereotype of women as natural peacemakers or even as generally more moderate than men in their attitudes toward the Troubles. Morgan and Fraser, for instance, cite the work of E. E. O'Donnell, who says in *Irish Stereotypes* (1977) that the spectrum of women's views about the Troubles is essentially the same as that of men.[37] Furthermore, Ward and McGivern make the case that Northern Ireland media have assisted in stereotyping women as peacemakers by, for example, downplaying or ignoring less noble behavior of women in the peace movement, such as Corrigan and Williams's decision to keep the Nobel Peace Prize money for themselves rather than donate it to the Peace People Movement.[38]

IV

Troubles stories written by women frequently depict women, in the way that social science literature does, as helpless victims whose lives are controlled by the forces and circumstances of the Troubles. For instance, Nora, the elderly protagonist of Mary Beckett's "Failing Years," is prevented from returning home to Belfast, where she longs to go after years of unhappiness in Dublin, because a terrorist explosion has made her travel connections impossible. She decides to wait until spring to try again "when the weather was warmer or the Troubles were over" (BW 142). Anne Devlin's "Five Notes After a Visit" records the journal entries of a young Catholic woman who abandons her attempt to move from London back home to Belfast to live with her Protestant lover, also a Londoner. Pointed interrogation from an airport security official, barbed wire around her father's flower garden, tanks and police with bullet-proof jackets patrolling the Belfast streets, and anonymous, threatening phone calls to the lovers—all conspire to drive the woman, but not the lover, back to London, where, ironically, life seems no better. In Anne-Marie Reilly's brief story "Leaving," the narrator relates her mother's life-time desire to move from the family's rented house in

37. Morgan and Fraser, "Women and the Northern Ireland Conflict," 86.
38. M. Ward and McGivern, "Images of Women," 583.

the Catholic area of lower Falls Road to a better home "up the road." Ironically, the mother's wish comes true when the family is burned out by loyalist terrorists and relocated to the desired location. But so is everyone else: "'Up the road' became the new Catholic ghetto" (HW 248).

Several Troubles stories that treat the theme of woman as victim are about young mothers and their children. In analyzing the depiction of women in popular novels about the Northern Troubles, Bill Rolston identifies the mother as the most important of three major roles (the other two being whore and villain) that women play in these novels. The role of mother, he says, often puts these characters in an active, heroic position, as well as suggests that "women are peace-loving by nature": "As mothers, women care for children: they attempt to protect children from the ravages that life, especially life outside the domestic sphere, can bring. Violence, in particular, threatens children and the stability of family life and as such is abhorrent to mothers."[39] To the extent that mother characters attempt to protect their children, they take an active role in the Troubles; but in Troubles stories, as well as in some of the popular novels that Rolston analyzes, the mothers themselves become victims when the hostile forces they face are too great for them.

In Maura Treacy's "A Minor Incident," a group of Catholic mothers and children, some in prams, are harassed by British soldiers riding in a truck as they walk along a road lined with barbed-wire fencing. The driver forces the women to pull their prams onto the verge, and when the truck stops, the soldiers in the rear throw stones at "Captain," a dog belonging to one of the children. As a mother restrains the barking dog, one of the soldiers laughs, talks of shooting it, and maliciously suggests that his shot might "take two birds" (SH 128), or even three. He is referring of course to the women and children. As the truck drives off, the dog breaks free and chases it. Soon after, the mothers and children hear gunshots, and Sara, the child who owns "Captain," finds him lying still and bleeding at the bottom of the hill: "Blood oozed through his brown

39. Bill Rolston, "Mothers, Whores, and Villains: Images of Women in Novels of the Northern Ireland Conflict," *Race & Class* 31:1 (1989): 44.

and white coat in darkening patches and trickled onto the road and was absorbed in the dust" (SH 128).

The design of the conflict, pitting the powerful elements of the British army—truck, soldiers, and rifles—against vulnerable and helpless women and children hemmed in by barbed-wire fencing, risks plunging the story into melodrama. But Treacy avoids such a pitfall by underplaying the emotional aspects of the incident. Rather than giving way to utter fear for the safety of their children, the mothers seem to have grown adept at dealing with such harassment, considering it more of a nuisance than a dangerous threat, and the soldiers seem to act more out of boredom than evil intent, though assuredly killing the dog is a malicious act. Rather than mixing strong doses of malice and fear and thereby descending into melodrama, the brief narrative achieves emotional authenticity through its more subtle point that incidents such as this, though "minor," help to sustain the Troubles.

A young Catholic mother is also the victim protagonist of Fiona Barr's "The Wall-Reader." Mary spends her days pushing her baby in a pram through the streets of Belfast, occupied by British troops and armored vehicles. But instead of being the victim of these forces, as Treacy's women are, Barr's protagonist becomes the victim of an anonymous nationalist militant.

As she walks the streets of Belfast, Mary likes to read the ubiquitous wall slogans: "Shall only our rivers run free?"; "Is there a life before death?" (TV 46). Ironically, despite the ever-present violence that lies behind the graffiti ("four soldiers and two policemen had been blown to smithereens in separate incidents, and a building a day had been bombed by the Provos" [TV 49]), the slogans hold only academic interest for Mary. She fantasizes that she might someday write "a world-shattering thesis on their psychological complexities, their essential truths, their witticisms and intellectual genius" (TV 49). Ultimately, however, what seems impersonal and academic to her becomes all too real and personal: she and her family become the object of a threatening wall message.

One day while Mary is sitting on a park bench with her baby daughter, a British soldier in an armored vehicle parked nearby strikes up a conversation. Although she can see just "the tip of a rifle and a face peering out from the darkness" (TV 48), Mary, longing for company, enjoys talking with the soldier and so begins a kind of friendship. For weeks they innocently converse (the soldier always remaining hidden from view)— about their families, their hopes, and their views on life. Then one day her husband, Sean, discovers that someone has painted the word TOUT on the wall beside their driveway. Clearly, the anonymous writer—most likely a militant nationalist—has observed Mary speaking to the soldier and considers it an act of disloyalty to the nationalist cause. The wall graffiti that once held exclusively academic interest now has urgent, personal implications for Mary and her family. She and her husband decide that they must leave Belfast. One evening under the cover of darkness movers come to their home, pack their possessions in a van, and drive the family to safety in Dublin.

As the ending suggests, "The Wall-Reader" is built on an irony that sharpens the theme of victimization. Mary and her family are forced into exile, victims of the Troubles, precisely because she has attempted to live normally despite the war-like conditions around her. The irony drives deeper once we realize that Mary's normal behavior was, seen from another perspective, quite abnormal. The friendship with the soldier has, in fact, none of the human aspects that real friendships have: "No physical contact was needed, no face-to-face encounter to judge reaction, no touching to confirm amity, no threat of dangerous intimacy" (TV 49). She tells her husband that the relationship is "a meeting of minds" (TV 49), a phrase that is all too true and underscored by the insistence of Barr's narrator in referring to the soldier as "the voice" and to Mary as "the woman." Barr's point is that her protagonist, despite having a husband and a child, has been forced by conditions in Belfast to live a communal existence that is abstract; her intimate conversations are with a person she cannot see. Even as she looks at the wall message meant to threaten her life, Mary cannot help but examine it abstractly with her trained academic eye—which, ironically, helps her absorb the full emotional force of the message: "The job itself was not well done, she had seen better. The letters were uneven, paint splattered down from the cross T, the U looked a misshapen O. The workmanship was poor, *the impact perfect*" (TV 49; italics added).

Brenda Murphy also uses a young mother to explore the victimization of women during the Northern Troubles, but in this case the woman is victimized by her own husband, thereby raising the issue of gender relations. "A Social Call" at first appears to be exclusively a story of spousal abuse in a home in Ballymurphy, a Catholic area of Belfast, but Murphy links the abuse to the Troubles through her final, ironic sentence. The story begins when Teresa, the narrator, visits her friend Bernie, who is "a bit down and weepy and look[ing] very pale" (HW 270) after having her fourth child in four years. When Bernie's husband, Joe, arrives with two friends, he verbally abuses his wife and demands that she clean up the house and make tea for his friends. A short time later, after Bernie has gone upstairs to ask Joe for house money, Teresa hears shouts and thumps and then a child crying and begging his father to stop. When Teresa goes up to the bedroom to investigate, she sees Bernie, "lying on the floor, hands up over her face, knees drawn up close to her belly" (HW 271), and Joe standing over her about to kick her. Teresa pushes Joe down, and he in turn threatens her before he leaves the house with his friends. Bernie then reveals to Teresa that Joe became violent when she discovered he had a gun and demanded that he get rid of it.

The next morning while Teresa is reading the newspaper, she sees an article about an incident that happened the night before. A teenage boy from Ballymurphy was accosted and shot in the kneecaps by three men. The last sentence of the story links the theme of spousal abuse to the violence of the Troubles: "The local paramilitary group, who claimed they were responsible, said they shot the boy for repeated anti-social behaviour" (HW 273).

Despite its melodrama—complete with child screaming "Daddy, Daddy, don't" (HW 271) as the father beats the mother—"A Social Call" forcefully makes the point that the violence of paramilitaries like Joe and his friends is part of a pattern of anti-social behavior, rooted more in the need to dominate and abuse the weak and vulnerable, including their own wives, than it is in any admirable political goal. By linking male political militancy to violence against women, "A Social Call" also raises the issue of gender relations during the Troubles, an issue that dates back to the early part of the twentieth century when Inghinidhe na hÉireann called for sexual equality within the nationalist movement. But if the story is a cry for a halt to marital abuse, it does not call for sexual equality among militant nationalists. In fact, there appear to be no Troubles stories that portray women actively seeking to establish gender equality within either the nationalist or the unionist movement.

V

There is also scarce representation in Troubles stories of women playing active political and paramilitary roles in the Northern Troubles. This scarcity is most likely the result of complicating factors. One factor, mentioned previously, is the lack of data about women paramilitaries from which authors might draw representations. Another is the skewed perception society has about women terrorists. In "Myths in the Representation of Women Terrorists," Rhiannon Talbot explores the representations of women terrorists worldwide, including Northern Ireland, in both academic literature and the general media, but not in fiction. She finds these representations to be flawed in that either they emphasize the feminine identity of women terrorists, with all of the associated gender stereotypes (e.g., they act out of naïveté or because they are in love with a terrorist, or at the other end, because they are "extremist feminists"), or they portray women terrorists as having forsaken their feminine identity for male-associated attributes (violence, aggression, etc.). "The construction of a 'terrorist' is a strongly masculine one," she states, "whereas the perception of femininity excludes use of indiscriminate violence."[40] The result, according to Talbot, is that representations of women terrorists are almost invariably skewed in one direction or the other: "If the feminine is the focus, her complicity is minimized through a patronizing assumption of lack of intelligence or a naiveté about her

40. Rhiannon Talbot, "Myths in the Representation of Women Terrorists," *Éire-Ireland* 35 (fall/winter 2000): 165.

actions. If the masculine is maximized, the result is a diminution of the connection between feminine and terror. Either way, the notion of a woman *as* a terrorist is discarded; she is either a woman *or* a terrorist."[41]

Such a bias in public perception creates an obvious challenge for any writer of fiction, male or female, attempting to portray a woman terrorist as a well developed and balanced character—unless of course the writer has direct and personal experience, something that, apparently, none of the contemporary Irish writers, except Gerry Adams, possesses.

Nevertheless, there are two stories by women that take up the theme of women's involvement in terrorism: Mulkerns' "The Torch" and Anne Devlin's "Naming the Names." Mulkerns' story examines a young woman's response to an invitation, which turns into a threatening demand, to become involved with IRA terrorists, while Devlin's story relates the role of the female protagonist in a terrorist execution and examines her motives for being involved. Although neither Mulkerns' nor Devlin's portrayal may satisfy Talbot's plea for an integrated portrait of woman and terrorist, both provide interesting insights into the theme of women and terrorism.

The plot of "The Torch" involves the attempt by a Provisional IRA operative named Peadar O Lonargáin to engage Sarah, an art student in Paris, in a terrorist act. (Sarah is the absent daughter of Denis and Emily in "Four Green Fields," the terrorist story by Mulkerns discussed in the last chapter.) Growing up in Dublin as the granddaughter of one of the Irish rebels who fought in the War of Independence, Sarah became an activist in the nationalist movement, learning Irish and associating with people like O Lonargáin. But she has since broken off from them and has come to like the freedom she has found in Paris, with its remoteness from the Troubles. Just prior to the opening of the story, O Lonargáin has unexpectedly phoned her, and she has, out of respect for their former friendship, reluctantly agreed to meet with him.

Although she has distanced herself physically from Ireland and the Troubles, Sarah has not entirely rid herself of nationalistic feelings.

41. Ibid., 170; italics in text.

When they meet, she greets O Lonargáin in Irish, and the glances they draw from Parisians because of their "strange language" makes "Sarah proud" (AQ 65). But, significantly, she has drawn a sharp moral distinction in her mind between the nationalists of her grandfather's era and contemporary terrorists. She tells O Lonargáin that what he asks her to do (the task is not made explicit, other than that the terrorist tells her that she will not be directly involved in the violence) "is distasteful in the extreme" and that she "regard[s] [his] activities and those of the rest as loathsome and criminal." When O Lonargáin then asks her if she considers her "grandfather's fight for freedom as loathsome and criminal too," Sarah makes her sharpest point: "That generation offered their *own* lives, not those of innocent civilians. There's no point of similarity in what your lot are doing and their insurrection" (AQ 65; italics in text).

O Lonargáin appears to accept Sarah's refusal as final, but later that day he calls her as she is leaving work and insists on seeing her. When she again meets him, he tells her that O'Riain, the IRA man organizing the operation, has not accepted her decision. O Lonargáin warns Sarah not to return to her apartment or to her place of work the next day; nor, he says, should she return to Dublin. He then vanishes into the crowd, rather than asking Sarah to reconsider her decision, and thus makes credible the thinly veiled threat of violence against her. The story ends with Sarah coming to a sober realization: "It was only above a certain level of self-respect that one could operate at all, and she knew that running away from her job was not something she could do. . . ." Bravely, Sarah sets off to "buy bread and wine for supper" (AQ 68).

The portrayal of Sarah as brave and uncompromising, willing to risk her safety for her moral principles, is especially admirable since her refusal to acquiesce to the demands of terrorists requires that she be morally assertive. Mulkerns emphasizes this aspect of Sarah's character through a counter example. In a letter to her father, she admits to moral passivity in the job she has taken. "The surveying job," she writes, "turned out to be for a firm which schemes to knock down all the parts of Paris I cherish, but for the moment I don't care, which must be immoral" (AQ 63). Rather than exposing a serious inconsistency in her character, her passivity in this instance serves to emphasize the strength required in her refusal to cave in to the terrorists' demands. In this sense, Sarah is one of the strongest of the women protagonists in the Troubles stories.

Anne Devlin's "Naming the Names" is the only Troubles story—by female or male writer—that presents and explores the mind of a woman terrorist. (Although Gerry Adams' "The Rebel" depicts the conversion of Margaret, a Belfast woman, into a politically active nationalist when her son is unjustly jailed, Adams does not depict her engaged in violent activities.) Finnula McQuillen, the narrator of Devlin's story, recounts her role in the sectarian execution of a young Englishman, an Oxford University graduate student staying in Belfast for the summer while doing research on Gladstone and home rule. Finn, as she is called by friends, and the unnamed young man meet when, looking for books on Irish history, he visits the bookstore where she works. They develop a friendship that soon turns amorous. Nevertheless, when she is asked by fellow members of the Provisional IRA to lure him to a park at night so that they can kill him (he has been selected for execution because his father is a judge), she agrees to do so, perhaps in what might be called a version of the "honeytrap."

Devlin structures the narrative so that much of Finn's story comes out during a police interrogation. Finn willingly relates to the police much about her own involvement in the Provisional IRA, including her motivations for being involved, but she refuses to divulge the identities of her accomplices. Instead, when asked for their names, she recites the names of West Belfast streets, a favorite pastime she had as a child. In addition to what she tells the police, we learn more about her motives for belonging to the terrorist organization from what she tells us in the course of her narrative. By the end of the story we realize that Finn's motives for her terrorist involvement are a complicated tangle. They include a contentious family heritage of nationalist ideology, outrage provoked by sectarian rioting in West Belfast and the subsequent British policy of internment, failed relationships with two Englishmen, and, possibly, a feminist motive of giving women a larger role in the nationalist movement. Furthermore, her numb, perhaps even regressive state of mind at the end of the story, indicated by her rote and child-like recitation of the names of Belfast streets, suggests that Devlin's protagonist is caught somewhere between her two identities, that of the victim Finnula (Fionnuala, daughter of the Irish ocean god Lir, transformed into a captive swan by her evil stepmother) and the militant Finn (Fionn mac Cumhaill, hero and leader of the Fianna, legendary ancestors of the Fenians and the IRA).

In her account to the police, Finn dates the onset of her nationalism to 14 August 1969, when the streets of West Belfast erupted in violence following the Bogside riots in Derry two days prior. Roaming gangs of youths, petrol bombs, fire-destroyed shops, armored vehicles with gun turrets patrolling the streets, and people killed—all at first served primarily to provoke in Finn sympathy for the victims. She was particularly concerned with the plight of her grandmother who was, Finn later discovered, saved and taken to a refugee center by a man whose son some time afterwards asked Finn to become involved in the Provisional IRA.

It was, however, the British policy of interning suspected militants, which followed the outbreak of violence, that awoke in Finn a latent nationalist militancy that had, apparently, skipped a generation in her family. Finn's grandmother, who claimed to have "met De Valera [sic] on a Dublin train while he was on the run disguised as an old woman" (WP 98) and to have visited Countess Markievicz in prison (the deceased grandmother's picture of the Countess still hangs in her house, which Finn has inherited), must have eventually become a strong influence on Finn's decision to join the Provisional IRA. However, the grandmother's hardened nationalist attitude was not, apparently, shared by Finn's parents, as hinted in a cryptic comment by Finn: "father and grandmother didn't speak for years: because he married my mother" (WP 116). The implication is that the mother was Protestant and, therefore, anathema to the grandmother.

Perhaps because her parents did not share the grandmother's fervent nationalism, Finn's acceptance of her grandmother's ideology was not without serious psychological conflict, as suggested by a dream that she recounts late in the story. The dream took place shortly after the 1969 violence and while she was living with an English journalist, Jack McHenry, whom she met on the eve of the outbreak of the violence. In the dream, Finn is "horrified" when she is unable to fight off an old woman she does not recognize who comes to her with outstretched hands and attempts to pull her out of the Englishman's bed. Her struggle is so violent that it awakens her lover, who then tries to comfort her. When she falls back to sleep, the dream—and the struggle—resume, but this time it is clear that the woman is her grandmother. Still, Finn resists: "She pulled and I held on. She pulled and I still held on" (WP 116). The symbolism of Finn's dream is transparent: the old woman is Ireland herself, Cathleen ni Houlihan,[42] attempting to wrest the reluctant Finnula from the seductive clutches of England and enlist her in the nationalist cause.

Finn's love affairs with Jack McHenry and the Oxford graduate student further contribute to her terrorist motives. Both Jack and the young man tell Finn that they love her, but ultimately both betray her. Jack, after securing Finn's love, leaves for America, telling her that he is "ambivalent about [their] relationship" (WP 101). At the end of the story he returns to visit Finn in the police station and rebukes her for what she has done: "I ask myself over and over what kind of woman are you, and I have to remind myself that I knew you, or thought I knew you, and that I loved you once" (WP 117). She and the Oxford student fall in love during his summer stay, but when Finn, against her better judgment, confesses her love for him, he reveals to her that he is to be married when he returns to Oxford. He has, in fact, previously told Finn some things about the other woman, but he has done nothing to discourage Finn's feelings for him. After revealing his marriage plans, he tells Finn, "I can't give you up," and "I do love you" (WP 105, 106), an apparent attempt to confine her (like her mythic namesake) to a state of psychological captivity. Devlin's extensive treatment of the two entrapping love affairs suggests that Finn's decision to take an active terrorist role has as much to do with her need for psychological freedom as it does with nationalist ideology.

42. Michael Parker, introduction to *The Hurt World: Short Stories of the Troubles*, ed. Michael Parker (Belfast: Blackstaff, 1995), 6.

There is also a hint of feminism in Finn's motives to be involved in an actual violent act. When the police ask her whether, in 1969, she was "a member of an illegal organization," she responds: "What organization? There were a half dozen guns in the Falls in '69 and a lot of old men who couldn't even deliver the *United Irishman* on time. And," she adds, "the women's section had been disbanded during the previous year because there was nothing for them to do but run around after the men and make tea for the Ceilies" (WP 110). Although there are no other overt signs of feminist motives in Finn, her comment has a ring of feminist criticism of the nationalist movement, a scorn for both the ineffectuality of the men and for the subservient roles assigned to women in the movement. Finn may have been subconsiously motivated to take a direct role in the act of terrorism as a way of making women more centrally involved.

Finn's refusal to reveal the names of her accomplices in the terrorist act may seem at first to be an act of loyalty to the nationalist organization, but upon closer examination it appears that there is something else at work. Her litany of West Belfast street names—"Abyssinia, Alma, Balaclava, Balkan, Belgrade, Bosnia" (WP 118)—is performed in such a rote manner that it seems to reveal as much a numbness in her about what she has done as a strategy to keep herself from betraying the organization. The very names of the streets, taken from countries and areas of historical conflict, link the Troubles in Northern Ireland to conflicts around the world and hint at an endless cycle of violence—a sense of which has probably occurred to Finn. In the last paragraph of the story, addressed to the reader and not the police, Finn suggests that the way out of the cycle is through acceptance of personal responsibility. She says that she alone should be held responsible for what happened to her lover: "when the finger is pointed, the hand turned, the face at the end of the finger is my face, the hand at the end of the arm that points is my hand. . . . I only know for certain what my part was, that even on the eve, on such a day, I took him there" (WP 119).

Devlin's protagonist makes for an interesting study, particularly when viewed in light of Talbot's call for the integrated representation of women terrorists as both women and terrorists. As her name suggests,

Finnula/Finn has both feminine and masculine traits, and these are born out in her behavior. Her concern for her grandmother's well-being and her vulnerability in love affairs emphasize traditional feminine qualities, while her cold-blooded complicity in the execution of the Oxford student and her stoic responses to police interrogation reveal a masculine side. At the same time, however, her feminine traits, as well as her feminist concern for the greater involvement of women in the Provisional IRA, seem to fall into what Talbot considers gender stereotypes. If Finnula/Finn is represented as neither woman nor terrorist exclusively, it is also true that she is not a well balanced integration of woman and terrorist, entirely free of gender stereotypes. Nevertheless, as the only fully developed woman terrorist in the Troubles stories,[43] Devlin's protagonist represents a fine achievement.

VI

The representations of women in Troubles stories are varied, rich, and insightful, if not full and complete. Whereas male writers of the early stories depict female characters in the supporting roles of couriers, nurses, and the like (roles that their real-life counterparts actually performed), women writing about the Northern Troubles in the latter part of the twentieth century place women in the more central role of

43. Apparently, women terrorists are also scarce in Irish novels. In her extensive study of the novels of the Northern Troubles, Laura Pelaschiar finds just three representations of women terrorists. Two of these characters—Sharon McElwee in Maurice Leitch's *Silver's City* (1981) and a nameless woman in Maurice Power's *A Darkness in the Eye* (1987)—are, according to Pelaschiar, "depicted with strongly aggressive and violent male characteristics, as if their activism in political terrorism had necessarily forced them to define themselves in masculine or male terms and to give up their own female identities for more macho ones." Isabel Lynam, in Eugene McCabe's short novel *Victims* (1976), is, according to Pelaschiar, "the only fully developed female terrorist to be presented in a Northern Irish novel." In Pelaschiar's analysis, McCabe achieves his fully-developed characterization of Lynam by entangling and thereby blurring her motivation for a recent abortion (the father is an IRA commander) with her motivation for being involved in militant republicanism. Nevertheless, in the collision of feminine and masculine interests—motherhood and militant nationalism—the latter wins: "The sacrifice of female identity is the necessary price to be paid to the call of terrorism."

Laura Pelaschiar, *Writing the North: The Contemporary Novel in Northern Ireland* (Trieste: Edizioni Parnaso, 1998), 83–84.

victim, and occasionally in the roles of activist and terrorist. Together, male and female writers provide a fairly broad array of representations of women in the Troubles.

There are, of course, problems and gaps in the representations. Some of the early stories idealize women characters, thus perpetuating the myth of women as mother Ireland, while others fix women in the stereotype of handmaiden to the rebel. These stereotypes are all the more influential because of the absence in early stories of any realistic heroines that might provide counter images of women revolutionaries. More importantly, there seem to be no Troubles stories that address the issue of feminist aspirations vis-à-vis nationalist priorities, even though the theme of gender equality is found in many other contemporary Irish short stories. Since women's rights have been a concern of women nationalists from the inception of such organizations as Inghinidhe na hÉireann and Cumann na mBan, it seems odd that no short-story writer, especially a woman, has examined the issue of male dominance in Irish nationalism and the ways in which that dominance has suppressed gender equality in Ireland. Such a theme would provide an excellent basis for conflict in a Troubles story. Still another gap in more recent stories is the absence of loyalist women as protagonists, whether victim, activist, or terrorist. And, finally, there are no women characters except Trevor's Penelope Vade in "Attracta" who are portrayed as active in the peace process. Given the contentious nature of the peace process over the last several decades of the twentieth century, as well as the prominence of such women as the Noble prize winners Corrigan and Williams in the peace movement, it would seem to be an excellent topic for representing women in Troubles stories.

These problems and gaps notwithstanding, a reading of Troubles stories by or about women serves to remind readers that the Troubles are not an exclusively male phenomenon and that women have played significant roles.

Conclusion

The End of Cultural Identity?

And whatever you say, you say nothing.
Smoke signals are loud-mouthed compared with us:
Manoeuvrings to find out name and school,
Subtle discrimination by addresses
With hardly an exception to the rule
That Norman, Ken and Sidney signalled Prod
And Seamus (call me Sean) was sure-fire Pape.
—Seamus Heaney, "Whatever You Say Say Nothing"

I

By the end of the twentieth century, the stories of the Irish Troubles were again showing signs of changing in character, as they had continually throughout the century in response to new events and to shifting attitudes of the Irish people toward the Troubles. Political developments in the 1990s, particularly the declarations of ceasefire by the IRA and loyalist paramilitaries in 1994 and the 1998 Good Friday Agreement, held out the prospect of a peaceful resolution to a quarter century of conflict in Northern Ireland. The hope generated by these events, however, was attenuated by the sporadic violence of militant factions on both sides and by the daunting task of implementing the 1998 Agreement. The uncertainty of peace and unabated sectarian animosity guaranteed the continued existence of Troubles stories.

Whereas the Troubles stories of the 1970s and 1980s focus largely on sectarian violence and terrorism, the stories of the 1990s and early years of the new century focus on the root cause of the hostility and violence, i.e., sectarian identity and allegiance. If the stories of the 1970s and 1980s might be read as a repudiation of sectarian-linked violence, recent stories can be construed as a repudiation of sectarian allegiance. In some of these stories, characters seem willing to set aside sectarian identity in order to bridge the gulf between divided communities, while others flee from, and even renounce, their sectarian identities. Identity-formation and violence have, of course, been at the core of the Troubles from the beginning. But the revolutionary events that began the Troubles in the early twentieth century—the Easter Rising and the War of Independence—were sparked, and then fueled, by an Irish nationalism built to a significant degree on an Irish cultural identity implicitly inclusive of both Gael and Anglo-Irish, Catholic and Protestant, in keeping with a tradition stretching back through Parnell and Butt to Tone and the United Irishmen. Moreover, these events were carried out with a violence that, even though at times equivalent to terrorism, was interpreted by perpetrator and sympathetic citizenry alike as justified means toward the goal of an Irish nation.

By the end of the twentieth century, however, the circumstances and perceptions of the Troubles changed radically. Not only had the battleground shifted from the south to the north and the conflict from being mainly one of Irish against English to one of Irish nationalist against Anglo-Irish unionist, but the conflict between nationalist and unionist over the political fate of Northern Ireland came to be defined on the grounds of more narrowly constructed cultural identities. Now "nationalist" almost always meant a member of the Gaelic Catholic heritage, while "unionist" meant British Protestant heritage. Furthermore, such narrowly defined constructions made identification of members of the two groups, nationalists and unionists, a relatively easy task for terrorists. As Seamus Heaney makes clear in the poetic excerpt above, names, addresses, schools (he might easily have added places of employment, sports teams, churches, pubs: virtually any association or affiliation) are all overt signals of cultural identity.

Attitudes toward violence also shifted by century's end. In *Anomalous States,* Lloyd explains that Irish violence has always been interpreted in two opposing ways by historians: "For nationalist historiography, the violence of Irish history is symptomatic of the unrelenting struggle of an Irish people forming itself in sporadic but connected risings against British domination," whereas for imperial historiography "[v]iolence is understood as an atavistic and disruptive principle counter to the rationality of legal constitution as barbarity is to an emerging civility, anarchy to culture."[1] In the Troubles of the early twentieth century and in the early years of the Northern Troubles, the former view of violence as justified "unrelenting struggle" prevailed among Irish nationalists. Since the height of the Northern Troubles, however, the latter view of violence as "atavistic and disruptive" has strongly held public sway, even among many nationalists and certainly in the representation of violence in Irish short fiction since the late 1970s. The violence of nationalist rebels that was once viewed by a sympathetic citizenry, and promoted—if not graphically described—by Corkery, O'Connor, and O'Faolain in their romantic Troubles stories, as the necessary means of the freedom fighter has now come to be viewed by the Irish citizenry as the senseless brutality of the terrorist. Similarly, the counter-violence of Protestant paramilitary groups, itself first seen by loyalists as a legitimate response to IRA terrorism, has also come to be viewed as barbaric and anarchic. Unrelenting violence and counter-violence has brought about the complete discredit of any violence, nationalist or loyalist. Nevertheless, despite this prevailing view of violence, both communities continue to promote their distinct sectarian identities through loyalist and nationalist traditions and rituals, which helps to explain why violence has also continued as a part of life in Northern Ireland.

The effort to find political solutions to the vexing problem of sectarian-related violence in Northern Ireland has been on-going. Lloyd argues that the causal link between cultural identity and violence may be unbreakable as long as neither community gains hegemony. In *Anomalous States*, he speaks of "the implicit violence of identity formation, not so much in the sense that identity seems to provoke and legitimate a sec-

1. David Lloyd, *Anomalous States: Irish Writing and the Post-Colonial Moment* (Durham: Duke University Press, 1993), 125.

tarian antagonism towards the different, as in the far more fundamental sense in which the formation of identity requires the negation of other possible forms of existing."[2] In other words, the full realization of loyalist identity requires the virtually complete negation of nationalist identity, and vice versa. Thus, any assertion of one community's identity is likely to provoke violence from the other, as for instance, in the way that the annual Orange parades provoke violent responses from the Catholic community. The act of violence, in turn, promotes a heightened sense of identity in the attacked community (attacks on their parades increase the resolve of Protestants to conduct them) and further hardens the bond between identity-thinking and violence.

"[T]he end of violence" comes, Lloyd says, with "the legitimate state formation."[3] In other words, in Ireland's case it will come with either the realization of the nationalists' goal of a united Ireland that effectively subordinates the Protestant population or with the solidification of a Northern Ireland state that completely and permanently suppresses nationalist aspirations. The hegemony of one community, Lloyd says, will bring with it the "negation" of the defeated community's cultural identity, perhaps through "openly violent suppression," through "the liberal narrative of development which relegates [the negated community] . . . to 'premodern' or underdeveloped stages of humanity," or through some other means.[4] Those other possible means, not specifically mentioned by Lloyd, might include the virtually complete separation of the two communities, through either the repartitioning of Northern Ireland, ethnic cleansing, or both. Apparently, "the case for a repartition that would divide the province [of Northern Ireland] into distinct Catholic and Protestant territorial zones" was made by Northern Ireland politicians and academics in the 1970s and 1980s.[5] Moreover, the release to the public on 1 January 2003 of a 1970s secret British plan "to create a Protestant-

2. Ibid., 4.

3. Ibid., 125.

4. Ibid., 4.

5. Joe Cleary, ***Literature, Partition and the Nation State: Culture and Conflict in Ireland, Israel and Palestine*** (Cambridge: Cambridge University Press, 2002), 3. Cleary cites two plans for partition in an endnote: 226, n. 3.

only 'sectarian statelet'" made clear that ethnic cleansing has not been an entirely unthinkable solution. The secret plan for repartitioning called for the ceding of Catholic-majority areas in Northern Ireland to the Republic, as well as for the forcible expulsion of as many as 300,000 Catholics from the redrawn northern state. As many as 200,000 Protestants from the ceded areas would be moved back to the north.[6] The plan was eventually "abandoned as impractical and unworkable."[7]

A more positive and peaceful, though not necessarily a more probable, means of breaking the link between identity and violence has been proposed in the so-called "dual identity" theory, which may be seen to be at work to some degree in the 1998 Good Friday Agreement. As explained by Michael MacDonald in "Blurring the Difference: The Politics of Identity in Northern Ireland," dual identity theory proposes that unionists and nationalists discard or circumvent the "traditional notions of sovereignty [a united Ireland vs. a continued Protestant-dominated northern state], which have produced conflict and violence"[8] and instead begin the reconciliation process by "attributing the conflict to the different national identities and allegiances of Northern Ireland's two communities."[9] Possibly then, according to this theory, "the conflict can be mended through the symbolic inclusions of the embattled communities in expressive institutions."[10] That is to say, both Catholic nationalists and Protestant unionists would be granted institutional recognition of their political and cultural traditions in a governmental entity whose character would be shaped by the combined electorate. In fact, the 1998 Agreement calls for institutions, such as the RUC, to be reformed along dual identity lines.

6. John Crossland and David Lister, "Heath Drew Up Plan for Partition in Northern Ireland," *The Times* (London), 1 Jan. 2003.

7. Al Webb, "Document: U.K. Plan to Cede Land to Dublin," *United Press International*, 2 Jan. 2003.

8. Michael MacDonald, "Blurring the Difference: The Politics of Identity in Northern Ireland," in *The Irish Terrorism Experience*, ed. Yonah Alexander and Alan O'Day (Brookfield, Vt.: Dartmouth Publishing Co., 1991), 84.

9. Ibid., 85.

10. Ibid.

Dual identity theory is not without problems. MacDonald discusses the objections to, and flaws in, the theory, such as the fact that it "ignores the possibility that the communal identities of Protestants and Catholics are formed through interaction with, and not in isolation from, each other. That is, unionism and nationalism are not just pulled in different directions by Britain and Ireland; they also push against each other."[11] Consequently, if the continued existence of both communal identities requires that they "push against each other" in order to define themselves, then the potential for violent "pushing" will always remain. Nevertheless, as embodied in the 1998 Agreement, the dual identity theory holds out the possibility of a peaceful solution to the Troubles in Northern Ireland, one that will grant full and institutional expression to both cultural identities.

II

The question of literature's role in representing solutions to the Troubles has been one of keen interest to critics, particularly in recent years as political solutions have floundered. That role is problematic. Most literature, including much of the Troubles literature of all genres, is not overtly ideological, in the sense of advocating one political solution or another. Although some stories of the Troubles, such as those of romantic nationalism, openly advocate an ideological position, most simply portray the causes and effects of the Troubles and evoke, according to the literary modes employed, moral disgust, sardonic laughter, anguish, horror, and other responses less ideological and more "human." What Trevor has stated about his Troubles stories, that the political aspects for him are always secondary to the human relationships, may also be said of most of the other stories of the Troubles. Nevertheless, "new" historical and other cultural critics of literature have argued that literature does have a powerful ideological impact on society. According to these critics, the subtle techniques of literature, such as indirection, irony, and symbolic narrative, have the power to influence the

11. Ibid.

reading public, often unconsciously, and to bring about profound change. Troubles stories of the last ten years offer some insights into possible conclusions to the Northern Troubles, some with a more ideological bent than others.

The stories of Gerry Adams espouse a militant solution, rather like that of enforced hegemony explained by Lloyd. As president of Sinn Féin, the political arm of the IRA, Adams has fully committed himself to the unification of Ireland and, at least up until the 1998 Agreement, would seem to have approved the use of violence to obtain that goal. In *The Street and Other Stories* (1993), Adams attempts to cast militant nationalism, including the use of violence, in a romantic light. Stories such as "The Rebel," "Granny Harbinson," and "A Good Confession" reprise the old themes of romantic nationalism, including the sentimental connection between rebels and sympathetic citizens and the need for armed rebellion. In "Granny Harbinson," for example, the title character discovers that her grandson has hidden IRA weapons in her house. When the house is about to be raided by British soldiers, Granny, who has vivid memories of British oppression in the 1920s, moves the weapons to a safe place and later advises her grandson to take greater care, presumably so that he can continue as an active member of the IRA in the violent struggle toward unification. Despite the skillful use of romantic techniques, however, Adams' stories fail to inspire readers in the ways that the early romantic stories did. By the 1990s, terrorism had rendered the romantic view of violence insupportable and the story of romantic nationalism obsolete.

Other stories take a less overt ideological approach to the Troubles, requiring subtle analysis by ideological-minded critics. One such analysis is that found in *Literature, Partition and the Nation State* by Joe Cleary. Cleary analyzes cultural narratives that portray the Northern Troubles, such as Bernard MacLaverty's novel *Cal* and Neil Jordan's film *The Crying Game*. He maintains that these narratives play a potentially significant ideological role in ending the Troubles, even though the narratives almost invariably focus on the communal borders within Northern Ireland, rather than on the state border between north and south.

Cleary argues that, by focusing on communal borders, the narratives reinforce what he believes to be an erroneous conception, promoted since the 1970s by revisionist historiography, that the conflict results from sectarian problems internal to Northern Ireland rather than from the problem of partition. The distinction, Cleary says, is crucial because it promotes solutions to the Troubles that urge, ineffectually, a change of attitudes in the divided communities, rather than "some more radical reconstruction of the state order in the [British and Irish] archipelago as a whole."[12] Focusing on the latter solution, in Cleary's view, would more likely lead to permanent peace.

Cleary nonetheless reads some of these narratives in such a way as to assign them an important ideological role. In his view, they do not necessarily reflect a lack of interest in the traumatic impact that partition has had on the Irish psyche, as one historian has claimed.[13] Rather, they suggest that the issue of partition has been repressed and sublimated in the portrayals of communal borders and violence. When read in psychoanalytic terms, the narratives "disclose some dream or other of reconciling the divided communities they depict, and that dream inevitably resurrects, directly or otherwise, questions of state. That is, the dream of overcoming sectarian conflict requires as its inevitable corollary some conception, however vaguely delineated, of a state form that might accommodate such reconciliation."[14]

Employing Marxist literary theory, Cleary asserts that analysis of the forms of these cultural narratives reveals their ideological intent. He points out that "one of the more recurrent formal structures to appear in fictional narratives about the Northern situation is that of a relationship, or attempted relationship, between two characters from different sides

12. Cleary, *Literature, Partition,* 101.

13. Cleary says that Clare O'Halloran, in her book *Partition and the Limits of Irish Nationalism: an Ideology Under Stress* (Dublin: Gill and MacMillan, 1987), xiv, "suggests that the lack of a major body of Irish fiction about partition can be taken as evidence that partition was never experienced by the majority of Irish people as a national trauma of any sort." Cleary, *Literature, Partition*, 104.

14. Cleary, *Literature, Partition*, 109–10.

of the political divide." While this relationship is at times a male friendship, itself sometimes homoerotic, more often it "takes the form of a Romeo-and-Juliet-type heterosexual romance between Catholic and Protestant lovers, a romance in which the lovers, who desire sexual union, must struggle against the centrifugal forces that pull their respective communities apart." Even though such a narrative typically ends in frustration with the failure of the romance, it has the potential of raising the reader's hopes for an end both to the obstacles that stand in the lovers way and to the type of state that creates the obstacles.[15] In Cleary's judgment, however, most Northern Ireland narratives that employ the romance form ultimately fail to inspire the reconciliation of divided communities.

The same might be said of the few Troubles short stories that employ the romance-across-the-divide narrative. Rather than raise expectations for a peaceful resolution to the Troubles, these stories leave the reader with a sense of futility that easily overwhelms whatever hope has been stirred by the romance. For example, Kiely's "Bluebell Meadow," which portrays the Romeo-and-Juliet love affair between the Protestant boy, Lofty, and the unnamed Catholic girl, leaves the reader with the sense that personal relationships stand no chance when pitted against the communal forces of sectarianism. Similarly, Devlin's "Naming the Names," leaves the reader in despair after Finnula betrays her English lover to the terrorists.

More recently, Colum McCann has used the romance-across-the-divide narrative in a story entitled "Everything in This Country Must," from a collection of the same name published in 2000. In the story, a Catholic teenage girl named Katie and a British soldier stationed in Northern Ireland are attracted to one another, but Katie's father quashes the relationship before it has a chance to blossom. The story begins as six British soldiers risk their lives in a river, flooded by a torrential rain, to rescue a farm horse belonging to Katie's father. Grateful for their courageous act, Katie invites the soldiers, drenched and exhausted, into

15. Ibid., 112–13.

the farmhouse for tea. Her father, however, cannot abide the soldiers' presence in his home. Nor can he allow their generosity to overcome the bitterness he has harbored for all British soldiers ever since his wife and son were killed when an army truck accidentally hit them. Angered as one of the soldiers flirts with Katie, the father rudely tells the soldiers to leave. But their departure is not satisfaction enough for him; he must also reject their gift of saving his favorite horse. After they leave, he goes out in the rain and shoots the horse.

McCann takes the title of his story from the reflection Katie has as she watches Stevie, the soldier that she becomes fond of, risk his life to save the horse: "I was wearing Stevie's jacket but I was shivering and wet and cold and scared because Stevie and the draft horse were going to die since everything in this country must" (EC 10). Despite a few brief celebratory moments in the farmhouse after the rescue and smiles exchanged between Stevie and Katie that hint at possible peaceful co-existence of hostile communities, the theme of the story, signaled by the title and the poignant ending, is obviously dark. The astonishing act of the father killing his own beloved horse brings home to the reader how much stronger the bitter emotions of sectarian hate are than those of romance and love.

III

A more traditional, humanistic view of literature's role in bringing about an end to violence in Northern Ireland is that of Patrick Grant. In *Literature, Rhetoric and Violence in Northern Ireland, 1968–98*, Grant argues that literature can counteract the violence wrought by sectarian rhetoric through the moral agency of the imagination. "[I]maginative literature," he asserts, "gives us special access to the workings of violence, showing the mechanisms by which it perpetuates itself, and also the means by which the violent conceal from themselves and others the consequences of their actions."[16] Furthermore, by imagining an al-

16. Patrick Grant, *Literature, Rhetoric and Violence in Northern Ireland, 1968–98: Hardened to Death* (New York: Palgrave, 2001), 16.

ternative to the incessant cycle of violence, the alternative of forgiveness and reconciliation, literature offers a way toward liberation to those who perpetrate violence, as well as to those who suffer it.[17]

Grant recognizes that forgiveness and reconciliation do not come easily. He provides detailed accounts of how actual victims, their relatives, and some perpetrators of violence have wrestled with the issues of forgiveness and reconciliation. To be effective, Grant admits, literature must portray the difficulty, pain, anguish, and doubt that accompany the struggle toward reconciliation. Moreover, there is no "prescription" by which literature can do this; it must proceed through such means as "imagery and narrative."[18] Grant finds such a process at work in the poetry of John Hewitt, the plays of Frank McGuinness, and the novels of Robert McLiam Wilson and Bernard MacLaverty.

Curiously, forgiveness and reconciliation are not a common theme in Troubles stories. One might expect to find it in the stories of sectarian violence discussed in chapter 5, yet only Trevor's "Attracta" treats the theme in any depth. In relating the newspaper account of the brutalized Penelope Vade to her schoolchildren, and by telling them how she forgave her own parents' killers in the early Troubles, Attracta attempts to offer the children an object lesson in forgiveness and reconciliation, but her efforts fall on deaf ears.

Another story by McCann, "Cathal's Lake," published in his 1994 collection, *Fishing the Sloe-Black River*, does offer an interesting treatment of the theme of reconciliation achieved through an act of imagination. McCann's title character, living on a remote farm, is "cursed" to empathize with victims of sectarian violence. As the story opens, Cathal lies on his bed, smoking and imagining the last act of a fourteen-year-old boy whose death has just been announced on the radio. While demonstrating in the streets of Derry, the boy was about to toss a milk bottle full of petrol at British soldiers when he was hit by a plastic bullet fired by one of the soldiers. The bottle fell at the boy's feet and broke, ig-

17. Ibid., 122–23.
18. Ibid., 123.

niting the petrol and engulfing the boy in flames. Later, "still alive in his house of burnt skin" (FS 174), the boy succumbed to death.

Cathal's need to recreate the Catholic boy's death in his imagination does not stem from any sectarian allegiance on his part. His "curse" also forces him to empathize with the British soldier, "maybe . . . just a boy himself" (FS 175). Cathal, in fact, takes all sectarian victims—and perpetrators—of violence into his empathizing imagination:

> The girl from the blown-up bar looking like a twin of the soldier found slumped in the front seat of a Saracen, a hole in his head the size of a fist, the size of a heart. And him the twin of the boy from Garvagh found drowned in a ditch with an armalite in his fingers and a reed in his teeth. And him the twin of the mother shot accidentally while out walking her baby in a pram. Her the twin of the father found hanging from an oak tree after seeing his daughter in a dress of tar and chicken feathers. Him the twin of the three soldiers and two gunmen who murdered each other last March. . . . And last week, just before Christmas, the old man found on the roadside with his kneecaps missing, beside his blue bicycle. . . . (FS 181)

For each of these victims, Cathal performs the same strange and fantastic ritual. He takes a shovel out to the edge of his lake, on which many swans drift, and digs down three feet until he reaches the body of a swan. Then, "feel[ing] the heart flutter," he lifts the swan out, tosses it in the air, "and watches the wondrous way that the swan bursts over the lake, soil sifting off its wings, curious and lovely, looking for a place to land" (FS 183). The other swans then make room for the "newborn."

Cathal's ritual of transporting swans from death in the soil to life in the air is obviously one designed to bring about regeneration for the victims of sectarian terrorism, if not actual rebirth, then at least an imaginative, symbolic one. The story also suggests, particularly in the passage quoted above, that victims and perpetrators of both sectarian identities are really "twins" and that a peaceful reconciliation requires that they be imagined as such.

McCann's use of fantasy has interesting, if ambiguous, implications. On the one hand, the reader is tempted to view Cathal as deranged, living in a fantasy world, and to view his "solution" as confirmation that any solution to the Troubles is fantastic. On the other hand, Cathal's great act of imagination, surely one with a moral dimension, may be viewed as an inspiration. The story reinforces Grant's point that literature can awaken the moral imagination to forgiveness and reconciliation and thus offer a way out of the Troubles.

IV

A third possibility for the resolution of the Northern Troubles, one that sits somewhere between the violent negation of one sectarian community or the other and the peaceful reconciliation of the two, is suggested in stories by Jennifer C Cornell and Bernard MacLaverty. These stories suggest that the end to the Troubles may come about from an unintended consequence of violence: the concealment and repudiation of sectarian identity.

In "Outtake," from her 1995 collection *Departures*, Cornell[19] dramatizes the danger of revealing one's sectarian identity to strangers. But, conversely, the story also hints at the advantage of concealing one's affiliations. Cornell's protagonist, Jim, carelessly lets slip his Catholic background, first to a young woman he meets in a pub and then to strangers in a taxi he shares on his way home. For his mistake he will be beaten by the strangers, Protestant extremists.

Jim, a young single man looking for women, goes to the Abercorn, a pub recommended by friends as "[t]he best bloody pickup joint in Belfast" (DP 73). What Jim doesn't know, or at least gives no indication of being concerned with, is that the Abercorn is also a Protestant hangout. Once there, things are almost too easy for Jim, who has not had much luck with the opposite sex. An attractive young woman named Angie approaches him. They share drinks, dance, and carry on an easy conversation, ranging in topics from "pop groups and videos, the best places in town to go for a meal" (DP 79) and other trivia to their jobs (he drives a fork-lift, she's a waitress in a Chinese restaurant). When their

19. Cornell, an American, is the only non-Irish writer treated in this study. However, she lived for a period of time in Belfast, an experience which led to the writing of the stories collected in *Departures*.

conversation turns to curiosities and superstitions, Jim mentions one about Rosary beads bleeding if the string is broken. He thus unwittingly reveals his Catholic identity. Angie abruptly excuses herself and, despite Jim's pleas to stay, leaves the pub with her friend Denise who, obviously having heard the news from Angie, "stab[s] two fingers in his direction and appear[s] to spit on the floor" (DP 83). Perhaps because he is by now hazy with alcohol, Jim gives no sign that he knows the reasons for Angie's departure or Denise's rude gestures. Shortly thereafter, he leaves the pub and searches the rainy Belfast streets for a cab to take him home.

Jim finally finds a partially-filled cab headed for the Shankhill, the Protestant neighborhood, from which "he could easily walk home" (DP 84), presumably to the adjoining Catholic Falls Road neighborhood. As he listens to the conversation of the male passengers about their evening's adventures of failed attempts to pick up women, he mentions his hard luck at the Abercorn, and then casually remarks that "there's good crack in the Rex on a Saturday night" (DP 86). Apparently a Catholic hang-out, the Rex is another clue to his identity. Again, Jim seems not to be consciously aware of his mistake, but as he looks out the cab window the signs of the Troubles are obvious: "He could see shops now, some with their shutters down, a few others standing empty, their windows smashed, their signs removed. On the gables of the houses that rubbed shoulders with the road he could see the murals, shadows of gunmen, weapons, flags" (DP 88). "His throat dry," a sign of his dawning recognition of his plight, Jim asks the driver to let him off at the next stop, but "silence . . . fall[s] over the men in the back of the cab" (DP 88) and the driver ignores his plea to let him out. As the cab speeds off into the dark streets, Jim fully realizes his mistake: "His eyes smarting, nearly blinded by tears, Jim turned away from the window and folded his arms, waiting for it to be over" (DP 88).

The reader can be certain that Cornell's protagonist—a young man with apparently no overt interest in his sectarian identity (his friends call him "Jimmy," not Seamus or Shamie)—will learn to better conceal the cultural markers that could lead to a repeat of the beating he is about to receive from the strangers in the cab. Indeed, the theme of "Outtake" is that survival in a world of sectarian hostility requires concealment of one's sectarian identity.

MacLaverty's "Walking the Dog," the title story of his 1995 collection, takes Cornell's theme one step farther. The story dramatizes a Belfast man's refusal to divulge—and his ultimate repudiation of—any religious or political affiliation in order to survive an abduction by extremists. Shortly after leaving his house on the outskirts of Belfast at nine o'clock one winter evening to walk his dog, MacLaverty's protagonist is forced into a car at gunpoint by two men who claim to be "from the IRA" and ask him: "Who are you?" (WD 5). What they really want to know, of course, is his sectarian affiliation. They are looking for a random victim and want to be certain that they choose one from the opposing community. In order to discover their captive's sectarian identity, they demand, in successive order, that he reveal his name, his school, his and his parents' religion, and his employer—any one of which might reveal his identity. They also ask whether he knows anyone from the Provisional IRA, and they order him to recite the letters of the alphabet, based on the belief (as he knows) that Catholics and Protestants each pronounce "h" differently.

Not at all certain that his abductors are, as they claim, members of the IRA looking for a Protestant victim, and fearful that they might, in fact, be Protestant extremists searching for a Catholic to murder, the man follows the advice offered in Heaney's poem ("And whatever you say, you say nothing"), answering their questions in such a way as not to reveal any sectarian affiliation. At each question he thwarts them: he gives an ethnically neutral name (John Shields); refuses to name the school he attended; claims that neither he nor his parents profess or practice religion; and denies that he knows anyone in the Provisional IRA. In reciting the alphabet, he deliberately pronounces "h" in both ways ("aitch" and "haitch"). He does, however, reveal that he works at the Gas Board, apparently thinking that it is not a decisive clue to his identity. Ironically, it is on this basis that they decide to let him go, and thus reveal their own unionist identity: "There's not too many Fenians in the Gas Board" (WD 9), one of them remarks.

With its innocuous title, nondescript protagonist, and simple narrative structure, "Walking the Dog" conveys with pointed irony the way in which terror has intruded on ordinary life in Northern Ireland. It also records in its details a series of more subtle ironies that hint at a range of related themes: the dangers of living in Belfast, the need to know where one is at all times, and the pervasiveness of sectarianism and identity-thinking. On leaving the house the man's only conscious fear of danger is that he might slip on the ice. At a traffic light in his abductors' car and with his head forced down on the seat so that he is unable to see where he is, the protagonist hears the beeping noise that allows blind people to "know where they were" (WD 9). Meanwhile, the terrorist driving the car dutifully obeys the traffic lights that turn "from orange to green" (WD 10), as if sectarianism were imbedded in mechanical devices. Even the last sentence of the story, which describes the freed protagonist returning home, contains an ironic reminder of the pervasiveness of identity: "The street was so quiet he could hear the clinking of the dog's identity disk as it padded along beside him" (WD 12).

But it is the irony that comes to us *after* we finish reading the story that stays with us. Although we think we know the man well because we have fully experienced his terror, we realize that we know nothing of his sectarian identity. We do not know whether he is Catholic or Protestant, nationalist or unionist, or if what he suggests is true—that he has no sectarian affiliation. We are not even certain his name is John Shields. He may, in fact, be shedding his sectarian identity in the short period of his abduction, perhaps beginning with a change in his name. When he tells his captors that his name is John Shields, one of them asks: "What sort of a name is that?" (WD 6), as if it is an oddity that someone from Belfast would not have a name that clearly indicates sectarian identity. Before he tells his captors that his name is John Shields, the narrator refers to him simply with the third-person pronoun "he." Thereafter, the narrator consistently refers to him as "John," suggesting that the protagonist has just chosen and has permanently assumed that name. Similarly, when one terrorist directly asks if he is Catholic or Protestant, he replies: "I'm . . . I don't believe in any of that crap. I suppose I'm nothing" (WD 7). The ellipsis marks in the text indicate a careful hesitation in an effort to say the right thing but perhaps also imply a repudiation of whichever tradition he has belonged to, while the word "nothing" reverberates with multiple meanings, including the idea that he now claims to be a kind of cultural and sectarian non-entity. MacLaverty's protagonist may very well now be a man with no cultural identity. But he may also be the future citizen of Northern Ireland—in which case, and in a kind of perverse irony, the Troubles might expire for a lack of sectarian identity in the citizens.

V

In the dedication of his 1847 novel, *The Black Prophet: a Tale of Irish Famine*, William Carleton expressed the wish to Lord Russell, British Prime Minister, that Russell's policies would make it impossible for the genre of the Famine novel ever to be written again. Citing Carleton's dedication, the Irish critic Fintan O'Toole notes that the Famine novel is an interesting example of "a fiction that has no interest in being read as part of a historical continuity because it longs for the obliteration of the conditions from which it emerged."[20] The Troubles are, arguably, second only to the Famine in painful associations in the Irish consciousness, but they have surely exceeded the Famine as the subject of fiction—in both quantity and quality[21]—and, it would seem, the authors of Troubles stories have had every intention of making these stories "part of a historical continuity," recording as they have the various phases of the Troubles through the twentieth century. Nevertheless, it could also be said about the Troubles stories what O'Toole says about the Famine novel: "[they long] for the obliteration of the conditions from which [they] emerged." Once the conditions of the Troubles are obliterated, there will be no more need, or desire, for stories of the Troubles.

20. Fintan O'Toole, "Trying Not to Awake," *The New Republic*, 15 October 2001, 62.

21. The Famine novel has, despite Carleton's wish, taken its place in the Irish canon: O'Flaherty's *Famine* (1937) and Walter Macken's *The Silent People* (1962) are two of the most prominent examples.

Glossary

Auxiliaries (Auxiliary Cadets): police force, comprised largely of former British Army officers, created during the War of Independence to assist the Royal Irish Constabulary in its attempts to subdue the Irish rebels. The auxiliaries were responsible for the brutal Croke Park killings and the burning of Cork city centre in late 1920.

Black and Tans: police force comprised of British ex-servicemen that joined with the Royal Irish Constabulary and the auxiliaries during the War of Independence in their brutal attempts to quell the rebellion and intimidate the Irish population.

B Specials (Ulster Special Constabulary, B Specials): part-time branch of Ulster police force formed in 1920 to counter IRA violence in the north. The force was disbanded in 1970 after being implicated in violent responses to the civil rights marches of the late 1960s.

Cumann na mBan ("Irishwomen's Council"): organization founded in April, 1914, in the cause of "Irish liberty." It became a supporting branch of the Irish Volunteers and, subsequently, the Irish Republican Army, providing aid to the rebels in the 1916 Easter Rising, the War of Independence, and the Civil War. The organization has supported both the Official IRA and the Provisional IRA in the Northern Ireland Troubles.

Inghinidhe na hÉireann ("Daughters of Ireland"): women's nationalist society founded in 1900 by Maud Gonne and absorbed by Cumann na mBan in May 1915.

Irish Citizen Army: socialist militia created in 1913 to defend workers' rights. The organization joined with other rebel forces in the 1916 Easter Rising and fought under the leadership of James Connolly, one the leaders of the Rising executed by the British.

Irish Free State Army: militia formed as a result of the Anglo-Irish Treaty of 1921. The army was made up largely of pro-Treaty members of the Irish Republican Army and led by Michael Collins against the anti-Treaty republican forces in the Civil War.

Irish National Liberation Army (INLA): a splinter group of the IRA founded in the mid-1970s as the military branch of the Irish Republican Socialist Party. The INLA has been responsible for numerous terrorist attacks and sectarian killings in Northern Ireland.

Irish Republican Army (IRA): major militant nationalist organization in Ireland. The IRA emerged in 1919 as the successor to the Irish Volunteers. Politically aligned with Sinn Féin, the IRA waged the War of Independence against the British and fought the Civil War against the Free State government. The organization was proscribed in 1936 but continued to conduct military campaigns, notably in England in 1939 and against the north in 1956–1962. In 1970 it split into the Official IRA and the Provisional IRA. Small splinter groups of the IRA include the Contingency IRA, the Real IRA, and the INLA.

Irish Republican Brotherhood (IRB): secret revolutionary organization also known as the Fenian Brotherhood. Founded by James Stephens in 1858, the IRB was involved in the Risings of 1867 and 1916 and was dissolved in 1924.

Irish Volunteers: militia founded by Eoin MacNeill in late 1913 in response to the formation of the Ulster Volunteer Force earlier that same year. In 1919, the organization became the Army of the Republic, thereafter the IRA.

Loyalist Volunteer Force (LVF): group formed in 1996 from disaffected members of the Ulster Volunteer Force. Refusing to endorse the 1994 ceasefire, LVF carried on brutal attacks against Catholics.

Northern Ireland Civil Rights Association (NICRA): organization created in the late 1960s to work for the civil rights of Catholics in Northern Ireland. NICRA organized protests and demonstrations that, at times, evoked violence from unionists.

Orange Order: unionist organization founded in 1795 to uphold Ireland's relationship with Britain and defend Protestant interests. Named after William of Orange, the Order celebrates the seventeenth-century Protestant victories over James' Catholic forces at Aughrim, the Boyne, and Derry with annual parades in Northern Ireland.

Provisional Irish Republican Army (Provos or PIRA): the dominant militant republican organization in the north. PIRA was formed in 1970 by IRA dissidents committed to violent opposition to British and Protestant control of Northern Ireland.

Red Hand Commandos: a small but brutal Protestant terrorist organization that emerged in Northern Ireland in the early 1970s.

Royal Irish Constabulary (RIC): chief law-enforcement agency in British colonial Ireland. Despite the fact that many of its members were Catholic with nationalist sympathies, they became assassination targets of the IRA because of the RIC's link to the Crown. It was disbanded in 1922 following partition and succeeded by the Royal Ulster Constabulary in the north and the Garda Síochána in the south.

Royal Ulster Constabulary (RUC): largely Protestant, Northern Ireland police force formed in 1922 following partition. The Good Friday Agreement of 1998 calls for its reform, specifically for greater inclusion of Catholics.

Sinn Féin ("Ourselves"): Irish party founded by Arthur Griffith in 1907 and later associated with Irish Volunteers in the 1916 Easter Rising. The party reformed after the Rising and won the 1918 general elections, proclaiming itself the Dáil Éireann (Irish Parliament). It reformed again in 1923 as the political wing of the IRA, which role it continues today for the Provisional IRA.

Tara: virulently anti-Catholic paramilitary organization active in the Northern Ireland Troubles from the beginning and responsible for savage sectarian attacks.

Ulster Defence Association (UDA): large umbrella unionist organization founded in 1971 out of smaller paramilitary groups. Reputed to have at one time as many as 50,000 members and to have been extensively involved in sectarian violence, the UDA was outlawed in 1992 by the British government.

Ulster Defence Regiment (UDR): Northern Ireland regiment of the British Army formed in 1969 to replace the B Specials. The UDR was disbanded in 1992 because of its extensive complicity with Protestant paramilitary groups.

Ulster Freedom Fighters (UFF): Protestant paramilitary group formed in 1973 by the Ulster Defence Association to carry out terrorist activities against the Catholic community.

Ulster Resistance: unionist group formed in 1986 to campaign against the 1985 Anglo-Irish Agreement which sought a consensual solution to the

Northern problem. The group acquired weapons but apparently has not been directly linked to violence.

Ulster Volunteer Force (UVF): militant organization originally formed in 1912 to provide resistance to home rule and, after the 1921 Treaty, a defense of partition. The group's name was revived in the mid-1960s by a unionist terrorist organization, whose members reputedly included the infamous "Shankill Butchers," a group responsible for the gruesome murders of Northern Catholics.

United Irishmen: nonsectarian, secret society of Irish patriots founded in Belfast in 1791 upon the republican principles of the French Revolution. Under the leadership of Wolfe Tone and Lord Edward Fitzgerald, the society instigated the insurrection of 1798. Its failed rebellion of 1803, led by Robert Emmet, brought on the demise of the society.

Young Ireland: cultural movement begun in 1842 to promote a nonsectarian, romantic nationalism. The views of its members, including Thomas Davis, John Blake Dillon, and Charles Gavan Duffy, were expressed in ballads, poems, and essays published in its weekly newspaper, *Nation*. Some of its members, notably John Mitchel, took part in the failed rebellion of 1848.

Selected Bibliography

I. Primary Sources

Adams, Gerry. *The Street and Other Stories.* New York: Sheridan Square, 1992.

Beckett, Mary. *A Belfast Woman*. New York: William Morrow, 1980.

Behan, Brendan. *Poems and Stories*. Ed. Denis Cotter. Dublin: The Liffey Press, 1978.

Boyle, Patrick. *At Night All Cats are Grey*. New York: Grove, 1966.

Burke, Helen Lucy. *A Season for Mothers and Other Stories.* Dublin: Poolbeg, 1980.

Carleton, William. *Stories From Carleton*. 1889. Reprint, New York: Lemma, 1973.

Corkery, Daniel. *The Hounds of Banba*. 1920. Reprint, Freeport, N.Y.: Books for Libraries, 1970.

Cornell, Jennifer C. *Departures.* Pittsburgh: University of Pittsburgh Press, 1995.

DeSalvo, Louise, Kathleen Walsh D'Arcy, and Katherine Hogan, eds. *Territories of the Voice: Contemporary Stories by Irish Women Writers.* Boston: Beacon, 1989.

Devlin, Anne. *The Way-Paver.* London: Faber and Faber, 1986.

Johnston, Jennifer. "Trio." In *Territories of the Voice: Contemporary Stories by Irish Women Writers.* Ed. Louise DeSalvo, Kathleen Walsh D'Arcy, and Katherine Hogan. Boston: Beacon, 1989.

Kiely, Benedict. *The State of Ireland: A Novella and Seventeen Stories*. Boston: David R. Godine, 1980.

Lavin, Mary. *The Patriot Son and Other Stories.* London: Michael Joseph, 1956.

MacIntyre, Tom. "An Aspect of the Rising." In *Tears of the Shamrock: An Anthology of Contemporary Short Stories on the Theme of Ireland's Struggle for Nationhood.* Ed. David Marcus. London: Wolfe, 1972.

MacLaverty, Bernard. *Walking the Dog and Other Stories.* New York: Norton, 1995.

Marcus, David, ed. *Tears of the Shamrock: An Anthology of Contemporary Short Stories on the Theme of Ireland's Struggle for Nationhood*. London: Wolfe, 1972.

Martin, Augustine, ed. *Forgiveness: Ireland's Best Contemporary Short Stories*. New York: Four Walls Eight Windows, 1989.

McCabe, Eugene. *Heritage and Other Stories*. London: Victor Gollancz, 1978.

McCann, Colum. *Everything in This Country Must.* New York: Picador, 2000.

———. *Fishing the Sloe-Black River.* London: Phoenix, 1995.

McLaverty, Michael. *Collected Short Stories.* Dublin: Poolbeg, 1978.

Montague, John. *Death of a Chieftain and Other Stories.* Dublin: Wolfhound, 1964, 1978, 1998.

Morrow, John. *Northern Myths*. Belfast: Blackstaff, 1979.

Mulkerns, Val. *Antiquities: A Sequence of Short Stories*. London: Andre Deutsch, 1978.

Murphy, Brenda. "A Social Call." In *The Hurt World: Short Stories of the Troubles*. Ed. Michael Parker. Belfast: Blackstaff, 1995.

O'Brien, Flann. *Stories and Plays*. New York: Viking, 1976.

O'Connor, Frank. *Bones of Contention and Other Stories*. London: Macmillan, 1936.

——. *Domestic Relations*. New York: Knopf, 1957.

——. *Guests of the Nation*. London: Macmillan, 1931.

——. *More Stories by Frank O'Connor*. New York: Knopf, 1954.

——. *An Only Child*. New York: Knopf, 1961.

——. *The Stories of Frank O'Connor*. New York: Knopf, 1952.

O'Faolain, Sean. *The Collected Stories of Sean O'Faolain*. Boston: Little, Brown, 1983.

——. *Vive Moi!* Boston: Little, Brown, 1963.

O'Flaherty, Liam. *Shame the Devil*. London: Grayson & Grayson, 1934.

——. *Spring Sowing*. London: Jonathan Cape, 1924.

——. *The Tent*. London: Jonathan Cape, 1926.

——. *The Wounded Cormorant and Other Stories*. New York: Norton, 1973.

Park, David. *Oranges from Spain*. London: Jonathan Cape, 1990.

Parker, Michael, ed. *The Hurt World: Short Stories of the Troubles*. Belfast: Blackstaff, 1995.

Reilly, Anne-Marie. "Leaving." In *The Hurt World: Short Stories of the Troubles*. Ed. Michael Parker. Belfast: Blackstaff, 1995.

Treacy, Maura. *Sixpence in Her Shoe and Other Stories*. Dublin: Poolbeg, 1977.

Trevor, William. *The Collected Stories*. New York: Viking, 1992.

White, Terence de Vere. "Someone's Coming." In *Forgiveness: Ireland's Best Contemporary Short Stories*. Ed. Augustine Martin. New York: Four Walls Eight Windows, 1989.

II. Secondary Sources

Abrams, M. H. "English Romanticism: The Spirit of the Age." In *The Correspondent Breeze: Essays on English Romanticism*, 44–75. New York: Norton, 1984.

Alexander, Yonah and Alan O'Day. "Introduction: Dimensions of Irish Terrorism." In *The Irish Terrorism Experience*. Ed. Yonah Alexander and Alan O'Day, 1–8. Brookfield, Vt.: Dartmouth Publishing Co., 1991.

Alexander, Yonah and Alan O'Day, ed. *The Irish Terrorism Experience*. Brookfield, Vt.: Dartmouth Publishing Co., 1991.

Aretxaga, Begoña. *Shattering Silence: Women, Nationalism, and Political Subjectivity in Northern Ireland*. Princeton: Princeton University Press, 1997.

Ashcroft, Bill, Garth Griffiths, and Helen Tiffin. *The Empire Writes Back: Theory and Practice in Post-Colonial Literatures*. New York: Routledge, 1989.

Averill, Deborah. *The Irish Short Story from George Moore to Frank O'Connor*. Washington, D.C.: University Press of America, 1982.

Barry, Tom. *Guerilla Days in Ireland: A Firsthand Account of the Black and Tan War (1919–1921)*. New York: Devin-Adair, 1956.

The Bedford Glossary of Critical and Literary Terms. Ed. Ross Murfin and Supryia M. Ray. Boston: Bedford, 1997.

Bell, J. Bowyer. "Case Study IV: The Irish Republican Army." In *Contemporary Terror: Studies in Sub-State Violence*. Ed. David Carlton and Carlo Schaerf, 215–26. New York: St. Martin's, 1981.

——. *The Irish Troubles: A Generation of Violence, 1967–1992*. New York: St. Martin's, 1993.

——. *The Secret Army: The IRA 1916–1970*. New York: John Day, 1971.

Bolger, Dermot. Introduction to *The Vintage Book of Contemporary Irish Fiction*. Ed. Dermot Bolger, vii–xxviii. New York: Random House, 1994.

Boyle, Ted E. *Brendan Behan*. New York: Twayne, 1969.

A Brief History of the UDA/UFF in Contemporary Conflict. Belfast: Prisoners Aid and Post Conflict Resettlement Group, 1999.

Brown, Terence. *Ireland: A Social and Cultural History, 1922 to the Present*. Ithaca: Cornell University Press, 1985.

Buckley, Suzann, and Pamela Lonergan. "Women and the Troubles, 1969–1980." In *Terrorism in Ireland*. Ed. Yonah Alexander and Alan O'Day, 75–87. New York: St. Martin's, 1984.

Butler, Pierce. *Sean O'Faolain: A Study of the Short Fiction*. New York: Twayne, 1993.

Cahalan, James M. *Double Visions: Women and Men in Modern and Contemporary Irish Fiction*. Syracuse: Syracuse University Press, 1999.

——. *Great Hatred, Little Room: The Irish Historical Novel*. Syracuse: Syracuse University Press, 1983.

——. *Liam O'Flaherty: A Study of the Short Fiction*. Boston: Twayne, 1991.

Cairns, David, and Shaun Richards. *Writing Ireland: Colonialism, Nationalism and Culture*. Manchester, England: Manchester University Press, 1988.

Cleary, Joe. *Literature, Partition and the Nation State: Culture and Conflict in Ireland, Israel and Palestine*. Cambridge: Cambridge University Press, 2002.

Coogan, Tim Pat. *The IRA*. Rev. ed. New York: Palgrave, 2002.

Coogan, Timothy Patrick. *Ireland Since the Rising*. New York: Frederick A. Praeger, 1966.

Corkery, Daniel. *Synge and Anglo-Irish Literature*. Cork: Cork University Press, 1931.

Costello, Peter. *The Heart Grown Brutal: The Irish Revolution in Literature from Parnell to the Death of Yeats, 1891–1939*. Dublin: Gill and Macmillan, 1977.

Crenshaw, Martha, ed. *Terrorism, Legitimacy, and Power: The Consequences of Political Violence*. Middletown, Conn.: Wesleyan University Press, 1983.

Cronin, John. "Ulster's Alarming Novels." *Éire-Ireland: A Journal of Irish Studies* 4 (winter 1969): 27–34.

Crossland, John and David Lister. "Heath Drew Up Plan for Partition in Northern Ireland." *The Times* (London). 1 Jan. 2003.

Dáil Eireann. *Official Report*. Vols. 67–68. 13 May 1937.

Davis, Richard. "Northern Ireland Political Papers and the Troubles, 1966–90." In *The Irish Terrorism Experience*. Ed. Yonah Alexander and Alan O'Day, 29–55. Brookfield, Vt.: Dartmouth Publishing Co., 1991.

Deane, Seamus. Introduction to *Nationalism, Colonialism, and Literature*, by Terry Eagleton, Frederic Jameson, and Edward W. Said, 3–19. Minneapolis: University of Minnesota Press, 1990.

Dillon, Martin. *The Dirty War: Covert Strategies and Tactics Used in Political Conflicts.* New York: Routledge, 1999.

Doyle, Paul. *Sean O'Faolain.* New York: Twayne, 1968.

Fanning, Ronan. *Independent Ireland.* Dublin: n.p., 1983.

Forkner, Ben. Introduction to *Modern Irish Short Stories.* Ed. Ben Forkner, 21–42. New York: Penguin, 1980.

Foster, John Wilson. *Forces and Themes in Ulster Fiction.* Totowa, N.J.: Rowan and Littlefield, 1974.

Freud, Sigmund. *Jokes and Their Relation to the Unconscious.* 1905. Reprint, New York: Norton, 1963.

Frye, Northrop. *The Anatomy of Criticism: Four Essays.* Princeton: Princeton University Press, 1957.

———. "The Archetypes of Literature." In *Fables of Identity: Studies in Poetic Mythology,* 7–20. New York: Harcourt, Brace, 1963.

A Glossary of Literary Terms. 5th ed. Ed. M. H. Abrams. New York: Holt, Rinehart and Winston, 1985.

Gramsci, Antonio. *Selections from the Prison Notebooks.* London: Lawrence and Wishart, 1971.

Grant, Patrick. *Literature, Rhetoric and Violence in Northern Ireland, 1968–98: Hardened to Death.* New York: Palgrave, 2001.

Gray, Katherine Martin. "The Attic LIPs: Feminist Pamphleteering for the New Ireland." In *Border Crossings: Irish Women Writers and National Identities.* Ed. Kathryn Kirkpatrick, 269–98. Tuscaloosa: The University of Alabama Press, 2000.

Gregory, Lady Augusta. "Our Irish Theatre." In *Modern Irish Drama.* Ed. John P. Harrington, 377–86. New York: Norton, 1991.

Grene, Nicholas. *The Politics of Irish Drama: Plays in Context from Boucicault to Friel.* Cambridge: Cambridge University Press, 1999.

———. *Synge: A Critical Study of the Plays.* London: Macmillian, 1975.

Guelke, Adrian. "Loyalist and Republican Perceptions of the Northern Ireland Conflict: The UDA and the Provisional IRA." In *Political Violence and Terror: Motifs and Motivations.* Ed. Peter H. Merkl, 91–122. Berkeley and Los Angeles: University of California Press, 1986.

A Handbook to Literature. 3d ed. Ed. C. Hugh Holman. New York: Odyssey, 1972.

Harmon, Maurice. *Sean O'Faolain: A Critical Introduction.* South Bend: University of Notre Dame Press, 1966.

The Harper Handbook to Literature. Ed. Northrop Frye, Sheridan Baker, and George Perkins. New York: Harper & Row, 1985.

Harte, Liam and Michael Parker, eds. *Contemporary Irish Fiction: Themes, Tropes, Theories.* New York: St. Martin's, 2000.

Hildebidle, John. *Five Irish Writers: The Errand of Keeping Alive.* Cambridge: Harvard University Press, 1989.

Jackson, Alvin. *Ireland 1798–1998: Politics and War.* Malden, Mass.: Blackwell, 1999.

Kearney, Colbert. *The Writings of Brendan Behan.* New York: St. Martin's, 1977.

Kearney, Richard. *Transitions: Narratives in Modern Irish Culture*. Manchester, England: Manchester University Press, 1988.

Kennedy-Andrews, Elmer. *Fiction and the Northern Ireland Troubles since 1969: (De-) constructing the North*. Dublin: Four Courts, 2003.

Kiely, Benedict. *Modern Irish Fiction—A Critique*. Dublin: Golden Eagle Books, 1950.

Kilroy, James F., ed. *The Irish Short Story: A Critical History*. Boston: Twayne, 1984.

Kilroy, James F. "Setting the Standards: Writers of the 1920s and 1930s." In *The Irish Short Story: A Critical History*. Ed. James F. Kilroy, 95–144. Boston: Twayne, 1984.

Krause, David. *The Profane Book of Irish Comedy*. Ithaca: Cornell University Press, 1982.

Lanters, José. *Unauthorized Versions: Irish Menippean Satire, 1919–1952*. Washington, D.C.: The Catholic University of America Press, 2000.

Lehan, Richard. *The City in Literature: An Intellectual and Cultural History*. Berkeley and Los Angeles: University of California Press, 1998.

Lloyd, David. *Anomalous States: Irish Writing and the Post-Colonial Moment*. Durham: Duke University Press, 1993.

Loftus, Richard J. *Nationalism in Modern Anglo-Irish Poetry*. Madison: The University of Wisconsin Press, 1964.

Long, David E. *The Anatomy of Terrorism*. New York: The Free Press, 1990.

Longley, Edna. *Poetry in the Wars*. Newark: University of Delaware Press, 1987.

MacDonald, Michael. "Blurring the Difference: The Politics of Identity in Northern Ireland." In *The Irish Terrorism Experience*. Ed. Yonah Alexander and Alan O'Day, 81–96. Brookfield, Vt.: Dartmouth Publishing Co., 1991.

MacKenna, Dolores. *William Trevor: The Writer and His Work*. Chester Springs, Penn.: Dufour Editions, 1999.

Matthews, James. *Voices: A Life of Frank O'Connor*. New York: Atheneum, 1983.

Matthews, Steven. *Irish Poetry: Politics, History, Negotiation: The Evolving Debate, 1969 to the Present*. New York: St. Martin's, 1997.

McMichael, John. Interview in *Marxism Today*. December, 1981.

McMinn, Joseph. "Contemporary Novels on the Troubles." *Études Irlandaises* 5 (1980): 113–21.

"Memorandum on British Atrocities in Ireland 1916–1920." *Interim Report*. Washington, D.C.: American Commission on Conditions in Ireland, n.d.

Mercier, Vivian. *The Irish Comic Tradition*. Oxford: Oxford University Press, 1962.

Moran, Seán Farrell. *Patrick Pearse and the Politics of Redemption: The Mind of the Easter Rising, 1916*. Washington, D.C.: The Catholic University of America Press, 1994.

Morgan, Valerie and Grace Fraser. "Women and the Northern Ireland Conflict: Experiences and Responses." In *Facets of the Conflict in Northern Ireland*. Ed. Seamus Dunn, 81–96. New York: St. Martin's, 1995.

Mulvey, Helen F. *Thomas Davis and Ireland: A Biographical Study*. Washington, D.C.: The Catholic University of America Press, 2003.

O'Brien, James H. *Liam O'Flaherty*. Lewisburg: Bucknell University Press, 1973.

O'Connor, Frank. "Synge." In *The Irish Theatre: Lectures Delivered During the Abbey Theatre Festival Held in Dublin in August 1938*. Ed. Lennox Robinson, 31–52. London: Macmillan, 1939.

O'Faolain, Sean. "About Myself." *Now and Then* 41 (Spring 1932): 35.
———. "Daniel Corkery." *Dublin Magazine* 11 (April–June 1936): 49–61.
———. "Don Quixote O'Flaherty." *London Mercury* 37 (December 1937): 170–75.
———. "Forward." *The Finest Stories of Sean O'Faolain*, vii–xiii. Boston: Little, Brown, 1949.
———. "A Portrait of the Artist as an Old Man." *Irish University Review* 6 (spring 1976): 10–18.
O'Halloran, Clare. *Partition and the Limits of Irish Nationalism: An Ideology Under Stress*. Dublin: Gill and Macmillan, 1987.
O'Hegarty, P. S. *The Victory of Sinn Fein*. Dublin: Talbot, 1924.
O'Toole, Fintan. "Trying Not to Awake." *The New Republic*, 15 October 2001, 61–65.
Parker, Michael. Introduction to *The Hurt World: Short Stories of the Troubles*, ed. Michael Parker, 1–8. Belfast: Blackstaff, 1995.
Paulson, Suzanne Morrow. *William Trevor: A Study of the Short Fiction*. New York: Twayne, 1993.
Pearse, Patrick H. *An Claidheamh Soluis*. 27 August 1904.
———. "From a Hermitage." In *Political Writings and Speeches*. Dublin: Talbot, 1952.
Pelaschiar, Laura. *Writing the North: The Contemporary Novel in Northern Ireland*. Trieste: Edizioni Parnaso, 1998.
Porter, Raymond J. *Brendan Behan*. New York: Columbia University Press, 1973.
Price, Alan. *Synge and Anglo-Irish Drama*. London: Methuen, 1961.
Putzel, Stephen. "The Black Pig: Yeats's Early Apocalyptic Beast." *Éire-Ireland: A Journal of Irish Studies* 17 (fall 1982): 86–102.
Rafroidi, Patrick and Terrence Brown, eds. *The Irish Short Story*. Atlantic Highlands, N.J.: Humanities Press, 1979.
Ranelagh, John O'Beirne. *A Short History of Ireland*. 2d ed. Cambridge: Cambridge University Press, 1994.
Roche, Antony. *Contemporary Irish Drama: From Beckett to McGuinness*. New York: St. Martin's, 1995.
Rolston, Bill. "Mothers, Whores and Villains: Images of Women in Novels of the Northern Ireland Conflict." *Race & Class* 31:1 (1989): 41–57.
Sales, Rosemary. *Women Divided: Gender, Religion and Politics in Northern Ireland*. London: Routledge, 1997.
Saul, George. *Daniel Corkery*. Lewisburg: Bucknell University Press, 1973.
Scanlon, Margaret. "The Unbearable Present: Northern Ireland in Four Contemporary Novels." *Études Irlandaises* 10 (Dec. 1985): 145–61.
Schirmer, Gregory A. *William Trevor: A Study of His Fiction*. New York: Routledge, 1990.
Storey, Michael. "'Not to be written afterwards': The Irish Revolution in the Short Story." *Éire-Ireland: A Journal of Irish Studies* 27 (spring 1993): 32–47.
———. "Postcolonialism and Stories of the Irish Troubles." *New Hibernia Review* 2 (autumn 1998): 63–77.
Tabor, Robert. *The War of the Flea: A study of Guerrilla Warfare, Theory and Practice*. London: Granada Paladin, 1970.
Talbot, Rhiannon. "Myths in the Representation of Women Terrorists." *Éire-Ireland: A Journal of Irish Studies* 35 (fall/winter 2000): 165–86.

Thompson, William Irwin. *The Imagination of an Insurrection: Dublin, Easter 1916. A Study of an Ideological Movement*. Oxford: Oxford University Press, 1967. Reprint, West Stockbridge, Mass.: The Lindisfarne Press, 1982.

Titley, Alan. "Rough Rug-Headed Kerns: The Irish Gunman in the Popular Novel." *Éire-Ireland: A Journal of Irish Studies* 15 (winter 1980): 15–38.

Tonge, Jonathan. *Northern Ireland: Conflict and Change*. 2d ed. Harlow, England: Longman, 2002.

Trevor, William. "The Art of Fiction CVIII." Interview by Mira Stout. In *Paris Review* 110 (1989): 118–51.

Vance, Norman. *Irish Literature, A Social History: Tradition, Identity and Difference*. Oxford: Basil Blackwell, 1990.

Ward, Alan J. *The Easter Rising: Revolution and Irish Nationalism*. Arlington Heights, Ill.: Harlan Davidson, 1980.

Ward, Margaret. *Unmanageable Revolutionaries: Women and Irish Nationalism*. London: Pluto, 1983.

Ward, Margaret, and Marie-Thérèse McGivern. "Images of Women in Northern Ireland." In *The Crane Bag Book of Irish Studies*. Ed. Mark Patrick Hederman and Richard Kearney, 579–85. Dublin: Blackwater, 1982.

Waters, Maureen. *The Comic Irishman*. Albany: State University of New York Press, 1984.

Webb, Al. "Document: U.K. Plan to Cede Land to Dublin." *United Press International*. 2 Jan. 2003.

Weir, David. *Anarchy & Culture: The Aesthetic Politics of Modernism*. Amherst: University of Massachusetts Press, 1997.

Wilkinson, Paul. "The Orange and the Green: Extremism in Northern Ireland." In *Terrorism, Legitimacy, and Power: The Consequences of Political Violence*. Ed. Martha Crenshaw, 105–23. Middletown, Conn.: Wesleyan University Press, 1983.

Wills, Clair. *Improprieties: Politics and Sexuality in Northern Irish Poetry*. Oxford: The Clarendon Press, 1993.

Wohlgelernter, Maurice. *Frank O'Connor: An Introduction*. New York: Columbia University Press, 1977.

Yeats, W. B. *W. B. Yeats: The Poems*. Rev. ed. Ed. Richard J. Finneran. Vol. 1 of *The Collected Works of W. B. Yeats*. Ed. Richard J. Finneran and George Mills Harper. New York: Macmillan, 1989.

Zola, Émile. "Naturalism on the Stage." Trans. Belle M. Sherman. In *Modernism: An Anthology of Sources and Documents*. Ed. Vassiliki Kolocotroni, Jane Goldman, and Olga Taxidou, 169–74. Chicago: University of Chicago Press, 1998.

——. Preface to the Second Edition. *Thérèse Raquin*. Trans. L. W. Tancock. Baltimore: Penguin, 1962.

Index of Primary Authors and Their Works

General Index

Representing the Troubles in the Irish Short Fiction was designed and composed in Galliard by Kachergis Book Design, Pittsboro, North Carolina.